TELL ME ABOUT IT

A BOOK OF MEMORIES COLLECTED BY

ST SUKIE DE LA CROIX

&

OWEN KEEHNEN

Rattling Good Yarns Press

33490 Date Palm Drive #3065

Cathedral City, CA 92235

USA

ISBN-10: 0-578-44239-6
ISBN-13: 978-0-578-44239-6

Tracy Baim for her support and inspiration

CONTENTS

PREFACE

We Asked You To Share Your Memories, And You Did

Everyone has great stories to tell — sometimes poignant, sometimes entertaining, and usually very interesting. As a pair of grassroots historians of the LGBTQ community we have been recording and collecting the memories, personal experiences, and anecdotes of queer folks for decades.

Listening to the stories of people is not only one of our favorite things to do; it is also important work. LGBTQ people have had their stories silenced and redacted from history for centuries. That legacy of censorship has had dire consequences that are still felt today. The result has been widespread isolation, misunderstanding, and shame; robbing us of something precious and necessary.

Connections are made through the exchange of personal experiences. Sharing stories not only helps us to understand one another, it can also help us to better understand ourselves by seeing how much we have in common — who we are, what we share, and where we fit in.

From the outset, *Tell Me About It* was meant to cast a light on the lives and experiences of others by sharing personal anecdotes drawn from answers to a specific set of ten questions. When we put out the call for LGBTQ participants to help us, we were overwhelmed by the enthusiastic response. We received dozens of honest, thoughtful, and funny answers. By far the most challenging part of this project came in choosing which answers would be included in the finished book.

We attempted to make *Tell Me About It* as inclusive as possible and to represent, as best we could, the diversity of LGBTQ experiences. Many thanks to everyone who participated. You have truly contributed to what we hope is a fun exploration of our community's unique perspectives on history.

Sharing and chronicling our stories has never been more important. As various malicious forces seek to divide us, erase us, and push us back into the closet, we need to be stronger, more vocal, and more bound to each other than ever. We hope *Tell Me About It* is a step in that direction.

– Owen Keehnen and St Sukie de la Croix

WHAT WAS THE FIRST GAY BAR YOU WENT INTO?

Sacramento, CA

Bojangles in Sacramento, CA. It was 1977 and I had come out to myself and most of my friends about 6 months earlier, including my friend Tim from 7th grade. He put me through agony for 6 months as I had written him about this deep secret, not knowing that he too was gay. Finally he got in touch with me when he visited from SF to Sacramento and we went out to the bar. I was so nervous at the bar, and cheap too, as I remember finishing off some abandoned drinks of others who had left. That night I met my first boyfriend, Frank, a self-described former gay now born-again Church of the Nazarene member. He was there with his friend Doug who hadn't swallowed the religious poison fully. Frank and I became pen pals and later long-distance boyfriends, him in San Diego and Sacramento, and me in Davis and Sacramento. About 4 months after his "conversion" back to being gay he had a major breakdown over his internalized homophobia and blamed me for him stealing novelty items from an adult bookstore in Sacramento. – Paul Harris

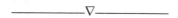

St. Louis, MO
East St. Louis, IL

1982, Martin's Bar in downtown St. Louis. It was right next to the abandoned Union Station which was famous because it was used in the film *Escape From New York* – later it turned into a shopping center. I was in

1

college, still 18, and a new friend from college was helping me find bars we could get in to. Back then there were no groups, social nor otherwise, that young people could be a part of, so the bars were the place to go. I was nervous as hell as we walked in past the door guard, into the regular bar section that had a jukebox and was full of people. (David Allan Coe's *Were You Born An Asshole?* and *The Rodeo Song* were staples). Then out into the hallway that was in the hotel part of the building, then into the dance bar. There was also a basement bar that catered more to the leather crowd. It was overwhelming, particularly when soon after entering, a guy my friend knew, Julio, sure zoned in on me fast. I didn't mind, as he was older and definitely my type. After Martin's, we went across the Mississippi River to Faces in East St. Louis, which was massive and exciting with the main dance bar and a basement bar (men only allowed down there). The basement bar closed at 6:00 AM! – Todd Jaeger

Redondo Beach, CA

It was the Lost and Found in Redondo Beach, during June 1978. I was 16 and you had to be 21 to get in. Fortunately for me, my CA driver's license listed my date of birth as 1957 so I was "officially" 21. My friend Siegfried took an X-ACTO knife to a copy of my birth certificate and moved some numbers around to make me appear older. The woman at the DMV counter only glanced at my birth certificate when I stood in line to get my driver's license.

We had a great time at that bar. People were friendly. The drinks were strong. They had the usual happy hour, well drinks, and awful draft beer.

The best part was that they played the *Time Warp* dance tune at midnight each night and every queen in the bar got up to dance to it. There were always 3 or 4 fag hags in the bunch of gay men back then and I was one of them. – Paul Regalos Urban (Born cisgender female during 1962. Transitioned to male at 26 during 1988)

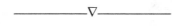

San Diego, CA

The Brass Rail, summer of 1972, heard about it from co-workers who were putting down the place as a tacky gay bar. – Art Healey

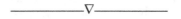

What was the first gay bar you went into?

Chicago, IL

The Loading Zone on Oak Street. I was working as a front desk clerk at the Continental Plaza, and one of the bellmen took me there. He had a beautiful bushy mustache, and I was completely smitten by him. He was very understanding, and while he declined to return my interest, he provided a wonderful and gentle introduction to my first gay bar. — Allan

———————▽———————

Chicago, IL

The first gay bar I went into was Shari's on Clark Street at Surf in Chicago. It was a hot summer afternoon in 1976, and I had just come from the suburbs and spent my very first day at the Belmont Rocks with Roy, my lifelong pal since kindergarten. I was 19 years old and I was so nervous not knowing what to expect. I imagined the bar was going to be some wild orgy-esque scene (we could drink beer and wine at 19 then, the law changed to 21 just before my 21st birthday so I was never deprived of my booze!) However, it was a quiet, pleasant, cozy tavern with a jukebox. The first person I met was Carl Sharp who I would maintain a friendly relationship with for the next 40 years! — Paul Mikos

———————▽———————

New Orleans, LA

Just out of college, I was visiting New Orleans checking out bars. I didn't know it was a gay bar until I noticed it was full of really good looking men and maybe one or two women. Of course, my male date got all upset and dragged me out. Maybe it was because nobody was checking him out. — Anonymous woman

———————▽———————

New York City, NY

1972. A lesbian bar called the Duchess. I wandered into it by mistake, and it was only after my eyes adjusted to the light that I realized a lot of very angry lesbians were staring at me. The bouncer directed me to Boots and Saddle across the street. — Sean Martin

———————▽———————

Chicago, IL

Alfie's on Rush Street. I was underage and in love with Aaron. He took me there and I danced to *Shame* by Evelyn "Champagne" King. I never felt prouder. – Gregg Shapiro

————∇————

Chicago, IL

The first BAR I went into was O'Banion's which was kind of gay but totally punk, when I was underage, in 1978. The first gay bar I went into on purpose was the Haig, at the corner of Dearborn and Chicago in the summer of 1980 when I wanted to eat my lunch, have a beer, and get a quick suck in the men's room. – R. M. Schultz

————∇————

Chicago, IL

My first gay bar was the Gold Coast. I had been whoring out at the Machine Shop across the street and wondered about all the tough guys going into that bar, so I went in and ordered a drink. The first one that spoke to me was more Nelly than Hedy Lamarr so that's when I (also) met my first big hairy woman. – Scott Strum

————∇————

Laguna Beach, CA

The Tiki Hut. It was kind of exciting because I was underage, but I got in with no problem. I met people from high school that I didn't know were gay. It was revealing to me. – Great Big D

————∇————

Springfield, IL

I can't remember if the first gay bar I went to was Smokey's Den on Fifth and Jefferson in downtown Springfield or Smokey's (aka Mary Lou Schneider) other venue outside the city limits on Peoria Road, called rather appropriately, Smokey's "Nu Den" which was a converted storage/warehouse. It was bigger and had more of a dance floor.

But in both of Smokey's bars in 1976, when jukeboxes were ubiquitous in taverns, bars and grills, disco hits still played. My favorite was *Sweetest Hangover* by Diana Ross.

I had never experienced anything so emotionally freeing as seeing same sex couples dancing together and expressing affection without fear, in an "our place" sort of feel; what is termed "safe space" these days. It felt different and very empowering. – Paxton Anthony Murphy

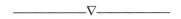

Chicago, IL

The New Flight on Clark in Chicago. I was just out of college in 1981 and was engaged to be married to my college sweetheart. I was scared and had no idea it was a hustler bar. It was just down the street from the Grand Ave. L stop, where I would catch my train home from work at Lake Point Tower. The New Flight was a convenient and easy stop. I remember a very cute Hispanic guy from the southside buying me a beer and trying to pick me up. I was too afraid, even though I was very attracted, to follow up on anything with him. I remember throwing his phone number on the L tracks after I left the bar, just so I wouldn't be tempted. Wonder where he is now? – Rick R. Reed

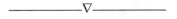

Chicago, IL

The first bar I remember the name of is Take One. It was on Clark St. just south of Wrightwood. A very small bar and I was underage of course. They did not ask for ID so it was an easy go-to bar. I was in college at the time, all my friends I hung out with were gay men. At the time I was, or so I thought, a straight woman. It was never crowded when I was in there. But now that I look back at that time it was the height of the AIDS crisis, 1986. We would go there to grab a beer or two. Now Berlin was the bar to go to but being under age, nope not going to happen. – Jake Cohn

Chicago, IL

1978, Piggin's Bar and Restaurant, (Clark and Diversity). My friend and I (we both attended Notre Dame High School. I was a senior) made the drive from Niles, Illinois. We walked through the Century Mall and grabbed a burger from Piggin's. But the second bar was the Glory Hole. I was 19 and dating a 30-year-old. He took me to the Glory Hole, a couple months later Carol's Speakeasy opened, that's where I got my membership card – gradually discovering Chicago Nightlife. I remember he also took me to the Gold Coast – I was awestruck. Friday Nites were my leather night bars and Saturday was my dance club nights. – David Plambeck

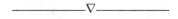

Atlanta, GA

Burkharts, Atlanta, GA 1991. – Roy Felts

Chicago, IL

The first gay bar was Shari's. It was at 2901 N. Clark at Surf. It was typical with the windows painted black to avoid outside looking in. That's all I remember except driving in 15-20 miles from the western suburbs. There was certainly nothing in or around Hinsdale, an affluent village where my family lived. – Tim Cagney

Dallas, TX

The Bayou Landing, sometime in 1973. My friend, Charlie Miller, asked me if I wanted to go to a party. I said sure. We were both students at Tyler Junior College, about 100 miles east of Dallas. Back in those days, gas was cheap and 100 miles was "down the road a piece." So, we jumped in Charlie's car and headed west. On the way, Charlie said there might be famous people at the party. "Like who?" I asked. Oh, maybe Paul Lynde. Or Nancy Walker. Those Hollywood B-listers would be starring in Dallas dinner theatre productions and would hang out in the local gay bars after their shows. I remember walking into the Bayou Landing for the first time and seeing cowboys slow dancing with each other. I thought I died and went to heaven. The BL became my home away from home when I lived in Dallas. – David Clayton

New York City, NY
Chicago, IL
Detroit, MI

I think the place was called Julius in Greenwich Village, or something like that. I went there during a multi-stop tour of lower Manhattan hosted by a friend from college who had moved to New York. I sometimes thought he was gay, but he's been with his lady for the last 30+ years in rural New Mexico, so I'd guess not.

Two things about Julius' stood out. One, the cobwebs hanging from the ceiling. Two, how "normal" it was – very fraternity/ preppy/ casual/ relaxed.

The second bar, but the first one I started going to in Chicago, was the Trip around 1970. That was accidental. I met a business colleague for lunch near his workplace. The Trip was a business lunch place. Some singer was rehearsing, I guess for that evening. Some weeks later, I went back to hear the entertainment. The rest is history. I still occasionally see and/or keep in touch with people I met (and sometimes did more) there.

I once stumbled by a bar in the basement of the Palmer House. I didn't go in, but it seemed clear that it was not for conventioneers.

I grew up in Detroit, but never went into any bars there. There was a place in mid-town that I noticed when driving by and saw people arriving or leaving. It wasn't too hard to guess what that was about. But I never went there. It was a dicey area to walk from a parked car.

Many years later I went to a movie theater in Detroit and met a kid with a VW bug. We had sex there. He was visiting from the University of Chicago. We never tried to maintain contact. – Anonymous

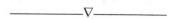

Fort Worth, TX

I came out in 1989, when I was 19 and living in the suburbs of Ft. Worth, TX. I knew some gay people from work but didn't go to a gay bar until several months after coming out. I had moved to Denton, TX, that fall for college, and had joined a gay student group at the University of North Texas. I went to my first gay bar with people from that student group. We had gone to dinner and then out to a bar called TJ's. I remember it was close to Halloween. I remember it had a big dance floor, and I danced with a guy I had met in the student group, who would become my first boyfriend. – Brent

Chicago, IL

The first gay bar I went into was Alfie's right there on Lincoln Park. I had gone for an evening with one of my best friends from the small town I grew up in, Wauconda. He was very out, and it was our senior year, and I had just turned 18. At that time beer and wine was then legal for 19-year old's but as you see, I was still not legal. The evening was with his boyfriend who was 21 or maybe older, and they had been together for a while. So, we first went to the Granada Theater, they were all PDA and such and trying to get me to cross over the line and admit I was gay as well. I mean, I knew I was, but had not been public or done anything of mention about it. So, the Granada had a double feature of *Norman is That You.*, which had a gay theme to it with Red Foxx, Pearl Bailey and Michael Warren. The second feature was *The Pink Panther* that was playing at that time, but we did not stay for that. They said let's go have a drink and we proceeded to drive to Lincoln Park. As we were headed there, they explained we were going to a Gay Bar. Well, I was a bit nervous but excited as well. And then there were the questions, what if someone wants to dance with me? Answer ... go ahead. And what if he wants to buy me a drink? Let him, was the response. But does that mean I have to have sex with him? If you want to, they said. It was a long time before I realized that buying me a drink did not buy you a roll in the hay. I was also instructed that I must order a drink, and it could not be beer or wine as they would then be prompted to card. So, what do I order, I asked? They recommended a screwdriver. What I remember of the evening was that it was exhilarating. A man talked to me, a much older man, or so he seemed, and he kissed me, and it was so exciting, I could not stop talking about it all the way home. They dropped me back at home in our small town and they were going on to a hotel. I told them I looked forward to going again and being a little bit more adventurous. – Dean Ogren

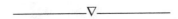

San Francisco, CA

I was in the Army in 1967 being held, because my wife was pregnant ... she was in Utah, I was at the Oakland Army base. I met this guy who was also in the Army and we became friends. He would disappear overnight sometimes. I finally talked to him and asked him what was going on. He said, "Well I go off to a bar and have drinks with people." So, I said, "Well, that sounds like fun." So, we went into San Francisco to Upper Grand Avenue, we went into a bar called the 527 Club, it was at 527 Union. He explained to me that this was a bar that was considered off-limits. So, it had a little bit of interest because ... this would not be looked on favorably by the Army. It seemed like a nice place, there was a female entertainer who sang, but, of course, everybody else in the house was male. My friend eventually explained that it was a gay bar. I said, "Oh, fine, I've been looking for something like this." I hadn't really come out. I mean, I knew there were gay bars and gay people in San Francisco. I was a closeted little Mormon, married and a baby on the way. So, I kept going to the same bar with him, and I ended up working there. – Steve

——————▽——————

Champaign, IL

My first solo experience to a gay bar was when I was going into my third year of law school in Champaign in the fall of 1976. Giovanni's was a small bar with a dance floor and a parking lot down the street where guys cruised in their cars. I was still dating a woman the first time I decided to go to Giovanni's, and I couldn't bring myself to go in; instead I slumped down in my seat in the parking lot, watching guys coming and going. The next weekend I finally got up the courage to go in. Almost immediately upon entering the bar I ran into someone with whom I had done summer theatre for several years in my hometown of Springfield, IL. He looked at me and got a big smile on his face before saying, "What took you so long?" – Tom Chiola

——————▽——————

Lafayette, IN
Champaign, IL

Technically I went into two. I was a sophomore at Purdue University when I came out. I was 18 and it was spring. Mind you, I had been in taverns and bars growing up in a small farming community in downstate Illinois, but my first gay bar, I was thrown out of for being underage. It was the Sportsmen's Bar and Lounge in Lafayette, IN. Now closed and converted into something else, it served as the queer watering hole for quite a while. It was split into three main areas; the bar where you came in, the pool table next to the bathrooms, and the dance floor in a small room with an even smaller stage opposite the bar. Coincidently, that is where my drag career started. Where it ended is another story.

I, and a few other underage friends, had a habit of hanging out, ok, loitering, on the front steps of the bar talking to patrons and friends that were old enough. There was nowhere else to go at the time. One evening, a patron, Richard, thought it was rubbish that we had to stand outside, so told us to grab hands and follow him in to the bar. We made it to the dance floor with him, and then we were promptly asked to leave. When I turned 21, the Sportsmen's was where I officially celebrated.

Until I was 21 though, weekends turned to travel as my friends had discovered a queer bar called C-Street Bar on Chester street in Champaign, IL. In Illinois, you could be 18 and be in a bar, unlike Indiana. Countless weekends were car trips, started at 9:00 pm for the hour and a half to Champaign on I-74 for dancing, flirting, being with other queers until close, a trip to Perkins for food, and then another hour and a half home.

So, while I spent a few years going back and forth to C-Street with friends, my first, and what I considered my home queer bar was the Sportsmen's Bar and Lounge in Lafayette, IN. – Cody Las Vegas

—————————∇—————————

Boston, MA

That probably had to be Boston's old 1270, at 1270 Boylston St. in the Fenway district. We figured out as teenagers that if you went on Sunday afternoon, before they were really open, you could go up to the rooftop bar and keep ordering soda from the bartenders as they arrived for work and got set up. And then the trick was to just stay put – and stay out of the bouncers' sight – until it finally got to be late enough for people to come. Being at a club when the lights are on and only a few people are there really takes the glamorousness away from your fantasy perceptions. By the time it got to be 11:00 at night I think I was sick of being there and had way too many cokes! We eventually became bold enough to head down the block and somehow (because we were so young perhaps) got in to the Ramrod, which is Boston's version of a heavy-duty leather bar. I always thought it looked like the set of a Cher video – too many silver chains and black bars. – Matt

—————————∇—————————

New York City, NY

Ty's on Christopher Street. I was living in Queens. I grew up there and I was about 16 or 17 and I drove into Manhattan. I knew I was gay, but I wasn't really out to anybody but myself. I heard about Christopher Street. I just decided to walk down Christopher Street and found this bar with dark windows. I saw guys coming in and out. I thought, they gotta be gay. And so, I went inside. The bar was busy. It was an innocent kind of bar. Guys hanging around the bar chatting away. A lot of people just like me. – Randy

What was the first gay bar you went into?

Warren

San Francisco, CA

I was 18 years old and it was the Savoy Tivoli. I went in with my friend Jeff because it had a dancefloor. The only thing memorable, other than the fact that we danced, was at one point I reached out and touched him and he jumped back and said, "You can't do that, the vice squad could be here. We could get arrested." That was probably in 1966. – Bill Barrick

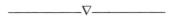

Palm Springs, CA

It was about '77-'78. I think it was called Manhunters. It was on Ramon Road near the drive-in. It's been torn down now. I was 23 at the time. – Randy

Detroit, MI

Backstreet. I was 16 and with my girlfriend. We had fake IDs and they let us drink. She was in a vintage 1940s-era cocktail dress and I was wearing a suit jacket that was a few sizes too big (it was the era of David Byrne's "Big Suit"). I'm pretty sure we weren't fooling anyone. It was located in a strip mall in what appeared to be a "dangerous" neighborhood for a bunch of white suburban high school students. Once inside, it was a banquet of light, sound, sights and music. A gay oasis in the middle of a desolate strip of empty and boarded up storefronts. – Misha Davenport

Denver, CO

I moved to downtown Denver in 1973 when I was 19, after growing up in a dull suburb there. My roommates were spectacular: an adjunct Cockette called Lily Rose who played piano and sang 1920s jazz tunes, a classical dancer named Roy who dressed around the house as a WWII WAC, and Maggie, an obese lawyer in her 30s originally from Philly. She'd recently returned from some years in the Levant, where she'd married a Bedouin and lived nomadically. She sported elaborate facial and hand tattoos, unheard of at that time. We and our other weirdo friends would all congregate at the Brew, a gay tavern a couple of blocks from the Capitol building. It was a 3.2 bar, meaning that 18-21year-olds could legally drink 3.2 percent beer. Lots of high school kids with fake IDs, a juke box that played the Three Degrees and Bowie, and a postage stamp "dance floor" surrounded on three sides by a white wrought-iron railing. All ruled over by Doris Douchebag, a very grand, very funny, drag queen. This was still the era of Quaaludes, so much bruising from falling off one's 3-inch platforms. – Steve Lafreniere

―――――∇―――――

New York, NY

1996. The Stonewall Inn. I was on a grad-school visit to NYU in 1996 and met up with my college boyfriend, who was taking a semester off and lived in Philadelphia at the time. I had a free hotel room and a stipend, so we endeavored to make a weekend out of it. I had yet to go to a gay bar and knew that the Stonewall was near the restaurant at which we ate dinner (El Teddy's).

I was beyond nervous, as my only exposure to gay bars had been from '80s and '90s film depictions. I fully expected to have my 21-year-old bones picked clean by a den of leather men, and I was not quite ready for that level of exposure.

Before we went in, I remember begging my boyfriend to hold my hand and demonstrate outwardly that I was with him, so I wouldn't be devoured.

It was an off night. Perhaps a Tuesday, and the bar was virtually empty, leading to an uneventful trip to the most historic gay bar on Earth.

Afterwards, we walked over a mile back to my hotel, not speaking one word the entire walk. – Kirk Williamson

―――――∇―――――

Madison, WI

As best I can remember, the first gay bar I went into was the Cardinal while I was in grad school, 1980-1982. I don't recall actually spending time there, but remember going in the front door.

I came out in 1978 in small-town Massachusetts, and after getting some professional advice I found *Gay Community News* in Boston, and the Harvard-Radcliffe Gay Students Association, and Gay Folk Dancing in

Philip Brooks House in Harvard Yard, and Clearspace in Central Square, Cambridge. None of that was bars. I don't drink, I detest tobacco smoke, and I'm no good at going up to strangers and starting conversations. So, I didn't try going into bars. When I moved to Madison I joined the United, a Gay & Lesbian political action group; folk dancing, overwhelmingly straight but a joy to dance and hear that music; and eventually the Madison Men's Chorale, a gay group. I may have gone to the Cardinal with someone from folk dancing or the singing group, I don't remember.

Also during my time in Madison, I went to the Club de Wash once, for the restaurant associated with it. I think it wasn't bar hours, but we were there for the food. I remember a hunky waiter who left the top inch of his jeans unzipped. – Rick

———————▽———————

Chicago, IL

I don't know. It was on Halsted Street in Chicago in 1985. I was in and out so fast I didn't get the name. I didn't *want* to be gay, and the bar didn't help my attitude. There was gay porn – a shocking novelty – on the video screens, lecherous older men, and a leather queen so aggressive I practically had to hit him with a brick. Not the best introduction to "the life." Fortunately, I found Gay Horizons, boys my own age, and dance clubs like Cheeks, Medusa's and Berlin. – Corey Black

———————▽———————

Lima, Peru

It was actually a quite recent first! I was taking a photojournalism class and my topic was LGBT spaces, so I decided to go the obvious route and go to a gay bar. It was called Lola, and it had a nice velvety front, I went with my girlfriend (we're both queer) early and sat there waiting for people to trickle in. Of course, I asked before taking pictures, but nobody said yes, so we eventually left empty-handed and I changed the angle of my assignment. It was kinda nice, since there were same-sex couples dancing and making out without fear – but at the same time my girlfriend and I aren't very party-y people so it was mostly for academic purposes. – Robb

———————▽———————

Norfolk, VA

The College Cue Club on Killam Avenue at 46th Street. I was all of 16 and (the legal age was 21) snuck in with my 20-something year old boyfriend. It was the first time I'd seen gay folks in a group and having fun. – Bud Thomas

————▽————

Chicago, IL

On purpose, Berlin. I was not quite 18 but before 10 on Saturdays, Berlin did not card. So if you went to Berlin, ordered water or soda until ten, and then they started carding it was OK to order drinks. Also, after ten you got a hand stamp so you didn't have to pay a second cover. In the late '80s a hand stamp was all you needed to avoid being carded at the next bar. Which is how I discovered Christopher Street and Manhole. – Mike Martinez

————▽————

Roanoke, VA

The first gay bar I went to was called the Horoscope Lounge in Roanoke, VA. It was one of those downstairs, no sign, paint it black bars. It had a dance floor that was lit up in squares that changed with the music. – Tom

————▽————

New Orleans, LA

It was the Parade in New Orleans in 1970. I was there on vacation in college with my fraternity. I snuck out and walked around the block a few times getting up the courage to enter the bar. – Anonymous

————▽————

Philadelphia, PA

My first gay bar was in Philadelphia. I was 26. I had recently divorced, was in a long-distance relationship with a man, and desperately wanted to sleep with a woman but hadn't yet. It was 1974 or 1975. I went to this bar with a gay woman I worked with. The bar was down a dark narrow street near central Philly. There was a neon beer sign in the window, no other indications it was a bar. It was owned/run by the mafia. A very butch looking bartender, very few patrons. It was sad-looking. We drank and talked until 1 in the morning. It was not what I would call a joyous introduction to the lesbian world. – Anonymous

Chicago, IL
San Francisco, CA

I don't remember the name of the very first bar I went into. I lived in suburban Chicago (DuPage County) and was convinced I was the only person who felt the feelings I was feeling. I was probably underage, so it would have been 1967/'68. Somehow, I knew that cruising happened in the bus depot in downtown Chicago, so I went into the city as soon as I was able and trawled the station until I saw someone "see" me. That was my plan. There was a lot of eye contact. He left the station and I followed him to a seedy little place somewhat close to the station but far enough that I was getting wary. He went in. I followed. There was a drag show going on. I was overwhelmed by the whole thing and a little afraid, actually. We connected and we went back to his apartment. I never went back, and I threw away the slip of paper with this name on it that he gave me. I felt loads of guilt.

The very *first* gay bar that I can *remember* the name of, that I went to knowingly, was the late, great, wonderful Stud in San Francisco. I was living in a hippy commune in Los Gatos, south on the peninsula, and was making my first tentative steps out of the closet in the safety of the non-judgmental group. One of the women told me about the Stud and told me where it was. I went as soon as I was able. The first time I went home with someone I didn't return to my home in Los Gatos for four days! My housemates thought they might have to call the police to find me! I went back to the Stud as often as I could and eventually moved into the City. The Stud is mythic in my mind ... and I'm sure in many others, as well. – Bo Young

Joliet, IL

The A Frame in Joliet IL. I was 18, it was one of two gay bars in Joliet. The other was the Continental West which became Maneuvers the following year. The A Frame was known for having the best dance music in town and it was always full on the weekend. So many wonderful memories of that place. The people, the music, the experiences all hold a special place in my memory. The building still stands but it is now a sports bar. – Jim Hensley

Portland, ME

The first gay bar I went into was Cycles in Portland, ME, in 1984. One of my coworkers at the time was a black guy (I later found out a drag queen who specialized in Diana Ross impersonation), who I think realized in a second that I was gay (I wasn't really out at the time, though I knew I was gay). He invited me out for a beer at a bar named Cycles. I'll never forget the moment I walked into Cycles, I felt instantly at home, like I belonged and could just relax. Cycles is no longer there (is now a straight bar called Brian Borg.) I did go back to Cycles a few times after that on my own, and kept having the strong, wonderful feeling of belonging. I never knew if my coworker asked me out because he was interested in me, or if he was simply prescient enough to know I needed to be taken to a gay bar.

If this counts: The first gay bar I ever actually SAW was Roland's, also in Portland, ME, and probably in 1978. But I never had the nerve to go in, and Roland's building is long gone. – Jeff

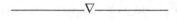

Honolulu, HI

Hula's Bar and Lei Stand, Honolulu. I was on vacation and heard a song I liked coming from the bar. I walked in and saw men dancing with men and women dancing with women and I knew I found my home. I was in college at the time in St. Louis, MO and ran into a lesbian I worked with at a part time job in St. Louis. – Eric Kuznof

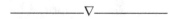

Minneapolis, MN

My first gay bar was the Gay Nineties in Minneapolis, in 1999. I was 19 and freshly out of the closet. I didn't have a fake ID, but someone in my small group knew the bouncer so he let us in as long as we promised not to drink. I was amazed by how big the place was. I had never danced in public before, but some cute guy ushered me out to the dance floor. I started dancing and soon got completely lost in the music and the crowd, and for the first time in my life I felt an overwhelming sense of freedom and belonging. The fact that I was able to do all this sober astounds me even today. – Shane K

———————▽———————

Kingston, Ontario, Canada
Toronto, Ontario, Canada

The Back Door, upstairs at a local stripper bar, early 1988. Smoky, blasting dance music. Probably why I didn't go to a bar again until 1992, another one in the same town (for one brief moment in the early 2000s, there were four in this rather small town – now there are none). The first gay bar I went to where I felt vaguely at home was in Toronto in 2002, the late Toolbox. Decent music, a venue that was smoke-free when that wasn't the law (had always been smoke free), and well-lit. From this, you may conclude I'm not really a bar patron. The fact that I don't drink also tended to make the places unattractive to me – grew up with alcoholics, so didn't want to spend my free social time around heavy drinking either. – Tim Murphy

———————▽———————

New York City, NY

Julius in Greenwich Village, 1967, when I was 19. I didn't even know such things as "gay bars" existed at that point, but an older (mid-20s) guy I met at an opera performance gave me my first "tour" of Greenwich Village and took me to Julius. It was both exciting to see all these gay guys in one place, and made me very anxious. – John D'Emilio

———————▽———————

Indianapolis, IN

First gay bar was the Hunt and the Chase, in Indianapolis. I was titillated and curious but for some weird reason I thought only guys could be gay and gay women were large square scary things that looked like men, which wasn't my thing. I don't remember much about it beyond dancing wildly and doing poppers, but my friend Charles had come out to me and we went clubbing and it was loud and fun. There was a small intimate bar at the top of the place called the Capture, but I never got up there. I think it was guys only. This would have been in 1976 or so. – Anne

17

———————∇———————

Hickory, NC

I am not a very social person, so to speak, but when I was 18 I was invited to the local gay bar. It was (and still is) the only gay bar in town. It was aptly named Club Cabaret. It was an intriguing night because I had just gotten off work and we went on a female to male pageant night. It was the first time I had experienced anything like it. What made it interesting for me was the performers and the owner, an older gay man, were quite friendly and welcomed me and my friends warmly. There was this big queen at the door, taking the IDs and money, one of the nicest people you could meet. Now the rest of the patrons on the other hand, were catty and rude, but it still didn't ruin the way it made me feel, which was wanted and fantastic. – Christian Bane

———————∇———————

Chicago, IL

The Loading Dock, I was 17 years old, afraid. I got in, I ordered a beer and got it.

I stood in front of the speakers on the dance floor and some guy walked up to me and said, "You're not old enough to be in here." I threw the beer in the garbage and ran out of there. – Joseph G

———————∇———————

Chicago, IL

Augie & CK's! I was underage and home from college for break. A girl I was dating took me there with a group of friends. I was so nervous that we'd get turned away because I looked so young and didn't have a fake ID. Luckily, they let me in. It was a blast! – Chicago T

———————∇———————

Chicago, IL

Big Chicks. My friend George _____ lived in Edgewater then, so Big Chicks was his neighborhood bar and he liked the not-Boystown vibe. I was married to a woman at the time. A very talented artist, a painter. I was in deep denial about my own sexuality. I remember feeling nervous being with George in a gay bar. I remember carefully calculating my every step and word, avoiding eye contact (even with Giorgio!)

A few days later I was downtown at the old stand-up bar at the Berghoff. Lunchtime. The place was jammed and as I elbowed a spot among the crowded bar and started in on my roast beef sandwich, I looked around. In those days, the Berghoff bar clientele was still mostly men (the joint had prohibited women for the longest time.) I noticed every guy among the sea of men crowded there that afternoon was avoiding eye contact, as well. "So," I remember thinking, "What's the difference between the Berghoff and a gay bar?" I swallowed a mouthful of beef. "Well," I thought again, "Besides the one rather big difference, I mean."

When I finally came out to George, we walked back over to Big Chicks to celebrate.

Now, George has passed away; a fact that breaks my heart every day. And my husband of 24 years (4 years legally) and I live in Edgewater about two blocks away from Big Chicks. – Michael Burke

Boston MA

The 1270, the early '70s. Back then the Boston bars could only be identified by a street number. And then a very nondescript door that you'd have to know to enter. Gay bars were still a bit of a secret due to homophobia. – James S

San Francisco, CA

Bradley's in the old Haight-Ashbury. 1972. Bradley's had the feel of a local neighborhood bar and meeting place for locals. I had just turned 21 and I thought the bartender would card me. He did not. Across the street was also a famous bar in San Francisco, Maud's. Maud's was one of the few lesbian bars in the SF bay area. My friends would go to Bradley's and my women friends would sometimes go to Maud's for drinks. – Dale Williams

New York City, NY

I'm pretty sure the first bar I went into was sometime in the winter of 1987,

right when I'd moved to New York to go to NYU. I'd followed a pack of new dorm friends, after a night out, to Uncle Charlie's on Greenwich Ave. I must have been just 19 years old. The first gay bar that felt like home, though, was Julius', which I started hanging out in with my friend Joey late at night, shortly after that first trip to Uncle Charlie's. I remember we had a regular table, kind of, and is it possible that the guy brought us our drinks *to* the table? Also, the hamburgers. The walls were chalked with graffiti and names of the customers which even to me then felt like ghosts. And the jukebox – it was the first place I ever heard Bobby Darin sing *Beyond the Sea* – an education in so many ways. – David Zinn

—————▽—————

Utica, NY

That Place in Utica, NY. A filthy hole of a place and I was scared shitless. – Dave Russo

—————▽—————

Quincy, IL

It was Irene's Cabaret and it closed a few years ago. I was in the closet and my straight friend took us to meet girls there. He said they go there to dance where guys won't hit on them, but he was going to change that! I was shy and sat at the bar and got wasted. I wouldn't go back until 6 years later after I came out. – Anonymous

—————▽—————

San Francisco, CA

I don't remember the name, but I was taken there to see Charles Pierce – in San Francisco. I was taken by my first lover. It was a whole new world to me, but it was related to entertainment and wasn't meant to be a "pick up" place. I was nervous leaving the bar because I felt that everyone would be looking at me and knowing that I was gay – which, of course, was foolish because most of them would have been gay as well! – Brian

—————▽—————

St. Louis, MO

Magnolia's on Vanderventer Ave. in St. Louis. October 1986. I was 23. I sat outside in my car in the parking lot for two hours watching to see what type of people went in, while trying to build up the courage to walk in myself. The worst part was giving them my ID, as they looked me up and down. I looked very young for my age. Stood against wall on dance floor all night drinking cranberry and vodka to calm nerves and just watched the cruising. – Robert Bender

—————▽—————

Darlinghurst, NSW, Australia

Ruby's in Darlinghurst (Sydney, Australia). Was a theatre restaurant that became a lesbian bar after 10 pm. – Susan H

—————▽—————

Northbridge, Perth, Australia

The first gay bar I went into was a pub called the Red Lion in Northbridge, Perth. I can't remember much about it. I was at a very fashionable straight club and I was extremely drunk. I couldn't find the friends I had come with, so I decided, in my drunken state, to nip down to my first gay pub. I did and was picked up almost immediately. I think I was only 17 at the time. – Mansfield

—————▽—————

Chicago, IL

The 21 Club (later renamed the Legacy). I remember they had a buzzer, but I didn't know that, and I pulled on the door so hard my head cracked against it. – Rick Karlin

—————▽—————

Chicago, IL

There was a gay bar (name long forgotten) that was next door to my apartment when I was in graduate school. I had heard rumors that it was a gay bar. When I realized I wanted to go to a gay bar I walked around the block many times for many weeks before I got up enough courage to go into the gay bar. I stood in a corner alone for many nights and ran out if anyone talked to me. It was months before I was comfortable letting someone talk to me. – Bob

Boston, MA

Early in my first year in law school, I fell in with some classmates from California. They took every opportunity I gave them to let me, a Midwestern farm boy, know how backward I was. When they partied on Halloween, one of them produced a joint, which eventually made its way to me. "Is this what I think it is?" I asked. "Go ahead, Ron," they replied. "You'll love it!" I did. They'd not only found a dealer, they'd also discovered a queer bar in Boston. None of them was a faggot, needless to say, but they had to go see the place in any event. It turned out to be the most popular gay bar in the city in 1961. The costumed holiday crowd immediately recognized my friends for what they were – tourists. They also seemed to figure out, almost as fast, the hayseed with the gawking California boys wasn't the least bit straight. One of the regulars drove me back to Cambridge, after, of course, a prolonged stop at his place. "Did you know that guy?" my West Coast friends asked me the next day. "Not until last night," I replied. – Ron Fritsch

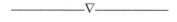

Cardiff, Wales, UK

To be honest, I don't remember the name of the club. It isn't there anymore. I was working for one of the co-owners (who also owned the solicitor's firm I worked for). There was a cocktail bar downstairs and a bar upstairs which was all black leather booths, red walls and dark lighting. I was pretty naive back then and I was wary of going up there. Although I was exploring my dominant nature it was mainly at small parties with people I knew, so I found it quite intimidating among all the leather daddies and quite pushy subs, if I remember right. – Nephy Hart

What was the first gay bar you went into?

Binghamton, NY

I don't remember the name. Corner of Main and Front Street. I was very nervous because people kept looking at me! LOL. It was the summer of 1972. I was still in the closet. Hooked up though – terrible lay. – Fester

———————▽———————

Gainesville, FL

The Spectrum. 1983. Its existence was "common knowledge," either from being a college town or maybe just urban legend. Either way, I knew of it. I was 15 1/2 (drinking age was 19). I dressed in a button down shirt to reveal what chest hair I had to make myself look older. My older "straight" friend Steve took me, I think it was meant as a joke. – Eric Andrews-Katz

———————▽———————

Chicago, IL

It was a bar called Shari's. I think it was around Clark and Diversey, although I am not sure now. This dates back to my college years 1970-1974. It happened in 1973. I confronted a fellow student in college who several people said was gay. I got up the nerve to ask him if it was true. He said yes, with some hesitation (we both attended Lewis University in Romeoville, a Catholic institution). I told him I thought I was gay. He asked if I ever went to a bar. After telling him no, he took me to Shari's that week-end. He wanted me to hook up with someone for my benefit and so that he could find someone himself. I looked around at everyone, fascinated. I saw one guy who I thought was interesting but in spite of his attempts to get me to make the first move, I just couldn't. Back then, I wasn't aware that I was an introvert so things like making the first move were extremely hard for me. To my friend's disappointment, I didn't connect with anyone. It didn't bother me though. He took us back to the college. When I did get my own car, I made my way back to Shari's. I still never made any connections then. It was nice, however, to be in the company of men who were like me. – Peter

———————▽———————

Jackson, MI

The first gay bar I went into was called the Ropa, because a gay couple, one named Ron and the other Paul, owned it and they squabbled over the name until they came up with that compromise. This was on the shabby main street of my home town, Jackson, MI. It has always been the space where the gay bar or the strip club exists, and therefore it has burned down four times. Back in 1983, the Ropa was where you found out your fellow altar boy was also gay, or the high school career counselor (when it became a strip club, I got to see two of the lunch ladies from the high school earn a little extra money shaking their groove things). But mostly the Ropa was there for everybody to watch the ups and downs and other downs of Ron and Paul. They would start out arguing as they mixed drinks, and devolve into a volley, back and forth, of "I am so sick of your bullshit!" and the witty response, "I am so sick of YOUR bullshit!" To this day, when I watch in the distance as two gay men argue, I lip sync "I am so sick of your bullshit." – Alec Holland

————∇————

Southern California
Chicago, IL

When I was still struggling with being gay many years ago, I used to visit southern California to see a friend who was significantly "outer" than I. Our favorite dinner spot was the French Quarter, a sidewalk café in West Hollywood. One night, after dinner, as we strolled along Santa Monica Boulevard, my friend dragged me into the closest gay bar because he had to pee. As he abandoned me in the bar's vestibule, I panicked a little. "What if someone hits on me?" As he trotted across the bar to the men's room, he yelled over his shoulder, "Just say no!" I think my first self-motivated, go-it-alone gay bar, many years later, was Sidetracks in Chicago. Now I worry about someone NOT hitting on me. – Bill

————∇————

Dayton, OH

The first gay bar I went to was 1470 West in Dayton, Ohio. I was in college and wasn't out yet and was going with my straight friends (one or two that ended up also being gay.) I forget why we went exactly except to dance and have fun. I was probably too paranoid to have fun. – Mike Uetrecht

————————▽————————

Des Moines, IA
Chicago, IL

I think the very first gay bar I went into was OP (Our Place) in Des Moines. I had the address, but I drove around and around and around the block because I could not find the entrance. Finally, I pinpointed where the entrance should be, and by golly there was a little, dark (probably painted black) door hiding between a couple of storefronts. On the other side of the bar was this nice, spacious bar with a dance floor. But it was 1979 or 1980, and it was hiding (as we all were back then). The first bar I went into in Chicago was Christopher Street, on the corner of Cornelia and Halsted. I sat in the window and had a beer. – David

————————▽————————

Columbus, OH

Oh my god, Axis Nightclub in Columbus, OH. What a mess. I remember the stench of syrupy liquor and Axe body spray pervading the humid air. I owned very few stylish clothes and was still very body-shy at 19 but the rest of the crowd was, luckily, also very awkward and nerdy. The few who were not were shirtless and I most definitely stared, unashamed and envious. – Jordan

————————▽————————

Chicago, IL

The first bar this small town boy from Michigan ever went to was the Bistro, which was down by Dearborn and Hubbard. At that time, I was attending school. I overheard several students from Interior Design class say they were going to the Gold Coast. "I need to suck some dick," one of them said. Another one responded, "Take your kneepads and some Kleenex if you're going down in the pit." And they all laughed. That was all this newly-emerging gay boy needed to hear. I had just recently discovered Bughouse Square across from Newberry Library where queer hustlers did business with an endless line of cruising, circling cars. In addition, there were drug dealers who sold weed and speed. One evening a young black boy approached me as I was walking around the park. He pulled a small knife out of his pocket and said, "How much you asking? If you asking any less than $15 for blow jobs, you gonna make some of these whores mad." "Oh, I'm not doing that," I said. "I'm here to buy some weed."

"Sorry man," he said. "I thought you were working. See that tall guy over there? He's dealing," he said, putting his knife back into his pocket.

I left the park shaken but exhilarated. There was also the gay Newberry Theater on Clark Street and the lakefront, but that was all anonymous sexual encounters. My first gay bar experience requiring an actual conversation with another person came several years later. I intended to make Gold Coast my first gay bar, but it was not meant to be.

On a warm Friday night in 1975, I entered the Gold Coast bar. It was packed with men dressed in leather vests, leather pants with no ass, studded caps, and nipple clamps. It seemed like everyone had a tattoo. A Rod Stewart song was blasting. The cigarette and cigar smoke was overwhelming. I immediately became self-conscious and out-of-place. It was intimidating. I turned around and left. As I walked outside, I saw the Bistro. Music spilled out into the night each time the door opened. Is that *Fly Robin Fly* by the Silver Convention? I LOVE disco music! I walked in. The bartender yelled, "Hello! Welcome! What are you drinking?" The dance floor was packed. There was a big disco ball suspended among strobing lights. The dance floor was lit from below. There was fog that made everything dreamlike. The Bearded Lady was perched on a raised platform wearing a curious floral housedress and a silly little hat, furiously fanning himself as he danced. On the dance floor people were dressed in their disco finery but there were also people in various stages of "undress." I was smitten. I summoned up some courage and squeezed myself into the crowd and danced my butt off. I was offered a small brown vial by a guy dancing next to me. "Poppers?" he shouted." I just put my hands up in a "I don't know what that is" gesture. He unscrewed the vial cap, put his finger on my nostril and shoved the vial to my nose. "Take a hit!" he yelled again making a sniffing motion. OMG! My head exploded. My heart pounded and I thought I was going to collapse and make a scene. The guy put his arm around me as he bounced up and down to the music and yelled, "You alright sweetie?"

"What was that?" I shouted.

"What?" he asked.

"What was that you gave me?" I shouted again.

He cupped his hand around his ear and shook his head. He took my hand and motioned to follow him. We went out to the bar and he said, "I couldn't hear what you were saying. Don't you like poppers?"

"Never tried it before," I said. He bought me a beer. We talked. He was from a small town too. He took me to his apartment on Chestnut and Rush.

So, though my first gay bar was intended to be the Gold Coast, it ended up being the Bistro and I'm happy it was. Who knows how much of a more lengthy coming out process it might have been if I had just left the Gold Coast that night and never went anywhere else? I did eventually go to the Gold Coast and the pit. Went to other bars in that area too, Sundays, the New Flight, The Baton and another bar that was a Country Western bar. I don't recall the name. There was also the Machine Shop. Who doesn't love a glory hole?

It was a sad day when the Bistro closed. – Deschicago

————▽————

Chicago, IL

I don't know the name of the place and don't believe it even had one. Its exterior and windows were painted black and there was no visible signage or even entrance. It seemed like a cross between a juke joint and a last chance outpost. I was terrified going there because I remember hearing stories of patrons getting beat and left for dead in the parking lot, and it was rumored to be one of [John Wayne] Gacy's hunting grounds. There was nothing unusual inside. It felt vaguely exotic and sultry. I remember hearing disco music with an R&B and new wave feel. I think I was in there for no longer than three minutes. I walked very fast back to my car, got the hell out of there, and never went back again. The danger felt stronger than my curiosity. – Anonymous

————▽————

Fort Lauderdale, FL

My first gay bar visit was spectacular because the bar happened to be the Marlin Beach Hotel bar in Fort Lauderdale. I was there just after high school graduation in June of 1981. The crowd I ran around with and I had driven from Ohio to beautiful Florida for a boozy, beachy week. We stayed on "the strip," so the Marlin Beach was just a short walk from our hotel. I was out of the closet to my friends, so I made no secret of the fact that I was planning on going to the bar. I don't recall if I asked anyone to go with me or not, but I do remember that I was there by myself. I used the fake ID that I had to get in and buy myself a drink. This was oh-so-many years ago and I'm afraid I don't remember the specifics, but I do remember feeling as if 200 eyes were all devouring me as I walked through the place. At this particular place in time, the men here were most likely in their forties and up, so this teenager tried not to be wide-eyed and bumpkin. Must have been quite the sight! I was particularly amused by the windows that connected the bar to the pool and that you could watch the swimmers from the bar. Where the boys are indeed! – Brett Shingledecker

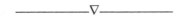

Chicago, IL

The first gay person I ever met was Greg. He just started where I was working and everyone was so glad to have us meet. The whole staff was straight. He was new to the Chicago area and was thrilled to meet me so we could go out-n-about. Greg decided to take me to the only lesbian bar he had heard of. It was CK & Augie's – where Charlie's is now. We arrived, Judy (always the bouncer) greeted us with a pool stick and pushed me aside to ask Greg for three picture IDs. She had no intention of letting him in. To everyone's surprise, he *actually had three* IDs, gave a swish towards Judy and we got to go in. Life was pretty darned good after that! – Anonymous

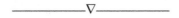

Indianapolis, IN

I was sixteen. Friends got me in. The doorman didn't ask any questions. We're sitting there for a while and one of the waiters came over and I said, "I was hoping you'd all be in these skimpy outfits." He said, "Honey, not with my body." That was my first gay bar. I don't remember the name of the bar, probably the Spike or something like that. – David Hardy

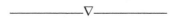

Chicago, IL

Chicago's Normandy Bar on Sheffield and Roscoe. My best friend and I were 14 and 15 years old in 1984 and we had heard that there was a "gay" area in Chicago. We rode the Belmont bus from the west side and noticed two well-dressed guys sitting next to each other, they were holding hands. We followed them to this small building under the L tracks with no windows. There was a bouncer who kept going inside, so when he was away, we ran in and went straight to the back of the bar. It was my very first time seeing a drag show and a room full of gay men. My friend and I eventually got fake IDs and went back often to all the bars in Boystown. – Ruben Cruz

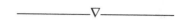

Orlando, FL

It was 1985 and I was 16 years old. The bar was the infamous Loading Dock in Orlando. Back then, they had a backroom for sex and the bathrooms all had glory holes. Now, let me explain who I was back then. I was a naive teenager whose only understanding of gay life was found in books from the library dated before 1960. I thought finding gay people would be hard and that my future as a gay man would be prostitution and insanity. That's what the books said.

I was shy and had a low self-esteem until I walked in that bar! Suddenly I had my choice of any man I wanted because they all wanted me. I was confused because my idealistic beliefs about love went right out the window. I didn't feel like I belonged in the gay community, any more than the straight world. I didn't understand "games" people would play. All I knew was that I loved the attention and desire. Oh, to be young again. – Bart L. Firsdon

———————∇———————

Blue Island, IL

It was this gay bar in Blue Island. I think I was 19. I was in BI for a friend's gallery opening and as often happened at that time I would just go to little dive bars with my friends as they were all 4 or 5 years older than I was and I could pass as older. I had come out shortly before I met this crew of artists and musicians that were my friends and they knew this little gay bar called The Edge (which is under a new name now) and we walked in and I was greeted by a twink in a thong dancing on a low stage. I got kicked out shortly after for being under age, but it was an exciting first taste. – James Conley

———————∇———————

Detroit, MI

The bar was called The Woodward Piano Bar, and while they had a piano, there was never a piano player. I had just graduated from college and purchased my first car, a Mustang convertible. I was a little nervous when I went in, but after I had a drink, Scotch and tall water, I relaxed a little. This very handsome older man sat next to me and bought me another drink. I ended up going home with him and spending the night at his place. I went back to that bar frequently. – Guy Sands

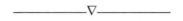

Los Angeles, CA

It was in North Hollywood. It was a piss-elegant dance bar. I was just twenty-one. I wasn't nervous about going there, more curious than nervous. A friend took me. I was amazed because it looked so normal. They just looked like regular people. I was expecting flamboyant hairdressers. It was 1972. It wasn't that long after Stonewall. They were feeling their way and discovering. The bar was Oil Can Harry's. It's still there. – Curt Miller

Baltimore, MD

I went to a bar called Mary's downtown in Baltimore city. It was downstairs in the basement. Flock wallpaper, red curtains, and I was living alone. It was 1967. I don't remember how I heard about it. It was older men. I was only 16. Met the owner Calvin Schumann, started dating him. He was a weatherman in Baltimore and Tallulah Bankhead's escort. I used to drive his Rolls Royce. – John Condon

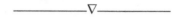

South Bend, IN

My first gay bar experience was terrifying. It was a place called the Image, in South Bend, IN. I was 19. I was renting shop space in the small repressed town in Southern Michigan where I had spent all my life so far. I was also dating a girl and working for a piano store in South Bend. The guy I rented my shop from had just divorced his nasty 4'6" 435lb wife, known around town as "Bubbles." He was in the process of "Coming Out," a very dangerous thing to do in the area at that time. He had heard about the Image, which had just opened. He did not have a car, so he asked me if I could take him down there. The plan was, I would drop him off and pick him up at 1am, outside the bar. When I came to pick him up, he wasn't there, so I decided to go in. I was very ignorant in sexual matters, but I was curious. (I was also unaware that though the drinking in Michigan was 18, it was still 21 in Indiana.) The bar was dimly lit with red and blue lights. All the walls were mirrored. There was all manner of hedonism and sexual activity going on. Quite a shock to me. Conjured up in my mind Peter Blume's painting of "The Eternal City," which gave me a sense of impending doom.

I sat down at a table. It wasn't long until this handsome long-haired hippie sat down next to me and offered me a drink. He started rubbing my crotch. I tried to hide my discomfort and reciprocate, but he picked up on it, sighed, arose, and walked away. I then spied my landlord, over in the far corner, in a state of ecstasy, being worked over by three very rotund drag queens. I wasn't about to pry him away. I got up and left. The parking lot was full of police cars. When I reached my vehicle, I was set upon by three huge officers. I was a scrawny kid. It was very intimidating. The first thing they asked me for was my ID. They passed it among them. By the look on their faces I quickly figured out that I WAS IN DEEP SHIT! They closed in tighter on me. "Do you like women?" asked one of the cops in a deep grumbly voice. I told them I had a girlfriend, explained the situation the best I could, and pleaded with them that this would ruin my life, etc. After a long lecture on the "Cancer of Homosexuality," they let me go. I was the excuse they needed to raid the place. How I avoided pissing and shitting myself, I'll never know. My landlord escaped the fracas and got a ride home. Next time I went by there it was boarded up. I've always felt bad about it. – Brian D. Thornton

Chicago, IL

It was a bar called Big Red on Clark somewhere near Belmont. A friend had to use a bathroom really fast and randomly went in to pee. He came out and said that the bathroom was covered with photos of naked men. I remembered where the place was and returned another day. I was young and naïve, and I met a hot muscular guy who had just gotten out of prison. He said he wanted me to teach him about college and he would teach me about the streets. – David Fink

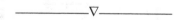

Eugene, OR

1979. It was called the Riviera Room, more commonly known as the Riv Room. I was working on the University of Oregon campus at the time and it was just common knowledge among most people that there was a gay bar and where it was. I was just getting divorced and I was so nervous about going into a gay bar, certainly of having sex with men. I'd never been in a gay bar. When I walked in, sitting at a table in a very dim backroom was a whole table from the university that knew me. And they all went, "Hi Tim! We wondered when you were going to be here." – Tim Parrott

————▽————

Boston, MS

CHAPS in Boston. It was a denim bar at the time and it was a place for meeting guys. It had a center bar and large barrels at one end filed with peanuts. So the floor was just covered with peanut shells. It was just part of the ambience of the place. It was fun. I was invited to go there to experiment and see what gay sex was like. Let's say it was a date. – Roy Alton Wald

————▽————

Milwaukee, WI

The first gay bar that I went to was named the Stud. It was the bar in a hotel on 5th Avenue off of Wisconsin Avenue, in Milwaukee. I was underage. I had friends who had heard that the Stud was a gay bar and that they didn't check ID cards. – Pat Cummings

————▽————

Greenville, NC

The Paddock Club in Greenville, NC, where I went to college. I wasn't out yet and went with two other gay guys. It was very strange at first being around that many gay people, but they were all so comfortable with themselves that it eased me a bit. – Bill

————▽————

Ann Arbor, MI

I recall the setting and circumstances vividly, as you'll see. Even after I came out at age 21, I was terrified by the prospect of walking into a gay bar. I didn't know what it would be like to enter a room in which I would not be a gay "solo act," reveling in my fabulousness, but one of a rainbow chorus. I secretly feared that, being among "my people," I would not measure up, and so I eschewed gay bars until my first boyfriend, a college love affair who we'll call M, almost literally forced me to have brunch with him at Autbar in Ann Arbor, Michigan.

This must have been August 2003. Having graduated from school that spring, I was due to leave town for Chicago, and he was staying in Ann Arbor. He worked at a local brewpub and was a celebrated member of their bar crew. He carefully avoided discussing our future plans, and so it never quite dawned on me that this would be our proverbial "last meal." I remember nothing of the interior of Autbar or anyone seated near us. As residual homophobia, I still flinched away from much about queer life. I ordered a veggie burger with cheese, and we chatted, ironically, about Madonna. M remained my galaxy and my guide to gayness, which placed a lot of pressure on one person; like so many cute rookies, swept off the queer market in a hurry, I placed too much emphasis on my first relationship.

The night ended with us at his place. He fucked me and then dumped me, as I lay naked in his bed, and fell asleep. I went to the bathroom and threw up the meal from the gay bar. I remember telling myself that I should just grab my shit and leave. But it also dawned on me that this would be my last chance to spend the night with a man who said he'd loved me for a year. So I slipped between the sheets and lay there crying for hours, tracing the cracks on his ceiling with my eyes and following their broken map. I pondered suicide. His shoulders rose and fell, and he occasionally murmured from a dream. When he rose that morning, refreshed, he drove me to my empty apartment, and I left Ann Arbor for good. – Robert W. Fieseler

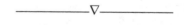

Calumet City, IL

It was in Calumet City, right on the state line between Illinois and Indiana. We went to a bar called the Our Way and ... they were playing *Gloria* and *Tainted Love* and *Hey Mickey*. – Honey West

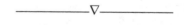

Atlanta, GA

I was 16 and my bisexual aunt took me to the Sweet Gum Head in Atlanta. It was a premier drag bar/disco. It was 1975 and the disco movement was happening. – Daniel Goss

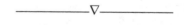

Chicago, IL

The first gay bar was in a basement on Broadway in Chicago in the early '70s. I went there with a young guy who picked me up in front of the theater across from Bughouse Square. I remembered the bar was very crowded, but we managed to find a table at the back. I was very nervous and overwhelmed by the crowd and the noise. I was not a drinker and I don't remember what I drank but after a few sips my head started swimming and pounding, I got scared and rushed out of the bar. I remember stumbling into a tall guy standing at the bar on the way out, I looked up at him and he greeted me with a hello and a smile. My date followed me out the bar and took me back to his apartment. – Chen Ooi

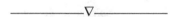

Boston, MA

Well, there's the first gay bar, when I wasn't aware that I was interested in women, and then there's the first lesbian bar ... I used to hang out with several gay men through high school and my early days of college, so I'd go out with them all the time to gay bars/dance clubs, but the story of my first lesbian bar experience is much more interesting!

After high school, I decided not to go straight to college. Instead, I moved to Boston with a friend who was going to BC [Boston College] and worked and lived in a tiny little studio apartment by myself. I took a part time job in a record/comic bookstore called Newbury Comics, and that's where I met the first lesbian I ever knew. She was my manager and we ended up working alone in the store together for almost every shift I had. We chatted constantly and I was very intrigued by her.

One night she asked me if I wanted to go out to a club with her after work. I was big into the club scene back home but hadn't been out to many places in Boston yet, so I eagerly accepted her invitation. I learned that the club was called Indigo and that it was a lesbian bar.

I was only 18 at the time, and I had never considered sleeping with women before, and wasn't really considering it then! I almost couldn't handle the looks I got as we entered and found our place in the club. In retrospect, I know that I was "fresh meat" to the women there, and that's how they were looking at me! It was terrifying and exhilarating all at once.

We drank and danced until the wee hours of the morning, and then we went back to my place. I strategically placed myself in my doorway, blocking her entrance, and she moved very close to me and leaned in for a kiss. I turned my face away but didn't pull my body away from hers. I told her I wasn't a lesbian, that I liked men. She smiled and chuckled, and gave me a look that I now know was the, "Yeah, OK" look! – Kit Welch

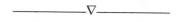

Chicago, IL

In 1980. It was on Rush (where a Swiss Chalet cheese shop would later go). I was in Chicago on business. I walked past the door about four or five times, then bolted in. I was very disappointed. In my head, I was imagining a bright place where people would be laughing and having fun. Instead, it was dark, with a small dance floor and men were either ignoring each other or staring intently at each other. I struck up a conversation with the guy next to me at the bar; he reacted as if I'd grabbed his crotch. Eventually, I just walked up to someone who was staring at me, asked him to dance, and then asked if we could go to his place. It was my first time having gay sex. It was awkward and he picked up on it. I admitted it was my first time and this seemed to boost his ego (why me? ... I flattered his ego, truth was that anyone close to my age and in reasonable shape would have fit the bill). I walked back to my hotel and wondered if I had possibly picked up an STD (VD then). – Bernard

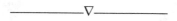

Champagne, IL

The first gay bar was in Champagne. It was the only one in town, and I was taken there by a couple of guys who had been my first (and only) three-way. I was 30 years old, as close to a virgin as possible, and the encounter was pretty much a failure. I was so far in the closet, mainly because this was the '70s, I was a newly-minted professor, and was sure that the truth would get me thrown out on my academic ass. Still, curiosity, and I'm sure a deep desire to be truthful and known for who I was (rather than speculated about) made me willing to go. But nerves. It turned out to be mild, and I went on my own reasonably regularly after that. I did get a phone call from a student, who called to say, "Just wanted to welcome you to the tribe." I pretended I had no idea what she was talking about. It takes a long time to get over cowardice. – Ripley

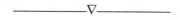

New York City, NY

A country bar in New York. I was wearing corduroy pants, and a plaid shirt; typically butch. Went well, met a cute Scarsdale boy, Bob, and we wrote songs together for a year. – Ralph Lampkin

—————▽—————

Chicago, IL

The 1st gay bar that I ever went to was the Lucky Horseshoe located in the gayborhood of Boystown right here in Chicago. I was 16 and with one of my gal pals from high school. We went on a Sunday afternoon and stayed all day. I was running around trying to find a boyfriend most of the day in addition to meeting and greeting the patrons inside. It was one of the most thrilling days of my life. I left there just wanting more. Needless to say, I was not a wallflower at that age and my gay bar career took off within a short time. – Natasha Douglas aka Joey Kiening

—————▽—————

State College, PA

It was called Mr. C's. In State College, PA. (My undergrad is from Penn State). It was small, almost a hallway, and most of the men were much older than me. It was pretty boring! – Melo

—————▽—————

New York City, NY

My first lesbian bar was the original Cubbyhole in the West Village (NYC). It was the mid-eighties, and there were very few bars for women in New York at the time – not at all my idea of being gay in the Big Apple. I was new to the city, an 18 year-old freshman at NYU. On Friday nights, my roommates would go off to clubs and straight bars, and I would hike over to Hudson Street in my little patent leather flats passing hopping gay bar after hopping gay bar. It bothered me that my choices were so few and so dimly lit. The Cubbyhole – again, the first iteration – was straight out of the '50s. It was dark with a hushed, subterranean feel to it complete with the requisite pool table in the back room. The signage on the door listed the

36

minimum age requirement as twenty-three and specified four to five types of ID you'd need to enter. There was also a bouncer – a scowling, leather-clad, physically imposing woman. A girlfriend of mine called her The Giant. I called her Liz, because that was her actual name and because she always let me in – though she sometimes rolled her eyes and even sighed at the sight of me. I was underage and dressed like the drama major I was. Liz clocked my comings and goings with various women and never batted an eye. On one occasion, though, I left the bar with someone to smoke a joint around the corner. After a minute, we were both staring down a furious Liz. "You want the bar to be shut down?" she said. Apparently, the Cubbyhole was always on tenterhooks with the authorities – probably as much due to sexism as economics and politics. We stubbed out our joint, and it was a while before I had the nerve to return. – Robin Chaplik

—————▽—————

Chicago, IL

The Daisy Patch, a juice bar on Broadway at Granville. It was the summer of '69. I was 18. I had heard about it from gay friends at Indiana University, where I was a freshman. It catered to an underage clientele; during the week it was a popular hangout for neighborhood straight kids, but on the weekend it "went gay." It had a dance floor in the back room, where we could dance to songs we played on a jukebox. The decor was Day-Glo flower petals. Very '60s. – Bill Williams

—————▽—————

New Orleans, LA

At the beach on Lake Pochatrain in New Orleans, I was so very fascinated by the gay people. I watched with intensity and wanted so much to join them. Finally, a butch named Lois and labeled "Big Lewey" approached me. She invited me out. She had to pick me up on the corner so my mother could not witness my first date with, as she would have referenced her, a "queer." I was only 16 but we went to Tony Bacino's. A flamboyant queen worked the bar and I had never had so much fun in all my life. Big Lewey had bleached blond hair and dressed in boy's clothing. Nonetheless, she would pick me up at school in a white Cadillac convertible.

I never experienced taking a ride in a paddy wagon until I came to Chicago. Sorry, I don't recall the names of the clubs that "Big Lewey" took me to. But I went for more rides than I can count. Once, I spent the night in jail because my new partner had pants on with a zipper in front. The strip search was done by an evil woman that scared me to death. – Janan Lindley

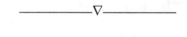

Minneapolis, MN

I was in my sophomore year at the U of M in Minneapolis when I heard about this bar called Sutton's. It was a block or two off Hennepin Avenue, the neon-lit row of theaters, strip clubs and 24-hour restaurants downtown. It said, "Sutton Place" in small black letters on the door, no neon, no windows, no welcome sign to say, "You made it!" to a 19-year-old long-haired kid with a fake ID that said I was 35 and six foot four.

"Sutton Place" was such a pretentious name, I thought, as if it were a gated community in the suburbs. It was actually three store-fronts. The first room had a long bar where I bought a 65 cent Budweiser and left the change of a dollar for a tip. We worked our way to another room lined with old vinyl booths where everyone was dancing in the middle. I think it was a Chinese restaurant at lunchtime. The third room was a bank by day. I remember setting down my bottle of Bud on a marble counter outside a gated teller's window. I think we danced in that room too. It's been a long time since I was 19, but that's what I remember. – Mark Abramson

Providence, RI

It was in Providence in 1986. It was referred to as "The No Name Bar" ... not because it was actually called that but because it actually had no name, no sign. I went with my straight galpal who was a regular and I dragged my 16-year-old sister and made her go as well. We all got in. I think 18 was the drinking age at the time. I was petrified and thrilled. – Mitchell Fain

—————▽—————

Calumet City, IL

My first gay bar was on 99th and southwest highway. It was owned by a gay woman, but it was kind of a straight bar, but the gay girls can use the side entrance and stay in the backside of the bar. We could not slow dance though. After a while I found out about a bar, or should I say a couple of bars in Calumet City. The Music Box and right next door was the men's gay bar, owned by Dick Bronkowski. So, I left Lill's and went to Calumet City. The rest is history. – Marge Summit

Long Island, NY

The first gay bar I went to was in Hempstead, Long Island. My family had just moved from Brooklyn, NY and I was 17. I was taking some college courses and going back and forth by bus. Hempstead was the connecting bus point and I had heard about this place from one of the people on the bus. It was a Mafia run establishment on one of the dark side streets, but I needed to check it out. Once inside there was a long bar with a bartender and a back room. They never asked for my ID and I took a seat at the bar near the front door. After about a half hour of sitting there a group of drag queens entered and I was quite impressed by the one who I later learned won a competition earlier that evening. I think she eventually picked up on my glances as she sauntered over and bought me a drink. Later that evening we left together and our relationship grew over the coming years. She eventually taught me that the T in LGBT also stood for Transitional. – Philip Raia

New York City, NY

I don't recall its name. It was in Greenwich Village in 1961, Tennessee Williams had a table across the dance floor from me. He and a very handsome youth kept eyeing each other but had no way of connecting. The whole crowd was involved in wishing the two could meet. Suddenly a man dancing crashed to the floor twitching and gurgling. The handsome youth, shoving everyone back from the stricken dancer, fell to his knees and did some medical motions to the fallen man. An ambulance arrived and took the dancer away. It was now perfectly proper for Mister Williams to send the heroic youth a drink and an invitation to his table. Alas, I had an office job to get to the next morning and had to leave without seeing what else transpired. – Robert Patrick

Milwaukee, WI

It was 1974 in Milwaukee. I can't even remember the name of the place. I met a gay man at work, Bill, where I worked in the stockroom at GE, 2nd shift, and we became friends. At first, I had no idea he was gay. Folks back then were much more guarded about something like that than today. He also had no idea that I was transgender. Eventually our occasional nights out after work, when we hit straight bars, led to a loosening of tongue after a few drinks, and Bill came out to me.

Admittedly, I was rather surprised because I had no clue whatsoever about Bill and he was the first gay man I had knowingly ever met in life. I was twenty years old at the time and the drinking age in WI back then was eighteen. Bill suggested we visit a gay bar next time we went out and for a moment I hesitated because I was afraid, but then asked myself afraid of what? I was transgender and attracted to women, but how did that make me any different from Bill who was simply trying to express himself in his own way, so I agreed.

So, after work on a Friday I went with Bill to his favorite gay bar to not only have a few a drinks, but to meet his steady beau, Gary, who was also a factory worker. The place was humming with hard core disco as we went in and for a while I was very afraid, but soon got over that. It was likely because of the stiffest drinks I ever had in my life, plus being with Bill, meeting Gary, and seeing how others in the bar all seemed so happy. I noticed some women in the bar too; some were queens, some were fag hags, as they were called back then, but all in all I had a really good time. I was quickly becoming educated in the whole scene and wondered if there was a place for me in it?

However, what I really liked was seeing Bill so free. In the straight bars Bill was always so reserved and guarded no matter how much alcohol he slammed, but not here! Bill was out and free and I just loved seeing him like this. We never went to a straight bar again after that night and even though the gay bar scene turned out not to be my path, I will always have Bill to thank for introducing me to Queerness in Milwaukee, back in 1974. – Denise Chanterelle Dubois

Detroit, MI

The first gay bar I ever went into was called the Casbah. It was a dyke bar on Warren Ave. in my home town of Detroit. I was accompanied by Michelle Crenshaw, a high school friend, and her girlfriend at the time, Devoria. It was in January 1975. I was in all my glitterkid/discoqueen finery and had just turned 18. The first song I got up and danced to was *Rock Your Baby* by George McCrae. When I went to the bar to order my first drink, the woman next to me clocked my nervousness, and offered to buy it for me. Her name was Carol and she was a "bulldagger," as we called them then. She wore a powder blue three-piece suit, slicked back hair, and a toothpick in her mouth. She told me that she would be honored to buy me my first drink in a bar, and I promptly ordered a Singapore Sling, which made her laugh out loud. When I got the drink, I knew why. Nasty, way, way too sweet, and if a drink could be gay, this was it. – Terence Smith aka Joan Jett Blakk

Chicago, IL

I had pretty much just arrived in Chicago to attend college. I was 18 ... right out of a Western New York farm town of 600 ... not very worldly. Everyone seemed to be talking about Berlin, an alternative/gay nightclub, in glorious tones. From what was being said, I was sure it was going to be this multi-leveled, cavernous warehouse with some kind of post war Germanic flair. Hell, I was probably expecting Joel Grey dressed as the Emcee from *Cabaret* to greet me at the door. To say I was excited about visiting this place would be an understatement. I had to stay in Chicago for most of winter break due to rehearsals – I was a theater student – and one night my best friend, who was from a small Appalachian town himself, decided it was time for us to go. We took the red line to Belmont and, soon enough, we were outside the door of the club. We were both underage and nervous as farmhouse colts, sure that we were going to be caught and thrown out. We took deep breaths, gathered up our courage, and rushed in, hoping that we were going to be lost within a swarming crowd and no one would suspect our youth. And ... not only was it the smallest space I had ever seen ... no one was actually there either! We must have hit the back wall within seconds ... the bartender and the two people he was serving, just stared at us with confusion and, most likely, humor. Surprised and dejected, we plopped our asses down, unceremoniously, on the edge of this stage piece and wondered what we should do. My friend really wanted a beer and I kept telling him to go get one, but that I wasn't going to get it for him. He kept on insisting that I should be the one to ask for it ... and I kept on refusing. Dejected, knowing that they would never serve us, we finally got up and left. So ... a lot of build-up and a huge let down ... and a pretty amusing story make up my first jaunt to a queer watering hole. – Brian Kirst

Chicago, IL

My first gay bar was my first bar. On my 21st birthday I took my girlfriends

to SPIN in Boystown in 2013. There happened to be a shower contest that night. After we enjoyed watching the boys compete, we hit every single gay bar in the neighborhood. I was desperate to see them all. Nowadays I don't even like to say, "gay bar." I call them bars, and everything else is a "straight bar." – Devlyn Camp

—————▽—————

Chicago, IL

The first gay bar I went to was Carol's Speakeasy. I was underage and my friend got me in on Friday dollar drink night. I had way too many screwdrivers and doubled down on the poppers. God help me. It was magical. Six months later I moved to Chicago, and like they say, the rest is history. – Terry Gaskins

—————▽—————

Carbondale, IL

Native New Yorker in Carbondale, IL. I must have been 16. – Jeffery Meskenas

—————▽—————

Chicago, IL

My first gay bar was Loading Zone on Oak St. It was my 18th birthday and all of my roommates from college were gone. I'd heard they did not card heavily, so I walked up there. I was so naive as to how to pick up a guy, I just went up to a guy, after a few shots of tequila, a white guy which I'd never been with before other than high school ... and asked him if he wanted to leave and go fuck. He was into it, so we went to his place on Delaware. – Malone Sizelove

—————▽—————

East St. Louis, IL

The first gay bar I went to was Faces in East St. Louis, IL. Truly a fun place in its day. A place to go and dance until four in the morning. I was underage but fake IDs were pretty easy to get. It also had a dark room downstairs where everything went on. Good times. I did drive my mother crazy coming in at all hours. – T.C. Burfield

——————▽——————

Rochester, NY

The first gay bar I went to was in Rochester, NY, my freshman year of college. That was when I came out. It was named Friar's. It was a neighborhoody type of bar and had a dance room along the side. It was mainly wood decor and the music of the late '70s. That's the first place I heard the B-52's and I vividly remember dancing to *Rock Lobster, Planet Claire*, and that's also where I heard Blondie for the first time with *Rapture*. I was a fresh faced young-un and the bar was mainly an "older" crowd. My schoolmates and I liked to go and dance and blow off steam from the conservatory where we studied music. – Leo Schwartz

——————▽——————

Houston, TX

My first gay bar was called Baja's. It was a tropical themed place in Houston. I take it Baja referred to Baja California. – Edward Thomas-Herrera

——————▽——————

Chicago, IL
East Orange, NJ

I had two gay bars enter my life at about the same time – one in Chicago, one in East Orange, NJ. It was 1980 and I was a freshman in college.

The moment I arrived at Northwestern, I quickly surrounded myself with a coterie of fresh-out-of-the-closet gay men of every ethnicity. We looked like a Benetton ad, if you remember those. Black, white, Asian, Jewish, Italian, Irish. We called ourselves "The Northwestern Army."

Every week, we would take our fake IDs – our college identification cards altered with an X-ACTO knife, a glue stick, and some Scotch tape – and take the El train from Evanston to Chicago to go to the Bistro for fifty-cent drink night. I think it was on Thursdays.

We never befriended anyone new there. And, rarely did any of us hook up with anyone. We had no self-esteem, or maybe we had too much! I still can't decide. Instead, we danced to *It Feels Like I'm In Love* by Kelly Marie and Lime's greatest hits and celebrated being gay and young and finally

43

being fully ourselves and surrounded by friends.

Meanwhile, on break back in New Jersey, I often would go to a place called Charlie's West in a rundown neighborhood to see a drag queen named Mimi.

Her signature number was *Where the Boys Are*. When she got to the line, "I wait impatiently," she'd make the up-and-down hand motion that is the international symbol for masturbation. Other drag queens did splits or twirled batons; Mimi jerked off to Connie Francis.

I remember two incidents that happened at Charlie's West: A butch lesbian bouncer threw out a straight couple who were making a big display of kissing on the dance floor. She said, "Do that somewhere else!"

And, I remember taking my friend's mother with me to the bar one night. She was very colorful and she liked to wear a different wig every day. Well, that night, she was wearing this big blonde cotton candy "do" that looked like it came from Dolly Parton's garage sale. After we'd been there a few minutes, a really hot guy came up to me. I was so excited as he approached because I was not used to that kind of attention. He leaned in really close to my ear, and over the disco din, said: "Is that your father?"
I only wish it had been. – Frank DeCaro

———————∇———————

WHEN DID YOU FIRST HEAR ABOUT AIDS?

Washington, DC

I was living in Washington, DC, in the period 1981-'86. There were unknown afflictions hitting gays, particularly in New York. I had friends in NY, one of whom became my first close AIDS death in 1984. I knew he was having a series of every tropical disease known to medicine in 1981 and beyond. He spoke of "my special interest" which he'd never specify, but it was easy to guess. I probably was less attentive in 1984 than I should have been because my mother was in a 9-month dying period from liver cancer at the same time (1984) and my attention was on her (and still needing to do my job in Washington). I think the designation of GRID happened after I knew something was going on, so my awareness came quite early. My own sex life became sharply curtailed in the early-to-mid 1980s and has been nearly non-existent for the past 10-15 years. (An aging body brings about changes, too.) – Anonymous

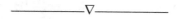

St. Louis, MO

1981, just barely into college. News reports on TV that were vague and scary. Being in the Midwest, St. Louis, there was just no information locally and no doctors that had any idea of what was going on. There was no gay group on campus for support (when one tried to form, strangely it was the Black Student Union that set up a table to get signatures to not allow funding for a gay group, and people were being a bit hostile towards the gay community at that time in general and on campus). This just made it more difficult to inquire or get more information, as people would give you "the look" as if you were part of "the problem." – Todd Jaeger

—————————▽—————————

Illinois

I first heard about AIDS long before it was called that. I first heard about it when it was mistakenly assumed to only afflict gay males. During that early period of time it wasn't even on the radar of conventional, mainstream medicine. It was only covered in gay publications such as the *Advocate* and other gay news mags.

As the crisis wore on, I became more and more concerned and fearful because despite research there was little enough known about its etiology, pathogens and transmission. Then after a short while it seemed that months and years went by where it was mentioned daily in the news. It came to the point where everyone knew an AIDS patient or knew someone who knew an AIDS patient. I remember the ghastly pictures of terminal AIDS sufferers which reminded me of pictures of victims of genocide in Nazi Germany. The AIDS crisis impacted me emotionally – galvanizing the movement as it was simultaneously decimating our numbers. It was a very dark time in LGBTQ history. – Paxton Anthony Murphy

—————————▽—————————

Texas

I remember hearing about AIDS on the news when I was about 13 or 14, so this would have been 1983 or 1984. Our family always had the TV on at the dinner table so my whole family was there. I don't remember my parents commenting on it at all, but I remember thinking that I was lucky I was so young because I knew that I was one of "them" and that I would be at a high risk for contracting it. It terrified me. – Brent

—————————▽—————————

Chicago, IL

I was going to college in Redlands, I had chosen it because, California, free from parents and judgement, lots of gay people because you know … California. I started my 1978 college year here after receiving my associate degree in Communication. Fast forward, I was now very out, and reading the *Advocate*, the *New York Native,* and, of course, when the first articles started showing up in 1981. Hidden in the back of the papers and buried.

My boyfriend at the time, Mike _____, worked for *Gay Life* and started to talk more and more about it, and was worried because he knew I had been, well let's say active in LA, and did not miss a chance to be with people. As the numbers started to rise in LA, and NYC, and San Francisco and then Chicago, of course my concern was, "Well, when is my time up?" And then, those around me started to get sick, and die, and then it seemed like it was never going to let up. The time was dark and sad as we watched those around us die. It seemed like there was no way to stop it or get the help we needed. It certainly was not coming from the government. – Dean Ogren

————∇————

San Francisco, CA

It wasn't called AIDS when I first heard about it. My first memory of thinking about it was in the early 1980s. There were articles in the B.A.R. newspaper in San Francisco about a gay disease that affected gay people and Haitians. Reading about it in the bar for the first time is when I became aware of something going on in the gay community with people getting sick. – Steve

————∇————

Chicago, IL

It wasn't called AIDS at that time. The first acronym I remember is GRID – Gay Related Immuno-Deficiency. The first person I knew who got sick was in my bowling league. Word went around that he had a stomach disorder, but I found out it was pneumonia. It all happened in a matter of weeks and suddenly he was dead. I can't put an exact date on when this occurred, but my recollection is late 1982. – Tom Chiola

————∇————

Illinois
West Lafayette/Lafayette, IN

I believe I was in middle school. I was briefly aware of what was called a "gay cancer" but was too young to really pay attention. In high school, I was versed on how AIDS was transmitted, but again, too young and too isolated to really have any activism around the disease. It wasn't until college that I really became aware of the proximity of AIDS in my life.

One of the friends I made while hanging out in front of Sportsmen's had come onto tough times and needed a break. I let him crash on my couch for a couple of weeks to get his life together. We had plenty of heart to hearts in that time. In one of those conversations, he revealed his positive status. I knew life would be an uphill battle for him. After him, I met others, older men usually, who hadn't been in the first or second wave of affected people but didn't escape the dormancy period of the disease. I spent the next few years watching some of the pillars of the community crumble and slip away as AIDS took its toll again.

Those experiences pushed me towards being a safer sex advocate and definitely had me pull in the reins a bit on casual sex. Typing all that, I didn't realize how much AIDS had affected me beyond a community reference. Friends long past, I miss you and hope you traveled well into the afterlife. – Cody Las Vegas

—————▽—————

Chicago, IL

As a junior in high school. (1984). I was taking college level biology and the teacher brought up the subject of "gay cancer," we followed the rise of AIDS the entire year. – Mike Martinez

—————▽—————

New York, NY

I had a boyfriend and we went to Ty's. We were sitting at the bar and he tells me he had been diagnosed with G.R.I.D. At the time it was G.R.I.D. Gay Related Immuno-Deficiency. At that time they really didn't know that much about it. Then, if you've ever seen *Longtime Companion*, I used to go to Fire Island and just like the character in that story, I was sitting outside somewhere and opened up a paper and read about it, that's exactly what happened. We heard about this disease that was spreading in the gay community. They later changed it to AIDS. But the first time I heard about it, it was G.R.I.D. and I didn't know what it was. But my boyfriend said he was diagnosed with that. It scared me and he said he didn't think there was any cure for it. – Randy Warren

—————▽—————

When did you first hear about AIDS?

San Francisco, CA

The first time was probably from my partner at the time. Jim had heard about this thing called Gay Flu and he was a big radio nut. He began voice recording what was coming out of mostly the newspapers about the epidemic. There wasn't much in the medical journals yet. The appearance of this strange pneumonia called pneumocystis carinii in New York. He started doing thirty-minute segments on cassette tape and putting it on an answering machine. Then advertising it as an information source. That was the first time I heard about it. Then the epidemic hit San Francisco. Then I became involved. – Bill Barrick

——————▽——————

Chicago, IL

I think it was sometime in 1982, but really didn't pay much attention, since it seemed all centered in NYC and San Francisco. – Jack Delaney

——————▽——————

Palm Springs, CA

Around 1980, after the first few people were reported. I heard about it on TV. – Randy

——————▽——————

Laguna Beach, CA

It was at the Tiki Hut, they had posters about it. Watch out for the gay plague, the gay disease. – Great Big D

——————▽——————

USA

I was 15. We walked into the grocery store and I saw the display of *People* magazines with Rock Hudson on the front. The photo of him was not flattering. I don't remember what the copy on that cover said but I just knew, like a feeling in the pit of my stomach, this was something that was bad – something bad that could affect me and something that was just beginning. My whole world tilted at one glance of a magazine cover.

Probably because I knew that I was different and I wondered if I was different in the way that Rock Hudson was. Was being different deadly? – Matt

————————▽————————

Chicago, IL

A *Chicago Tribune* article on a mysterious "cancer" targeting gay men. – Steve Lafreniere

————————▽————————

Madison, WI

It was a very slight murmur, a tale of trouble far away. I worry a lot, but at this time I didn't worry about safe sex. I didn't use a condom with the guy I was seeing in 1981-1982. When I moved back to Boston in 1982, I decided that I should practice only safe sex, and I've kept to that.

I didn't know people dying of AIDS until 1984. The first was my cousin, a hemophiliac. Within a few months my good friend and co-worker from college died; he'd been a born-again Christian and couldn't explain his impulses for anonymous sex with men in the bushes. Next came the brother of my cousin who had died, also a hemophiliac. Then friends from the Boston Gay Men's Chorus, and a former roommate. I joined a MAC study [Multicenter AIDS Cohort Study] but for years declined to learn my status. – Rick

————————▽————————

Lima, Peru

I think it was elementary school. As a class we were reading a story about poverty in Africa and the main character mentioned AIDS. I didn't get it, I thought it was like the word "aid," it took me several years to understand the gravity of the condition and even more to find out the impact it had on the LGBT community. It's kinda cool that they taught me about it so early on, though. I think it fully dawned on me when I was told Freddie Mercury died of AIDS. I was like 13 years old and he had died over a decade before, but I had grown up on his music, so it still struck me. – Robb

————————▽————————

Indianapolis, IN

In an article in *Newsweek* in 1983. – Corey Black

————————▽————————

New York, NY

I cannot remember the actual date. I had escaped Virginia to go to art school in NYC in 1982 and it was somewhere around then. I do remember a friend being hospitalized with what they, at the time, called "Gay Bowel Syndrome." They hadn't even come up with GRID yet. – Bud Thomas

————————▽————————

Chicago, IL

It was in the early '80s. I was in a local gay bar and people were talking about this "gay cancer" that had started to pop up around the country. – Kbro

————————▽————————

Atlanta, GA

I first heard about AIDS while living in Atlanta. It was actually called GRID then. My partner at the time began getting sick. Not long after we were both a couple of the first two diagnosed positive when we tested there anonymously. We were given numbers at the Atlanta Gay Center on 15th Street. – Tom

————————▽————————

New York, NY

I grew up in NY. The early '80s (I was a junior in high school) when the news broadcasted the closing of the NY bathhouses (I didn't know what a "bathhouse" was), due to the "gay cancer." – Frederick

————————▽————————

Chicago, IL

My best friend was a doctor in the ER at Cook County. She would tell me stories of gay men who came into the hospital with strange symptoms and diseases. No-one knew what it was or even if was contagious. This was sometime in the early 1980s before I even heard a name for the disease. – Anonymous

———————▽———————

Chicago, IL

It, like most else for someone who came of age in the 1960s, happened to me in real time. It was the summer of 1981, but they didn't call it by that name yet. It was "gay cancer." Then it became HTLV 3, then HIV/AIDS. The Chicago gay press covered it in more detail after it became news, but the lack of solid information and answers made it very scary and frustrating for years. – Anonymous

———————▽———————

Chicago, IL

I heard about AIDS when it was first called GRID. I worked as a volunteer at Howard Brown Health Center. – Bob

———————▽———————

New York, NY

My roommates and I lived in Manhattan and got the *New York Times* delivered to our door. We passed it around over breakfast and coffee each morning. One morning in June or early July 1981 there was an article – I think it may have been the first ever written – about this mysterious condition that was showing up in homosexuals in NY, SF, and LA, and that some had died. So, I was aware of it from the time it first went public. And pretty soon, there were public meetings in NY of mostly gay men. – John D'Emilio

———————▽———————

Madison, WI

1991. I was peripherally aware that AIDS existed when I was young, just from the news on TV, but no one in my life talked about it. I knew it was bad and I knew it meant death, and because of the passing remarks made by my father, I thought that people with AIDS deserved it. It wasn't until Jeffrey Dahmer was caught in 1991 that I became acutely aware of AIDS and homosexuality, and those two things were inextricable from each other as far as I was concerned. Because he lived in Milwaukee, Dahmer got continuous coverage in the Wisconsin press, and I was horrified and transfixed. AIDS was constantly brought up in articles about him. I mentioned AIDS at the dinner table once and my father was furious. It was also around this time that I started to suspect that my father was wrong about people with AIDS, but it still took years for me to unravel the truth about AIDS and homosexuality. It really wasn't until MTV's *The Real World: San Francisco* came out in 1994, with Pedro Zamora front and center, that I was able to really understand the toll of the AIDS epidemic and fully humanize people with HIV/AIDS. – Shane K.

————————∇————————

Los Angeles, CA

I was living in Los Angeles and my friends and I became aware of "gay cancer" via the newspaper (*Los Angeles Times*). I had been working as a press secretary for the No On 6/Briggs Initiative campaign, which we had just won, so I know it was November 1978 and my first reaction to the news was that it was yet another attack on the gay community, another attempt to smear us, further isolate us and otherwise stigmatize us. We were scared, too. – Bo Young

————————∇————————

Hickory, NC

Our area has a local AIDS awareness chapter which goes out into the community and speaks about AIDS and its dangers and how to prevent it, etc. During a health class in my freshman year of high school (2001) they came to talk to us and hand out safe-sex packets. Granted, at the time, there were only three openly gay students, they talked to everyone about the risks and dangers. – Christian Bane

————————∇————————

San Francisco, CA

Star Pharmacy 18th and Castro, there visiting, saw a flier about gay cancer.
– Virgil

——————▽——————

USA

I was watching the news in 1981 and they reported about a cancer that was
popping up in gay men in New York and San Francisco. I had a second
cousin who was gay and lived in San Francisco, he was the first person I
knew personally who died from AIDS. – Eric Kuznof

——————▽——————

Joliet, IL

It was on flyers around the bar, they talk about the new gay cancer that was
spreading. It was known as HTLV3 or GRID at that time if I remember
correctly. In 1985, I moved to San Francisco after working in Yellowstone
for a season. It was here that I learned about AIDS first hand. Meeting
people who had been diagnosed. Up till that point I did not know anyone
personally. I took part in the candle light march on City Hall in Nov. of
'85. I stayed there for three days getting petitions signed, taking my turn
being chained to the Federal Building and making signs of the name of
those that had already passed. They were taped to the side of the federal
building.
    Long before the red ribbon, we passed out a small piece of green
ribbon that was safety pinned to a small piece of chain that was bent to
have a hook on the end. If I remember correctly it represented breaking the
bureaucratic pain that was holding back the money that was needed for
research. I still have one of those pins all these years later. It is a piece of
gay history that I can proudly say I was part of. – Jim Hensley

——————▽——————

Milwaukee, WI

AIDS crept into the public consciousness during a time when I was very
sexually active but I was completely scared of pregnancy, so I was fanatical
about condoms. I kept going to planned parenthood and asking for

sterilization and they, very paternalistically, told me I would change my mind and I couldn't get sterilized unless I already had kids or got married and got my husband's permission! And it didn't occur to me till years later that having threesomes with male couples or bisexual men could have exposed me except for my condom use. So, in retrospect, Planned Parenthood may have saved my life. I do remember the first time I heard some asshole in a bar tell some gay jokes (and not in a good way) and how it was like a slap in the face, hearing the ugliness in the jokes. I read *And the Band Played On* and that is when it hit home to me. Later I worked at the AIDS Resource Center in Milwaukee. On a side note, I will never forget when my brother in law came in as a client. We were shocked to see each other and it was very awkward. I knew he was enthusiastically bisexual, but I had not known he was sick. He died of AIDS related illness a year or two after that. – Anne

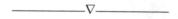

Ottawa, Ontario, Canada

An article in a magazine at my doctor's office, and given that I moved from there in 1984, either that year or 1983, in terms of discussing a mysterious ailment. I can't recall if it was still being called GRID then. I would have been 16/17, and though I wasn't aware of my own sexuality, I certainly had gay friends by then. – Tim Murphy

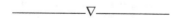

Sydney, Australia

I was a producer/broadcaster with Gaywaves, a gay radio program that broadcast from Broadway (Sydney, Australia) and heard about AIDS when it was referred to as GRID. Having trouble recalling the exact year but was very late 1970s. I remember we did a news broadcast that was very controversial because many gays believed the news about GRID was a homophobic conspiracy. – Susan H

—————▽—————

Santa Cruz, CA

1982, an old roommate moved to San Francisco and called me about gay cancer. – Glen

—————▽—————

Chicago, IL

About 1996, I had heard about it but after being diagnosed with it, I really understood what it meant. – Joseph G

—————▽—————

Chicago, IL

I was in high school. It was making the news in the mid-eighties. I recall news footage of Ronald Reagan making a comment about "fags" and AIDS when he thought the mics were off. It was horrible. – Chicago T

—————▽—————

Los Angeles, CA

1981 when reading LA newspapers at my employment at the Bulletin of Atomic Scientists where we regularly read newspapers from all over. Of course, it was not called AIDS. – Anonymous woman

—————▽—————

San Francisco, CA

I think around 1982 but not mainstream until '83 when friends started getting sick and dying quite suddenly. – James S

—————▽—————

Stockton, CA

1981. A small news story appeared in the *San Francisco Chronicle* about a new disease that was just affecting gay men. – Dale Williams

—————▽—————

Portland, ME

I don't really remember when I first heard of AIDS, but it must have been in the early '80s, from an occasional news broadcast. Shortly after that I moved overseas for a few years and heard about AIDS mainly in US news magazines. When I returned to the US in 1987 I was amazed how big the AIDS story had become – it seemed like it was all over the news, constantly. – Jeff

——————∇——————

Elk Grove Village, IL

Very early 1980s. Can't recall whether I initially learned about AIDS through friends or the news or work.

I was working in public relations for the American Academy of Pediatrics, which was then headquartered in Elk Grove Village, a Chicago suburb beyond O'Hare. The AAP was participating in meetings at the US Centers for Disease Control – and we encountered AIDS activists in the Atlanta airport who were handing out leaflets and information cards. "The government needs to do something about AIDS," shouted a protestor. "We agree," one of the pediatricians replied in an equally loud voice. Later, at a national pediatric conference, we handled a flurry of national media attention when we released official guidance for pediatricians and families.

Who was my first friend or family member who got sick? I recall a small bunch of guys in the circle of people I knew – one-by-one I started hearing their news, and I mostly recall the whispers and the worry and, ultimately, the grief.

"When did you first hear about AIDS?" This is such an evocative question; thank you for asking it. Time and sorrow, I've come to realize, have a way of blurring my memories. – Michael Burke

——————∇——————

Chicago, IL

There had been rumors floating around about some kind of disease that was coming out of Vietnam in the late '70s, but I don't think it was the same thing. I had by that time begun a relationship that eventually lasted 40 years before my partner died of Parkinson's-related dementia. We were exclusive almost the whole time, but I had made the huge mistake of straying early on – just once, but it was unprotected. So, when the stories started to come out, I was terrified that I might have it. Fortunately not, but I never again had sex outside our relationship. And now that I'm alone, I'm too old to be interesting to anyone, and I still don't know what it's like to have sex with a condom! – Ripley

—————▽—————

St. Louis, MO

July 1981. I heard they had found a cancer in gay men on TV. Suspect was a pilot that was visiting in SF, CA. Health authorities thought it was being transmitted by monkeys, but couldn't make the connection with the pilot and monkeys. Think they called it GRID? – Robert

—————▽—————

Indiana

Sometime when my sister was at the same hospital as Ryan White. – Daniel

—————▽—————

Seattle, WA

It's weird that I don't remember exactly – it must have been on the news. But what I do remember was that I used to walk by the newsstand on the Seattle waterfront and kind of dare myself into buying the *Seattle Gay News*, which I finally did in the spring of … 1982? I was in 7th grade? 8th grade? And the main headline was about the first case of AIDS diagnosed in Seattle. – David Zinn

—————▽—————

San Francisco, CA

I was in San Francisco when the rumors started. I would say that I became most acutely aware of the disease in the mid to late '70s. – Brian

—————▽—————

Iowa

After watching the movie *Philadelphia*. I was probably 21 or so, in the closet, and still homophobic to an extent. – Anonymous

—————▽—————

Cardiff, Wales, UK

To be honest, the AIDS epidemic never really hit the Welsh Valleys and even if it did no one heard of it. The valleys are very insular and no one travels far, even now. I heard whispers of something going on in London on the Cardiff scene, but I'd never known anyone who died of AIDS, so it didn't really hit home until much later. In around 1992 my brother started dating someone who was HIV positive and I read everything I could get my hands on. – Nephy Hart

————▽————

Perth, Australia

I can't remember when I first heard about AIDS. I was in junior high school when it first reared its ugly head. There was a very scary advertising campaign here featuring the Grim Reaper and a bowling ball. It is actually quite legendary here. But it scared the crap out of me. I didn't meet anyone with HIV until many years later. – Mansfield

————▽————

Chicago, IL

Some friends and I took turns hosting orgies. The acid was in the punch. The deeper you dipped the ladle in it, the higher you got. Early in 1981, an orgy friend got sicker than shit. Night sweats and severe pneumonia-like problems were two of his many symptoms. The doctors couldn't explain it. He died. A couple of other friends came down with the same illness. The orgies stopped. Then we heard some gay men in Los Angeles had died from a similar disease. Was it the acid? The poppers? Surely, it wasn't the sex. The first name for it was gay-related immune deficiency, GRID. Within the next few years, most of my orgy friends died. – Ron Fritsch

————▽————

Chicago, IL

I was with my partner, Arthur, at the time. He came home to tell me that a friend of ours was in the hospital. Frank had some sickness the doctors couldn't diagnose. It was puzzling to them. Frank didn't last too long. To my embarrassment, I couldn't visit him in the hospital or attend his funeral.

Arthur was furious with me. I just was so frozen, I couldn't function. Eventually, I did start attending classes at Howard Brown Clinic. I worked as a volunteer there for three days a week, doing various functions such as lab testing, answering the switchboard, and data entry. Howard Brown was very helpful to me in overcoming my fear. – Peter

————————▽————————

Binghamton, NY

1981, about the time John Paul II was shot. One of the faculty at Binghamton University was "taken ill." The administrator of the Catholic Hospital he was in put a sign on his room door that said something like "Do not enter. You don't want what this patient has." Another faculty member confronted the administrator – a nun in full habit no less! – in the hallway and Read. Her. Out. Shouting, tears, near violence. The nun backed down. AIDS was suddenly very real. – Fester

————————▽————————

Evanston, IL

I remember an article in the gay newspaper while in college, and they called it GRID. I wouldn't believe it for quite a while because I thought somebody had conjured it to create a scare about gays. It wasn't until I moved to San Francisco in 1985 that I first met people who were suffering from it. I must admit, I spent quite a bit of time in disbelief; it felt like a frame-up. We didn't call it fake news back then, but I might have called it fake news if it happened now. – Alec Holland

————————▽————————

Chicago, IL

I think I'd heard people talk about, or made mention of, "gay cancer" on television in the '80s when I was a kid, but I remember first really hearing about it while watching *The Golden Girls*. That episode, which I still think is very powerful, did a lot of dispel the stigma that was so prevalent, and educated me on what AIDS was, and that it wasn't some punishment for gay men. It was years before I heard a President or national government representative talk about it openly. – James Conley

————————▽————————

Chicago, IL

I'm pretty sure I began to learn about AIDs through the news media in the
'80s when I was finishing grad school. Then I began to see the plays that
focused on AIDs – *Falsettos, Jeffrey, The Night that Larry Kramer Kissed Me* –
and I began to understand AIDs at a deeply emotional level. The single
moment when I understood most powerfully the scope of the AIDS
epidemic was an afternoon when a few panels of the AIDS Quilt were
displayed at my college in the '90s. I volunteered to be one of many faculty
reading the names of AIDS victims from a podium beside the panels. I
think each of us read for only 15 or 30 minutes. Still, the drumbeat of name
after name after name after name after name – it shook me to
my core. Even now, as I write this brief memory, I cry. – Bill

Illinois

1982. I suppose I heard about it along with the rest of the mainstream
world, after this mysterious cancer had been discovered. I do remember it
being called "GRID."

I was 7 or 8 years old, so it did not touch me personally for many years
afterwards. I can say that I was raised very Catholic and sheltered and the
idea that this was God's punishment for sin was taken as fact in my
household. I do remember thinking that was bullshit, though. One of the
first sparks that the religious indoctrination and ignorance that shaped my
early development were just a load of bullshit. – Kirk Williamson

New York, NY

Around 1980. I had been living in New York City in the late '70s. NYC was
a sexual Disneyland in the disco years of the '70s and I used to go to the St.
Mark's Baths and the live sex shows at the Adonis Theatre, with headliners
such as Jack Wrangler. I celebrated St. Valentine's Day at Studio 54 in 1979.
But then people started getting sick with what was first called "gay cancer"
and GRID. – David Clayton

Chicago, IL

My cousin Karl was diagnosed early on and I remember my parents picking me up from the airport and telling me. This was very early on and not much was known about it. My Dad said something like, "Your cousin Karl is a homosexual and, as a result of that, has AIDS." It sounds harsh now but at the time I think that was the thought. I must have heard about it before as I remember correcting my father and saying it was because of unsafe sex, not because he was homosexual that he had AIDS. I also don't know if he really had AIDS at that time or was just HIV Positive. After this, he came to visit, and I remember my parents having a conversation about what to do with dishes and other things he would use. Not much was known about how it was transmitted at this time and they were still just small town folks. Looking back with what we know now it sounds naïve but then, that they would welcome him in our home and simply try to figure out how best to handle it was lovely. – Mike Uetrecht

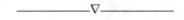

Florida

Late 1983. I had an older friend (platonic) that was 42 and became my mentor. He educated me on gay history, people, heritage, and the "new cancer" that gay men were contracting. Living in Florida at the time, I heard about it hitting the Haitian community as well. The joke at the time was, "What's the worst part of getting AIDS? – Convincing your mother you're Haitian." I never found AIDS jokes funny. – Eric Andrews-Katz

Chicago, IL

True story. I was in the pit (downstairs at the Gold Coast). I heard two guys talking about a new disease happening in San Francisco and New York. I didn't change my promiscuous behavior. – David Plambeck

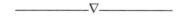

Chicago, IL

I think it was in the Cross Hall at Man's Country where they had the pictures of Franny and nurse Wanda where we were talking this or that and someone mentioned this disease going around with gay men; that was in

1981, that I learned of the seriousness of this news. – Scott Strum

———————∇———————

Atlanta, GA

It was the Rock Hudson *Newsweek* cover (1985). – Roy Felts

———————∇———————

Chicago, IL.

The first image that comes to mind is a *Time* magazine cover about the outbreak. This would have been mid-1980s. I may have heard something about it before, but it's that magazine cover that comes to mind. – Rick R. Reed

———————∇———————

Chicago, IL

I first heard about AIDS in 1981. I was working as an instructor at a gay gym in Chicago called The Body Shop at the time. It was all we were talking about, this mysterious thing that you could get that would kill you. We'd hear about a friend we hadn't seen in a while, only to find out that he had died. Died?? From a cold? That's what it was like. If you got a sniffle, you began to worry. As I write this, names and faces pass through my mind, and it is daunting. – Terence Smith

———————∇———————

Highland Park, IL

I will never forget this. I was in my daffy aunt's kitchen. She was making tea for my father, herself, and I. We were seated at the kitchen table as she busied herself putting on the tea kettle. She was telling us about an article she read about a gay cancer, that gay men were dying at a very high rate. I was 16 at the time, I thought it was the most bizarre thing she read. She was known to come up with bat shit crazy crap, so this would be one more item to that pile. I really thought she was full of shit! Because at the time I was reading *Drummer* magazine, *Blue Boy*, and *Playgirl*, and any other gay porn mag I could lay my hands on with big cocks in it, and fiction. *Drummer* was my favorite. I would go to the news stand in Evanston IL and go to the back southwest corner of the store. That's where all the gay porn mags were kept. I was not reading about this gay cancer in my magazines, so she was full of shit. No, sadly she was right. It took a few months for it to pop into *Drummer*.

So, the question is why is a 16-year-old girl reading *Drummer* magazine? Well a few days before my 16th birthday, Bill (not his real name) came over to my house, he lived a couple blocks away. We were in my garage. He was the first boy I ever kissed. We were making out, he put my hand to his hard cock in his pants. It was the first time I ever did anything like this. He asked me to give him a blow job. I had no idea what he was asking. No clue zero!! I did not say no but that was it, I had to have him leave. I was embarrassed I did not know what a blow job was. I opened the garage door and he took his leave. A few days later I asked my friend Lisa what a blow job was. She said you suck his cock. I was disgusted, piss comes out of that thing! I am supposed to suck on it? That is dirty, why would you put something that piss comes out of in your mouth?? I needed to do research, on the topic. Pre-internet meant a lot more leg work. So, I headed out to learn about how to give a blow job. I found gay porn magazines were a great way to learn the ins and outs of cock sucking. I had this edge above my peers in my knowledge of gay sex and what was going on in the gay community. – Jake Cohn

——————▽——————

Chicago, IL

I couldn't have been more than 4 or 5 years old when I first heard about AIDS, but I was born in the mid-'80s so it was something both of my parents saw happening in real time. My mother and I were walking down the street to my grandparents' house when we saw an abandoned, used condom on the ground to which I was warned: "Don't touch that if you ever see one or you'll get AIDS. It's a disease no one has survived because there is no cure." Years later, I certainly forgave the hyperbolic warning I received about HIV/AIDS because at that age a gray area isn't something a toddler can deal in very well, and also because my mom was acting with the information that was available at the time, fresh out of the crisis. What really surprises me, looking back, is how people have let their views on HIV/AIDS stagnate despite the breakthroughs in science. Fear is so powerful. – Jordan

——————▽——————

Long Beach, CA

I worked as a record store clerk from 5/78 until 2/80 at Licorice Pizza in Long Beach, California. My store manager, Michael Hayes, and I were about the same size, 5'7", 130 pounds. I was 16 when I started working there and he was 26. He was gay and our assistant manager, Siouxzen Smith, was a lesbian. During May 1979, Michael complained that he felt like he had the flu. By July, he went out on disability. I passed him on Broadway Ave. in the gay area during August. It was 90 degrees and he was wearing an electric blue puffer jacket unzipped with his long blond hair flowing around him in the breeze. I said, "Hey Michael, how are you?" He replied, "Awful, I am so sick, I can't get rid of this cough." Then he turned and walked away. It was unlike him. The smiling, socializing, Michael was gone and in his place was a skeletal young man who looked gravely ill. I walked into work two months later to hear Siouxzen crying, "Michael is dead. He died of pneumonia." He was 27. Other men were getting sick with similar symptoms during the late 1970s but we didn't know yet that it was HIV.

I would drive up to visit Bill and Don in San Francisco at least every other month and stay with them for the weekend in their apartment on Eureka Ave. in the Castro. Bill and I would go dancing at the I-Beam or the Rawhide, but sometimes we just met friends for drinks at Badlands. Across the street from Badlands and down the block was Star Pharmacy. I can't remember exactly when this occurred, but it was sometime between 1979 and 1981, Bill took me over to Star Pharmacy and in the window was a typed note with two Polaroids of a man showing his bare chest and forearms and another of his back. He was covered in Kaposi's Sarcoma. We didn't know what it was until a year or so later. The note begged people to be aware that a handful of the men in the Castro had this disease and no one knew what it was or if it was contagious. The man who posted these pics of himself was Bobbie Campbell. Bill turned to me and said, "Order beer in a bottle. Watch the bartender open it. Don't let the bottle out of your sight. No mixed drinks. We don't know how this is being spread." Bill was like my older brother. Almost 11 years older than me, he was the son of my immigrant parents' first friends in the US.

Back home in Long Beach around this same time period, Andy and John moved into the Broadway neighborhood from the Castro in San Francisco into the four-plex apartment building that sat next to my friend David's On Broadway Hair Studio. I was sitting at the dinner table talking with Andy when John came home early from his job at Akai Electronics. His voice was whiney and he complained of stomach cramps. What Andy told me years later was that John was battling amoebic dysentery. John was 6'2" and underweight. He had the beginnings of Kaposi's sarcoma with small brown cigar shaped lesions on his face and arms. I was married with a husband at the time and a few months after meeting Andy and John, Chris who lived across the street from them, had his annual gay Thanksgiving meal in his large apartment. It was the Friday after Thanksgiving. We lined up several tables and decided to do our version of Norman Rockwell's Thanksgiving. As the only woman, I put on an apron and held the platter with the turkey as my husband stood behind me with the carving knife and fork. Everyone held up their glass and said, "cheers!" The picture was taken. I had a 5"x7" copy of it hanging on my refrigerator, dog eared, faded, and torn, for three decades. I am the only living person left in that photo. – Paul Regalos Urban (Born cisgender female during 1962. Transitioned to male at 26 during 1988)

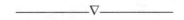

Davis, CA

First heard about **GRID** living in Davis, CA. Was out and politically and sexually active and started reading about this strange disease that was killing gay men in New York, LA, and SF. I remember the fundamentalists with their slogan, "Got Aids Yet" later on. I'm guessing this was about 1983? The whole beginning was scary but also a case of ignorance is bliss coupled with bouts of terror and inevitability. – Paul Harris

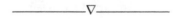

Chicago, IL

I first learned of AIDS while attending AGLO [Archdiocesan Gay and Lesbian Outreach]. It was a Catholic ministry for gay people in Chicago. My residence was 3330 N. Kenmore apt 3-B where I lived May 1988 to May 1990. There were two apartments on each floor. A & B. A gay man older than I lived across the hall. I knew little of him. And there was Anna. A crabby old lady in 1-A. She always grumbled at "the queers" when she would see us. The apartment was very nice. I was in the AGLO Men's Chorus. We were practicing in some church basement in Boystown. My best friend at the time, Michael Gillespie, took me into the men's room and showed me a purple spot on his leg. Back then we frequently jumped to conclusions. He was panicked, thinking it was KS. Turned out no. – Tim Cagney

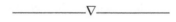

Chicago, IL

Reading one of the gay newspapers (don't recall which one) at Man's Country. There was an article about something called "GRID," which had two cases appear in San Francisco. This was disturbing to me, as I was planning to move to San Francisco at some point. As events turned out, my parents found out I was gay and politely kicked me out of the house and moved me to San Francisco, where I arrived in early 1981, just in time to watch the HIV pandemic unfold at one of three Ground Zeros (the others being New York City and Los Angeles). – Allan

———————∇———————

Chicago, IL

The first time I heard about AIDS was in 1985. Several of my friends were buzzing about the 'Gay Cancer' spreading from New York. Within a year the reality sunk in as more and more of my close running pals were struck down in their prime. My partner and I were soon tested for what was then called the HTLV-3 Virus. I was negative, he was positive. We struggled to stay together despite this terror but broke up in late '86 when he moved back home to Cincinnati. He lived until June 1993. He died exactly one week to the day after my then partner Johnny Ortiz (manager of He'vin and bartender at AA Meat Market in Chicago) died in my arms. It was a dark, terrifying, and horrible time which seemed to continue unabated until the mid-1990s when the anti-retroviral cocktail was introduced. The sadness and horror of that time haunts me to this day. – Paul Mikos

———————∇———————

New York, NY

I remember my friend Eduardo. He was from Venezuela, from Caracas. He was in a hospital in New York. My next door neighbor, Gary, called me up. We were all friends in Fire Island. Gary said, "Eduardo's sick in Roosevelt Hospital and we don't know what it is. Do you want to come with me?' So I said, "Yes." They made us put on caps, gowns and everything. So I'm thinking, "Well what the hell is this?" It wasn't flu, obviously. And when I saw him, his cheeks were sunken in. This was a guy in his twenties, full of life. He couldn't lift a spoon of yogurt. Afterwards we were going to the elevator and I was crying. I said to Gary, "What is going on?" I didn't hear the words AIDS, probably for another five or six months. It was GRID and there were other names for it. Things kept floating around. Oh have you heard there's a gay disease, something that people catch? But how? Do you get it by kissing? So, it was probably another year or so later that friends said, "Well maybe you should go and get tested." This was around 1986 or 1985 when the test came out. Someone said it was a sexual disease, so now we knew it was dangerous to have sex. Gay men had never heard of condoms. What did I do about it? I didn't stop. – Richard Pass

Montgomery, AL

I'm not sure where I was when I first heard about AIDS (before the term AIDS) – it was early 1980s and I learned that a dear friend in college had died from the "gay disease." The first of MANY over the years. It was in 1990 when my first relationship ended and I went to Mabel's (Beauty Shop and Chainsaw Repair). That night I met my second husband and found out that he was HIV positive. We were together for 6 years before he died with AIDS in 1996. – T

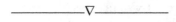

San Francisco, CA

We'd all read the article in the *New York Times*, and it scared us all shitless. No one knew anything, of course, and if the slightest thing felt out of order – a night of insomnia, heartburn from the meal the previous night – we all ran to our doctors, completely sure we'd somehow contacted it. – Sean Martin

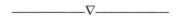

Chicago, IL

There were news stories about the gay plague that was alarming medical professionals in San Francisco and New York but seldom anything pertaining to Chicago – so I didn't pay too much attention. After that, a very close friend told me he had tested positive for HIV. Then other friends I knew became ill and started to pass away or move from Chicago to return to their family home because they needed to be cared for. TV news began to cover more news stories about AIDS and HIV cases. I went to TPAN and took a class on HIV. In 1994, I had a mild case of shingles. My doctor urged me to be tested for HIV since shingles was a common symptom of a compromised immune system. I tested positive. I informed my partner. He also tested positive. At that time, treatments were limited and ineffective. We both assumed we had a year or two to live. It was a frightening and depressing time. You literally could not have a social interaction without a discussion about HIV and AIDS – isn't it awful that so and so is sick? Did you hear what celebrity has HIV? Oh poor dear, he won't go out anymore because he can't drink with his meds. Have you seen him lately? He's got those fatty deposits on his neck and face. What's it called? Lipo something? He looks horrific. There are new drugs coming down the pipeline. I hope he can just hang in there.

Today, I look through my album of the Halloween parties I hosted. So many ghosts stare back at me. So many ghosts. – Deschicago

—————∇—————

Chicago, IL

When I read *The Leatherman's Handbook* in 1982, they had a section on G.R.I.D. (Gay Related Immune Deficiency). It said that only bottoms seemed to get it so avoid receiving semen or to make your top wear a condom. – R. M. Schultz

—————∇—————

Detroit, MI

I was married and first heard about it when Rock Hudson was diagnosed with it. Then two dear friends of mine died from it. I was devastated by that and began practicing safe sex. – Guy Sands

—————∇—————

Los Angeles, CA

Some friends of mine from Northern California were visiting, probably around 1981. They said, "There's some new Jewish cancer and a lot of gay men are catching it, it's an immune-deficiency thing," and I'm like, "Well, whatever." They thought it was Jewish because a lot of Middle Eastern guys were coming down with Kaposi's sarcoma. They were calling it the Jewish Plague first. – Curt Miller

—————∇—————

Los Angeles, CA

When Tom Descamp, a really good friend of mine, was in hospital and covered with Kaposi's sarcoma and I didn't recognize him. I didn't know what it was. Someone told me and I went to see him, and it was really sad. He was so healthy and muscular and then you see him lying there in a hospital bed and all you can recognize are his eyes. Really tough. – John Condon

———————▽———————

Boston, MA

I was living with my partner Bob. It had to have been about 1980. It was just men becoming ill and dying and they couldn't find any cure. Supposedly only gay men got it. – Roy Alton Wald

———————▽———————

Los Angeles, CA

I was in love with an older man, the actor Barry Robins. Our relationship was never consummated. He had gotten very ill. When we found out it was AIDS, he stopped talking to me. And to this day I regret that I didn't try harder to see him. But as I got older, I understood that he was protecting me. But it broke my heart. – Jason Stuart

———————▽———————

Chicago, IL
Paris, France

I had read about the "gay virus" in *Christopher Street*, I think. It was more or less dismissed as a joke (this had to have been late 1980 or early 1981). After that the first time it really came up was in Paris in July 1981. I was in bed with a gorgeous American (the son, who was 20, of a friend of mine). He thought he had the "gay virus" – I pointed out that his father was a world famous microbiologist so he should know that a virus can't tell if you're gay. His quick response was, "well this one can." – Bernard

———————▽———————

Chicago, IL

It was 1982 and I was working my first full-time job. A bookkeeper in my office had a sister who received a blood transfusion giving birth, contracted AIDS, and passed away quickly. – David Fink

———————∇———————

Athens, OH

I was in grad school in Athens, Ohio (kind of sheltered from the world) when the *New York Times* article appeared in the summer of 1981 – I was reading the NYT pretty often, but I missed that article. I was aware of it by the time I moved to Chicago in 1983, but I don't really remember the first time I heard about it. – David

———————∇———————

Chicago, IL

1984, I was 14 and watched a news report on PBS. A few years later I noticed the first person with Kaposi's Sarcoma. I was at the Melrose diner in Chicago and a young man walked in, in the advanced stages of illness. – Ruben Cruz

———————∇———————

Chicago, IL

The first time I ever heard about AIDS was when I was in middle school. It was the early '90s and they started to educate us about how it's contracted, spread, and its devastatingly fatal nature. I could feel the pain coursing through the community even then, though I was not yet out of the closet. They scared the shit out of us so we would do everything possible to protect ourselves. I remember there being a stigma about it for the gay community but by this time it had reached members of the straight community as well. It was very scary. – Natasha Douglas aka Joey Kiening

———————∇———————

Chicago, IL

AIDS was prevalent in every aspect of my daily life back in 1980. I had so many gay male friends and it was extremely scary, tense and nerve-wracking. I'll never forget a guy I met at Hunter's who got diagnosed that day and said he was going to have unprotected sex with someone that night because if he had to have AIDS, he didn't care who else got it. – Anonymous

———————▽———————

Chicago, IL

It was here in Chicago and it was in the early '80s. I remember that it was something happening far away. Or it seemed. We heard about LA and NY and it seemed like we were safer somehow? But then we found out we were not. I had several friends that went through a horrific end. – Honey West

———————▽———————

Rochester, NY

The first time I heard about AIDS was when I lived in Rochester, NY, with my first roommate after college – a gay man that I worked with at the time. We hung out together all the time and talked about the epidemic and how careful he had to be. It was 1991. I was devastated a year later when he told me he was HIV+ and was going on the "cocktail." I began my days of activism and have never looked back. – Kit Welch

———————▽———————

New York, NY

I heard about the dreaded disease while I was talking to my old friend, GT, whose job was as doctor at the emergency ward at New York's St. Vincent's Hospital. It took us all for a loop. I was living in Chicago by then, and started to perform at various AIDS benefits. A devastating time for all of us. – Ralph Lampkin

———————▽———————

Russian River, CA

It was the early '80s. I had moved up north from San Francisco to bartend at the Woods, the biggest gay resort in the Russian River boom in those days. Guys came up from the city and packed the place every weekend.

People started talking about friends getting sick with weird symptoms, some of them even dying. The first rumors were that it was caused by poppers. Then there was the scare about a certain kind of deodorant. One week when I was down in San Francisco to see friends, I saw the now-famous pictures in the window of Starr Pharmacy of "gay cancer." – Mark Abramson

───────────▽───────────

Chicago, IL

I was a young DJ at Dugan's Bistro and working for IRS Music Pool. Patrick Cowley was an up and coming artist when he was diagnosed with AIDS. It sent chills around the DJ community. – Daniel Goss

───────────▽───────────

Naperville, IL

I learned about AIDS, homosexuality and sodomy in one swoop on the car ride to the funeral of my uncle – a man I'd been taught to call uncle. Uncle Kenny was actually the brother of my aunt by marriage and thus of no biological relation. But I'd grown up calling him uncle at holidays and family gatherings, and his loss was no less profound.

I was 13 years old in January 1995 and just starting to acknowledge who and what I desired, and I learned on the car ride, by asking my parents, that there had been another person like myself. But he was gone. This man, who loved Neil Diamond and looked like Freddie Mercury and would philosophize with my grandmother for hours about her Christmas tree, had made love with men and evidently fallen in love with one man and caught AIDS and died young. I wondered if this would be the equation of my life, perishing in my forties. I lived in a conservative suburb called Naperville, where to be called "gay" was to become a freak and a joke, reduced to something like an animal.

Yet I'd never seen a funeral so well attended. Kenny, a supervisor at Inland Steel in northwest Indiana, had made a multitude of friends, straight and gay, who mourned him loudly and without inhibition. As my aunt gave the eulogy, it pained me to consider that someone so near to me, who shared my secret, left before I could ask him anything. And I grew up believing myself to be the last of our rare species. – Robert W. Fieseler

───────────▽───────────

Texas

I really don't remember when I first heard. But I do have a clear memory of asking my boyfriend if he was "worried" about anything before we had sex for the first time (this would have been in 1985). That was the euphemism we used. When Andrew said he wasn't "worried," we proceeded to have unsafe sex. I was a foolish 21-year-old; Andrew would have been not-too-much-wiser 24." – Edward Thomas-Herrera

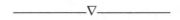

North Carolina

In high school. Even though I wasn't out I had already discovered a cruising spot at the mall and had jerked off with men and let another guy perform oral on me. I kept thinking I could possibly have it even though I hadn't really done anything. I didn't know anyone with it, but did see a guy on the local news who had been diagnosed with it and the media was trashing him. – Bill

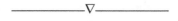

Chicago, IL

I first learned about AIDS when a dear friend that lived in my apartment building died of AIDS. I didn't realize what it was at first because I was told he died of pneumonia. His partner later confirmed it was AIDS. I tried to help in my small way by hiring those I knew had AIDS. I knew they needed the help with insurance. – Janan Lindley

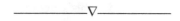

New York, NY

I had first heard about the immune deficiency, sexually transmitted virus affecting gay males in the late 1970s before it was called AIDS. Dr. Joseph Sonnabend was a friend and frequent visitor. To my husband, Joseph was one of his physicians, and for me Joseph would often accompany me on piano as I was learning a new opera role. On a number of occasions we would sit and discuss the catastrophic implications of the potential plague. By the early 1980s I began to experience its devastating effects on many of my friends, associates and teachers. – Philip Raia

—————▽—————

Chicago, IL

I first heard about AIDS in 1984-ish when articles began to appear in the print media I was reading. I began to meet people with ARC not too long after that. – Pat Cummings

—————▽—————

Puerto Rico

'84-'85. I was 19 or so. I don't remember the precise moment, but I remember my father – I was not out to him at the time – making sure I was using condoms (though we never discussed if I was having sex). 1985 was the year I became conscious of AIDS, though I didn't start using condoms until later. – Melo

—————▽—————

New York, NY

It was a Sunday, I was at NYU and had just bought the *New York Times*. I was sitting outside Rubin Hall, my dorm, and read about a "gay cancer" that was being discovered among a large portion of gay men in the city. Years later I realized it was THAT *New York Times* article that's referred to in many movies and documentaries. – Malone Sizelove

—————▽—————

San Diego, CA

It had to be around 1983 or so. I was living in San Diego, was a major coke dealer by then and attended a lot of late night, after bar, parties in homes where it had become a topic of discussion. Sadly, there were jokes about it too. Not funny at all to me and yet I never spoke out because I was still deep on the closet.

I just wanted to scream at some of those straight, horrible people, but the cocaine trade was a very macho, straight world, and the money rolling in back then corrupted any chance to be brave. You kept your mouth shut and let people get away with it.

Interesting in that I always considered myself to be a cheerleader on the sidelines for LGBTQ issues back then, (and even earlier), never

75

expecting to find myself out on the playing field these many decades later as a published author, but here I am and proud of it, to finally speak up.

I will never be silent again. – Denise Chanterelle Dubois

Tennessee

I first heard about AIDS in about 1983. A bunch of friends and I were having dinner and we were watching a Geraldo Rivera special talking about the gay cancer. – Jeffery Meskenas

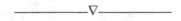

East Randolph, NY

I grew up in a small town – East Randolph in Western New York. It was a farm town of about 600 – and seemingly, especially to me as I aged and yearned to be free, a place at the edge of the world. It was the early '80s and information, while available, reached us at a slower pace. Therefore, while AIDS has been something I've been aware of since I've been sexually active – I probably heard about it when I was a junior in high school – I can't actually recall the exact time and place that I learned of its existence. I'm sure I knew it was true and a horrible phenomenon. It also probably felt like something that was happening someplace else to other people in a city that seemed almost impossible for me to reach. I'm sure it scared me and seemed like a threat – but it probably also seemed unreal, not a part of my life. It was only when I reached Chicago and I began to meet people who had contracted it or knew people who had died from it that it really affected me and changed my life. – Brian Kirst

Indiana

I heard about AIDS at some point in school in southern Indiana. I remember my class watching a documentary about another kid in Indiana, Ryan White, who had AIDS but wasn't even gay. It kind of felt like the doc was saying, "See, anyone can get AIDS, not just the bad guys." But I didn't fully understand what AIDS meant to the queer community until I was 14 and secretly watching the movie version of *Rent* in my bedroom. When I saw a transgender woman named Angel die just one year after forming this family and meeting her love who also had the virus, I realized Indiana schools were leaving out the cultural impact of the epidemic. – Devlyn Camp

—————∇—————

New York, NY

I was a flight attendant for over 24 years, from 1985 on. Being based in New York at the time, I started to have friends die. Call me stupid, I just did not understand. I was too busy flying around the world. So many regrets. – T.C. Burfield

—————∇—————

Chicago, IL

The first week of July 1981. I had just taken over as editor of *Chicago GayLife* newspaper. On July 3, the *New York Times* reported on clusters of cases of Kaposi's sarcoma among gay men in New York and California. My tenure as editor of Chicago's then-leading LGBT publication coincided exactly with the emergence of the AIDS crisis, though the mysterious "gay cancer" wasn't designated as AIDS until 1982. – Bill Williams

—————∇—————

Ohio

It was the early to mid-'80s, I was touring the 3rd National Tour of *Evita* on what is known as a Bus and Truck, costume buses to take us to two or three cities a week. The seats were very comfortable and when you have nothing to do but look out the window, sleep, or read, you read. There was a *Time* magazine on the bus with an article about "The Gay Plague" that was making the rounds of the company and I read the terrifying article while traveling through Ohio. It is a vividly uncomfortable memory. Beautiful green countryside and a bright sunny spring day and the "GAY PLAGUE." – Leo Schwartz

—————∇—————

New York, NY

Spring, 1982. Lobby of the Theatre for a New City in Greenwich Village. Actress Ann Harris walked through the lobby. She was the matron of a theatrical family. I asked casually, "How's the brood?" and she paused to say seriously, "Little George is ill." I automatically wished him well, but she grew more serious and said, "No, he's really very ill," and left with her forehead furrowed. Just days later I heard that George had died. He was George Harris III, also known as Hibiscus, creator of the troupe, "The Angels of Light," and he is also the blond-banged boy you see in the famous photograph, on the Pentagon steps, putting a flower in a soldier's rifle. – Robert Patrick

———————∇———————

Chicago, IL

I first heard about AIDS as a teenager. We all were learning about it. In high school there were jokes about it. I think as kids back then it was so hard to get a grasp of what was really going on. It had not really made its way to where I lived in Central Illinois. It was after I moved to Chicago and worked at Windy City Bar and Grill then for Marge at His 'n' Hers that I saw the toll it was taking. We lost so many friends and family so fast. – Terry Gaskins

———————∇———————

Rhode Island

ABC's 20/20 ... 1982 ... the year before I came out. – Mitchell Fain

———————∇———————

New York, NY

We were still in college, so this was before 1984, when we first started hearing about a gay cancer. It was scary, but it seemed so far off that it wouldn't affect my young invincible life.

But by the time I got to New York City in 1988, AIDS became all too real. I was writing about fashion for a newspaper called *New York Newsday* and my peers began getting sick and dying.

At one point in the early '90s, my Filofax date book was filled with memorial services, one every couple of weeks. Every time I heard someone eulogized, it might as well have been me in that coffin. These guys were my buddies, my acquaintances, my business colleagues. Somehow, my inner circle – my five closest college friends and I – were spared death, if not infection. We're all still here, thank heaven, still funny and biting and smart.

But I do feel like a war veteran, and it doesn't take much more than a mention of AIDS to make me weep. — Frank DeCaro

—————————▽—————————

WHAT'S THE WORST DATE YOU EVER WENT ON?

USA

Met someone through a classified (this was before we all had computers) and met for dinner after some phone conversations. He had a very sexy voice. When I went to pick him up on a rainy night, I was met at the door by his brother-in-law who he was staying with. My date was in the back room crying, wearing a mu-mu, convinced I was not going to show up! We then went to a nearby restaurant, after he changed of course, but he was drinking a bit much then flirting with the waiter! I knew then and there that nothing was happening this night, so I drove him home. His hands were all over me and I couldn't drop him off fast enough! As he left the car and walked across the grass I noticed his hairbrush on the front seat, so I promptly launched it out the sunroof in his direction. End of that date – Douglas

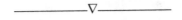

St. Louis, MO
East St. Louis, IL

In the late 1980s I went to Clementine's with a guy, then we went to Faces in East St. Louis, and shortly after getting inside he ditched me. This made it a terrifying situation because I had to walk through a dangerous part of East St. Louis at about 2 AM, walk ACROSS the bridge into downtown St. Louis (which was illegal to do). A guy in a pickup stopped to give me a ride when I was almost across, and of course he wanted to "get to know me" which was inconvenient as he was not my type and I didn't want to seem ungrateful for the ride. My car was parked at a Naugles I worked part time at, and that's where he dropped me off. I got home sometime after 4 AM or so, and just wanted to crawl into bed. – Todd Jaeger

———————∇———————

Chicago, IL

I've never had a "worst" date. I only remember ONE date in the sense that that term is used, and it was only afterward that he said to told me that that was what it was. I didn't know. It was fun. Short-lived (a few weeks). He began it and he ended it. I had no regrets. We still talk decades later. See him when he's in town, which is seldom these days since he moved to Seattle with his partner.

I don't remember anything date-like I initiated. I did "see people" after tricking. Still do, many years later. Were those dates? I didn't think of them that way. – Anonymous

———————∇———————

Illinois

I went out with someone very controlling, bossy and finicky. Her food never tasted right and her drinks were never mixed correctly. She even told me what to order and how to behave on the date. It was awful!

I encountered this individual about ten years later without recognizing her from our single doomed date, until she began to display some of the same behaviors as previously. It horrifyingly dawned on me that this was the same person from ten years ago! – Paxton Anthony Murphy

———————∇———————

Redlands, CA
Garden Grove, CA
Los Angeles, CA

So, at first, I thought I don't think I have one, and then I remember it. So, it needs the set up as well. I will try and keep it brief. Halloween party in LA at a fellow students. I think her parents helped make the arrangements. No one was of age … but they had a keg, and my 24-year-old roommate from college, of course was of age, and I had a car, so we drove in for this party.

Well it was lame, and then we smoked some weed, and said let's blow this party and go into West Hollywood. We went to an afterhours place on Melrose, I think it was the Spike … it had lots of dark corners and places you could close the deal so to speak. Well my roommate and I got separated, and of course I got something going, well needless to say, I was in love … what again Dean. My roommate found me going on and on about this guy who looked like Robert Redford and gave a blow job like I had never had before. He said no he did not look like Robert Redford, but I thought he was just saying that because he did not get any. Anyway, I had given him the number to the dorm, and he did call me and wanted to pick me up and bring me to his place the following weekend. Again, Rick my roommate said don't do it, but no I was convinced. I said the guy is picking me up in a Cadillac. I asked him to pick me up off campus as I did not want to be spotted getting into a fancy car with an older man. I don't know what I was thinking, so I had packed a small bag, and met him a few blocks away, the car pulled up, I looked in and oh no it was not Robert Redford, but I had said I would go with him, so I did. So, a weekend in his home just the two of us. He did take me out for a few meals, was very nice to me, asked me to wear nothing but my tightie whites when we were in his house, and he did give me several great blow jobs, and the reason was, as the Homer and Jethro song went … "her teeth were like the stars above because they come out every night" Yeah, that I think was the worst. – Dean Ogren

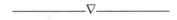

San Francisco, CA

We had invited a fellow over for a fourth at a bridge party. My boyfriend at the time didn't play bridge, wasn't interested in bridge. So this guy came over and during the bridge game we were playing footsie under the table. My partner was upstairs asleep in bed. The footsie kept going on and finally the game broke up and he was supposed to be staying overnight in the guest bedroom. Everybody went to bed and I went into his room and we were getting it on. My boyfriend showed up at the door with a can of cold water. Threw it on the two of us and stormed out. We broke up shortly after that. – Steve

Chicago, IL

I'm certain there are several that I put out of my mind, but I do remember going to the theatre with a guy who had a store which featured memorabilia of female film icons and femme fatales as well as many deco pieces. I love discussing a play after the performance to see what resonated with my date. Very quickly I realized that he had no idea what we had just seen. He was totally lost and couldn't recount the simplest of plot lines let alone discuss how it impacted him if at all. But ask him about the most miniscule fact about some old film star and he was off to the races. Needless to say we didn't have another date. – Tom Chiola

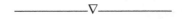

West Lafayette, IN

Oy, I had the worst date while I was still in the closet in my single dorm room. I was 18 and still figuring how to come out. It was fall. A fellow queer from my hometown area had set me up on a blind date with a friend of his at U of I. We ate take-out Italian in my dorm room, talked, went to bed, both of us too afraid to make the first move, and they left in the middle of the night. Ugh, horrible. – Cody Las Vegas

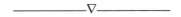

San Francisco, CA

If you mean a pick-up, he turned out to be a heroin addict and in the morning he was in withdrawal. It was not easy getting rid of him because he was disoriented and didn't know where he was. I finally got him out the door and locked it behind him. – Bill Barrick

New York, NY

If you consider one night stands, I picked somebody up. I was in a bad area. I walked down my street. I lived on 14th street, one side was Manhattan, the other side was the seedy side, with the Anvil. I brought him home and I went into the bathroom and when I got out, he was gone and so was my wallet. Other than that, I've never had a bad date. – Randy Warren

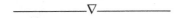

San Francisco, CA

I had some pretty bad ones with women. – Steve

————————▽————————

Chicago, IL

It was when I went home with this guy and he never shut up! He continually talked even during sex. SHUT UP! – Jack Delaney

————————▽————————

Chicago, IL

Dinner. Some dude edited his photo to look nothing like he did in real life. And on top of that, he wouldn't stop talking about himself. – Marc

————————▽————————

Palm Springs, CA

The most frustrating was when a Hollywood producer asked me out and I had just got a boyfriend a couple of days before. I had to turn him down, after he told me about all his clients, Candice Bergen … " – Randy

————————▽————————

Lansing, MI

In college, I went out with a college Republican who was pretty well connected with the GOP establishment in Lansing, MI. He took me to a party with a bunch of other closeted Republicans (some of them held office). I held my tongue the entire night. As he was dropping me off at the end of the night, he tried to force himself on me. His mouth tasted like bourbon and cigarettes. I managed to reach behind me, open the car door and somersault backwards out of the car. – Misha Davenport

————————▽————————

Chicago, IL

I had a date with a guy who is hearing impaired. He wore big hearing aids on both ears and read lips very well. We met for coffee at a busy Edgewater café – a café where the tables are fairly tight together almost as they are in a

New York City restaurant. This was an issue since my legally deaf date spoke with a very loud voice. I could hear him quite clearly; everyone could hear him quite clearly. I wanted to move to a more secluded table – if that were even possible – but I couldn't think of a tactful way to suggest it. The date took a sharp turn when he began explaining how he did not find me attractive and did not foresee any relationship developing between us whatsoever. He went into detail. Very loud detail. I was stunned into silence. I, and everyone, was forced to just hear him out. I tried to end the date by paying the bill but he protested, explaining (to everyone) that he felt he should pay since it was he who was rejecting me and he was sure that there was someone out there for me and how we were simply not meant to be.

To this day I wonder if he knew how very loud he was and if he realizes that everyone within 100 feet could hear him, though I have to assume that he did not want to embarrass me on purpose. That's a true story. – Matt

—————————▽—————————

Chicago, IL

I agreed to meet someone a mutual friend wanted me to meet. I got to the place and he looked up and said, "You are so much uglier than your photo." I think I replied, "FUCK YOU COCKSUCKER" and left. I never spoke to our mutual friend again either despite her multiple apologies. – Mike Martinez

—————————▽—————————

Chicago, IL

A friend from square dancing set me up on a blind date. He said I had a lot in common with this guy. I called him up and we agreed to meet on New Year's Day.

In the afternoon of New Year's Eve he called me. He was having a dinner party and had a cancellation, would I like to join them? Sure! I bought a bottle of wine to take along as a host gift.

It was a small group for dinner, and I quickly found out that they all had met through Alcoholics Anonymous. The wine was perhaps the worst gift possible. No criticism, I put the bottle with my coat, nobody mentioned it again, I took it away with me at the end of the evening. I don't drink, so either I used the wine for cooking or I gave it away.

The dinner conversation centered entirely on experiences with addiction, keeping the straight and narrow, and how important AA was. I came to realize that these men had substituted one addiction for another – alcohol for AA membership. AA membership is much, much healthier. But it's not fascinating conversation for the odd man out.

By the time I got home I decided that this wouldn't develop into a relationship. The only things that I could find that we had in common was that we were both single, and both gay men. I resolved to tell him when we met the next day.

I think we had lunch at the Melrose. He brought a friend to the date. He spoke as if we'd already agreed to date a lot, building up a great picture for his friend. Eventually I felt that telling him "no" then and there would humiliate him in front of his friend. So when I got home I called him immediately, and left a message that it wouldn't work out between us. – Rick

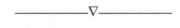

Chicago, IL

The extremely attractive schizophrenic I met at Berlin in 1990, who decided we couldn't have sex because his boss could see us through the walls of his apartment. – Corey Black

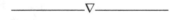

Palm Springs, CA

The worst date I ever went on, the guy took me to a casino for the buffet and spent the whole time there on the slot machines. I took a cab home. – Tom

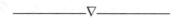

Lima, Peru

Oh boy, I haven't gone on many dates, actually, but the closest thing I've gotten to a bad date is my Prom night! The guy I invited out of peer pressure, was kinda overbearing and he kept trying to kiss me while we danced – but I didn't notice! I only know this because afterwards all my friends were like "holy shit you cockblocked that guy so hard." I just thought that was normal dancing distance! – Robb

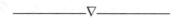

Chicago, IL

I went to a nice restaurant with a guy who could not stop looking at his phone and actually took two calls during our meal. That was our first and last date. – Kbro

———————▽———————

Chicago, IL

The worst date I ever went on was with a guy who ordered the most expensive thing on the menu and then continuously complained about everything and treated the staff like crap. – Giovanni

———————▽———————

Chicago, IL

His ex showed up and the two of them spoke outside for 45 minutes. This was before the age of Uber or smartphones, so I had to just sit there and finish the bottle of wine alone. – Anonymous

———————▽———————

Chicago, IL

One where a wealthy, attractive North Shore man 15 years my senior declared that I was to be "the other woman" to his wife. This was all news to me, as I had met him in a gay bar. We tricked and I assumed he had another story. Get me outta here! – Anonymous

———————▽———————

Chicago, IL

My worst dates were with aggressive women before I came out. After I came out my worst date was with an aggressive guy I did not find attractive. I should have never accepted the date. He badgered me so much I mistakenly thought that going out with him would put an end to things. I did not realize it would only make him pursue me even more. – Bob

——————▽——————

Madison, WI

2003. When I was 22, I went on a date with a guy named Andrew after he mysteriously attended a giant house party that my roommate and I had. No one knew who he was or where he came from, but he was hot and he asked me out and I was beyond thrilled. He owned a car and a small house, and I had never dated anyone who owned anything, so I was impressed. After our awkward dinner, I happily accepted his invitation to his house. The foul odor hit me first, before I even entered. Once inside I noticed mounds of garbage, old soiled newspapers, and large, dirty terrariums filled with tattered clothing. In his kitchen he proudly mentioned his collection of "rancid olive oils," and indeed, his counter was filled with murky bottles. There was a small path cleared to walk, sometimes only sideways, through the house and to the living room, where he led me by the hand. We sat on the couch, and on the opposite wall where a TV would normally be was instead a forty-gallon fish tank filled with crumpled paper. The smell was overwhelming, but I didn't want to be rude and cut our evening short. While we sat there and he lectured me about chemistry, I saw what looked like a large rat, dart across the room. The noise of rustling garbage was unmistakable, something was very alive in the corner. I politely interrupted him and told him that I thought he had "vermin," to which he angrily responded, "they aren't vermin!" He then explained that he had been rescuing mice and rats from the science lab that he worked at, and he no longer had space for all of them in the tanks, so they just roamed free in the house. I expressed concern for him, but he was proud of what he was doing; this was his animal sanctuary. I asked to use the bathroom and he snapped, "It had better be number one ... " and informed me that no one is allowed in his bathroom. He didn't even use it anymore himself, he claimed. So he told me to go in the backyard to do my business. I mildly protested, but he wasn't having it. It was well below freezing that February night, and there were no trees or shrubs to hide behind, so I just pissed in the snow in the middle of his yard. When I came back in, I told him I wanted to leave. But he was all over me, tugging at my clothes, undoing my belt buckle. He wanted me to come to his bedroom where he assured me the rats were "mostly not allowed," and I actually did consider it. No one this attractive had ever wanted to sleep with me before, and I found the attention flattering. But suddenly the smell just started making me feel nauseous. I wanted to leave, but I had no cell phone, there were no taxis or buses, no Uber or Lyft. He lived in the middle of nowhere. He told me that he'd take me home only if we slept together first. I said I wasn't feeling well, I said I was too tired. He wouldn't listen to me. I pleaded with him. He finally agreed to take me home if I agreed to have another date with him. "Yes," I lied. Our car ride back to my place was painfully silent, but I was grateful he took me back. Two days later I called him and told him I didn't want to date him because he was rude to the waitress. This wasn't a complete lie. I didn't even mention the rats and didn't know how to bring it up without talking about mental illness, and that just wasn't a conversation I was prepared to have with him. He called me repeatedly for a few days afterwards and then gave up, and I never heard from him again. – Shane K

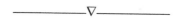

Crest Hill, IL

I was set up on a blind date by a friend. I showed up in a new outfit, rocking my new 1984 hair-do. I rang the doorbell and a man about 20 years older than me opened the door took one look at me and said, "I am sorry but this is not gonna work for me at all. I am sorry you came all this way for nothing. Good Night." Then he closed the door. Needless to say I stood there for a second a little shocked. I then turned around and went to dinner by myself. Does that actually count as a date? – Jim Hensley

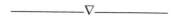

USA

I went out with a guy when I was 18. We met at a bar and there was an instant attraction. I am biracial and when my hair is short people often mistake me for White. We went to a bar and he turned to me and said let's get out of here there are too many N***** here. I was shocked and said to him, "What do you think I am?" and he said, "I don't know, Italian?" I said, "No, I am Black and this date is over. – Eric Kuznof

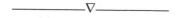

Charlotte, NC

I'm a big, cuddly bear guy, who's quite shy, and somewhat socially awkward, so I have a hard time speaking to people anyway without getting social anxiety. I met a guy online through Plenty of Fish, a nice Jewish guy who seemed to know what he wanted. We planned to go eat at the local Italian restaurant and then watch the new *Beauty and the Beast* movie. We drove separate cars and met up at the restaurant. He seemed fine at first, but later it seemed, he had an issue with my size. (It's the only thing I could figure out). Granted I'm used to this as I know a lot of people are shallow as a teaspoon, but this guy was rude about it. We started the meal and I ordered a grilled chicken alfredo, to which he says it's good I got the grilled, I could use less calories. Being my first actual date in 8 years, I let it go. He sat and talked about himself for a little over an hour. I ate like a bird, because I didn't want to have a mouthful of food when he inevitably asked a question. After he was finished, he asked me one question, to which I didn't even get to finish answering before he stopped listening. Then he insisted we rush out of the restaurant to the movie theater, despite the movie starting in an hour. We got to the parking deck of the theatre and walked through the square leading to the theater. It was a busy Saturday night. We get to where it tells the times of the movies and it says it will be ANOTHER hour. While we are standing in line he says, "I guess we can go get ice cream, not like your fat ass needs it." I just kept my mouth shut, I was determined to finish this date. Well it was a misprint as they had put up the next nights times prematurely. We get inside and he buys a soda and some candy and I get a water, to which he replies "good, water's good for fat people like you." Again, I was dead set on finishing this date. We watched the movie and during the whole time he sits beside me, he's acting like he has horrible indigestion, but we power through the movie and head back to our cars, where he shakes my hand and then just leaves. About a day later I message him and tell him that I'd like to give him another chance (hey we all have bad nights), to which he replies, it's best we don't see each other anymore. Worst date ever. – Christian Bane

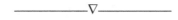

New York, NY

I've only dated two people, each long-term (one for ten years, the other for three and a half years). I suppose New York City in 2005, around the time I was realizing the first boyfriend and I probably weren't destined to be together forever. We had been out all day without eating, and I was getting faint and really had to eat soon or was going to be in crisis. He wouldn't stop walking and kept dismissing every place I wanted to stop. I finally said: "I am going to pass out and fall on the street if we don't stop NOW." He finally did. – Tim Murphy

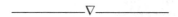

Riverside, CA

Stood up on my birthday in 1976. – Glen

————————▽————————

Chicago, IL

I was taken out to dinner. He was very attractive. He got completely drunk. I took him home, we had sex, and he pissed in my bed. – Joseph G

————————▽————————

Chicago, IL

Most awkward was a blind date arranged through an online dating site. I arrived at the bar where we agreed to meet only to find out that my date had arrived with three friends in tow. It was strange and a bit awkward – like I was taking part in a panel interview. I felt ambushed and there wasn't a second date. – Chicago T

————————▽————————

Utica, NY

I was just coming out and met a man at his home in Utica, NY. He was dull as dishwater and had nothing of interest to say. – Dave Russo

————————▽————————

Iowa

This guy drove one hour to meet me. We get in my car and drive to the movie *Wild River* when I realized he stinks like a cat litter box. I was polite the whole movie but it made me gag, he smelled so bad, plus his clothes were covered in cat hair. – Anonymous

————————▽————————

Chicago, IL

Oh, lord. My first thought was it had to be a "date" with a straight friend who didn't know we were on a date – you see, we were on a date in my mind only – when I was first coming to grips with who I am.

But now I recall a "date" from my teen years – when I was invited on a new friend's small sailboat, a dinghy he sailed on a tiny, man-made lake just outside of his family's condo building in the northwest suburbs of Chicago. I was the one who didn't realize that hot, summer afternoon was a date; looking back now I see it clearly was and I ache for my suitor ... and for myself. – Michael Burke

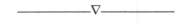

Washington, DC

I met a guy online who seemed interested in my profile, and photos, and wanted to meet for a drink. So we picked a bar and I got there a few minutes early. The guy showed up and I asked him what he'd like. He said he'd have a beer, so I got him one and sat down. But right then, he just blurted out that I was all wrong and he wasn't interested in talking. I was both amused and angered at his immaturity and thoughtless attitude, and asked him how am I different than what I was online? (I think my photos are actually pretty accurate). He just shook his head and repeated that he wasn't going to talk. He got up and said he was going to use the restroom in the back, but I suspected something was up. I paid for my drink, then caught the waiter and pointed out that my friend would pay for his beer. Sure enough, the guy tried to slip out the door past me, but I flagged him down for the waiter. The guy didn't look too pleased that he was out of the price of a beer, too. But I got him back: as I turned to leave, I said aloud to both him and the waiter, "And don't forget to tip your server!" – Jeff

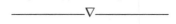

Chicago, IL

A guy who got drunk while at dinner, and then when I took him home he was hanging on me like bad drapes in a funeral home. Could barely move him to a spot where he could sleep it off. Called me in the morning to tell me how great the date was. – Robert

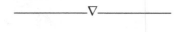

Chicago, IL

I tend not to remember those, but the bad ones usually just involve no rapport and as such, not great conversation. Although I admit asking a cop I was on a date with why cops put their sirens on to go through red lights, did not result in a great date. – Daniel

New York, NY

Is it weird to say I haven't been on a bad date? No disasters, certainly. I did go on a date once with a super nice South African guy that I had actually known for a little while, and when we went to sit and eat dinner my mind just … went blank. I was so nervous I couldn't think of anything to say, and just kind of disappeared in a miasma of self-consciousness. I'm sure it was a bad date for him. But we walked back to his apartment and he played me some George Michael and we sat in the kind of weird uncomfortableness of knowing we shouldn't probably get involved. And me still not really talking very much. And I pretended to like *Jesus to a Child* as much as he did, and walked the long way home late at night. – David Zinn

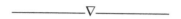

Chicago, IL

I met a college student cruising notorious Pine Grove Avenue in what was then called New Town. I asked him to go to my place, a block away, and have sex. He agreed. After we had our clothes back on, we exchanged phone numbers. He called a few days later, my heart went into overdrive, and he invited me to his place for dinner. "You cook?" I asked. "You're damned right I do," he said. Burgers for sure, I thought. What I wanted more than anything, though, was another taste of the cream he'd shot in my throat the night I met him. When I arrived at the address he gave me, I discovered the real cook was the man he lived with, one of his professors. I immediately let them know the three-way they'd hoped for was never going to happen. Well, they asked, would I stay for the meal anyway? Of course, I said. I could smell the roast in the oven. It was delicious. – Ron Fritsch

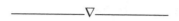

Pontypridd, Wales, UK

My worst date was going to a club in Pontypridd with my boyfriend and his friends who I hadn't met before. They argued all the way and I was pretty pissed off. My boyfriend ignored me entirely just staring out of the window. When we got to the car park the window fell out of the car and they refused to park and leave it, so we drove straight back home again (without a window – it was a side window not the windscreen.) We then ditched the friends who were still arguing and went to a local pub where he continued to ignore me. When I asked him what was wrong, he said all his friends arguing had made him think maybe he wasn't ready for a relationship, and he broke up with me. – Nephy Hart

—————▽—————

Chicago, IL

P.S. Bangkok on Clark Street. Summer of 1997. Blind date for dinner. He wouldn't stop talking. And all he could talk about was himself. For 90 minutes. I couldn't get a word in edge-wise. We didn't even say goodbye after dinner. We didn't even hook up! Never saw or heard of him again. Grateful. – Fester

—————▽—————

Northlake, IL

The worst date I ever went on had to be when I escorted my sister to her High School Prom at the last minute because her date was in a bad car accident the day before and was in the hospital. It wasn't that the company or the event itself was bad, it was just that we were upset over the situation and Susan and her friends were distracted and anxious all night. – Paul Mikos

—————▽—————

Chicago, IL

I met this guy, who I will call Tom. We had dinner at a restaurant at the corner of Clark and Wrightwood. I don't remember the name but I know it's closed by now. It was similar in scope to the Golden Nugget. The year was 1985. We had a nice dinner while we got to know one another. Then, after a certain amount of time, he said, "You know, you'd be an attractive looking guy if you only got your face scraped." The most sensitive part about me was my face, since I had acne scars since I was a teenager. Add that to the usual gay complex about being fit and handsome and there were self-image problems for me from day one. I was so offended but I didn't say too much to him after that. Obviously, we never met again. He later died of AIDS and I found out he was also a prominent member of the Chicago gay community when his obituary appeared in the Windy City Times. I always thought of myself as sensitive and caring, particularly since

I am now HIV+ (for over 27 years). However, when I heard of his death, I felt nothing. – Peter

——————▽——————

Chicago, IL

I should have known because he canceled the first date because he had to stay near the KILN in the CERAMICS studio because they were firing his ASHTRAYS when I had made a reservation. Then, when I went to his house to pick him up, I noticed that the only CDs he had in his extensive record collection were by Enya. Then during dinner he kept getting up to go to the bathroom and would come back very talkative and I didn't know much about cocaine then. I told him I was going to Paris in a month and was excited because it was my first time to Paris. He spent the rest of dinner explaining how to enjoy Paris, and only at the end of the meal did he reveal that he had never been to Paris. I went home with him anyway because I had sunk money into dinner. The bed was covered with stuffed animals. While we made out, he grabbed a rabbit and put it in my face and in baby talk, he said, "Hee's gonna getcha!" and then I went home. – Alec Holland

——————▽——————

Seattle, WA.

1997. I went on a date with a guy so "unnoticeable" my friends nicknamed him "Nebbish-Kenezer." He struggled with asking me out so badly, I felt sorry for him and said "Yes." We went to his friend's house for dinner (so he could show me off as a "trophy" date – I found out). This made for an uncomfortable introduction. He spent ten minutes in the bathroom squeezing pimples and returning to the dinner table with red welts across his forehead and cheeks. Dinner was seafood (I don't care for seafood), but I ate the vegetables. I excused myself to go to the bathroom and when I returned, I overheard them rating me on a scale. I was flattered, but very put off. I made an excuse and he took me home. His breath was foul but he pressed me against the car door until I kissed him goodnight.

I realized the next morning that somehow he gave me crabs. – Eric Andrews-Katz

——————▽——————

Chicago, IL

Gosh so many. The ones that stand out most though are those that you just had a horrible time and they call saying they had a wonderful time. You wonder if they were on the same date. One that stands out was painful as he was so nervous and anxious. I felt bad for him but it made me really nervous and anxious also. I just wanted it to end. It seemed to take him forever to finish his beer. I had finished mine. C'mon, hurry up. He was almost done. I went to the restroom relieved it was almost over only to come back to see he bought another round. – Mike Uetrecht

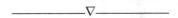

Chicago, IL

I'm actually going to answer this question for the person I went on a date. We were driving along Lake Shore Drive on our way to see a movie. It was our second date and I was falling hard for him. Suddenly my car engine started smoking and I had to pull over. When I opened the hood I saw that the engine caught on fire and within a minute or so, had a roaring Car-B-Q on my hands! Of course, this was in the mid-'90s and we didn't have cellphones back then, so I had to run and find a payphone. After a few minutes I could tell my date was growing more and more uncomfortable and excused himself and went home, but I could tell from the look in his eyes that it would be the last time I would ever hear from him again. I felt more devastated by losing him than my car, it was an accident after all.

About 12 years later, I was out in public running errands when I could feel someone looking at me. I didn't recognize him at first, but it was him, my date when the Car-B-Q happened. I'll never forget the look in his eyes, I could tell he was taking inventory of all the things he liked about me. I was in much better place in life, I felt great and I know I looked good for myself. Too bad, I had found someone, someone who would never have walked away during difficult moments in my life. – Anonymous

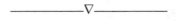

Chicago, IL

Labor Day weekend, 1994. I had been dating my boyfriend, George, for a year and things were going very well. The sex was great and we were very compatible. We used to hang out at the Lucky Horseshoe and enjoyed the go-go boys there, as well as the gregarious, moon-faced bartender named Sophie. So, George and I decided we would celebrate our anniversary with our first out-of-town date with a weekend excursion to San Francisco. I remember going to Carrie's LGBT bookstore on Clark Street and bought a gay guide to San Francisco and chose all the gay bars I wanted to visit on our trip. We booked ourselves into a cheap motel on the edge of the Castro district and arrived on the Friday night of Labor Day weekend.

My first clue to the disaster that was about to unfold was when George and I entered the motel room and he went straight for the San Francisco white pages to see if there were any other George (Miller)'s living in San Francisco.

I mean, who does that? Especially on their first trip to LotusLand. I learned the hard way that you never really know a person until you travel with them. He was rude to wait staff at restaurants and generally complained about everything. But the deal breaker was when we were on a bus, coming back from Chinatown, and he was imitating Chinese accents loudly. I was mortified. So, I decided to break up with him.

I probably shouldn't have done it in mid-flight on the way back to Chicago. He was stunned and heartbroken. And I had to find a different bar in Chicago with go-go boys. – David

———————▽———————

Chicago, IL

Two times – no shows. I met a guy at the short man's shop, and we were supposed to meet on Broadway and Surf. He was a no show (two times that happened). My second no-show, from a guy I met at the forest preserves and we were supposed to meet at the Fire Place on Wells Street. He called the restaurant and told me he's not coming. – David Plambeck

———————▽———————

Chicago, IL

The date itself was fine. We ate at Francesca's on Bryn Mawr. He had met me at Jackhammer the previous week and seemed very much into me. He was cute enough, so I agreed to meet him. The awkwardness was palpable, as I was beginning to age up (this is just before I turned 40) and he was the first in a long line of 20-somethings I continued to date/fuck. At one point, he remarked that his dream was to open a bar, which he described as, "A place where you can go if you're cool, or even if you're, like, 30." It was just a thousand little cuts like that.

We mutually split after a verrrry quick drink at the Granville Anvil, each with our own excuses about early work, etc. Lo, and behold, we saw each other about an hour later at Jackhammer. The last thing I remember was looking at him square in the eye and drunkenly asking, "So, how do YOU think that date went?" I don't recall him responding. – Anonymous

———————▽———————

Chicago, IL

Not a date, but a hookup via the phone sex lines that were so popular back in the days before online hooking up became a thing. It was in Chicago, probably early 1990s and I went to this guy's place in Rogers Park after we chatted on the phone sex line. When I saw him, I realized he wasn't at all how he'd described himself and I politely said I'd pass. He screamed at me as I left the building that he hoped I'd get AIDS. – Rick R. Reed

———————▽———————

Davis, CA

Date, date? What's that? Actually, it was with a woman I knew from high school. We both went on to attend UC Davis and lived in the dorms at 18. She liked me but I knew I was gay and there was no way this could become something. I took her to see John Waters' *Pink Flamingos*." I was loving it and she hated it, so she said she was leaving. I decided to stay. Maybe that wasn't a bad date after all. – Paul Harris

———————▽———————

Montgomery, AL

I don't remember which Shakespeare play we went to, but my partner of eleven years took me to a Shakespeare play on my 32nd Birthday. Afterward, when I was talking about the fun night we had ahead of us, he told me he had met someone else and that it was over. – T

———————▽———————

Chicago, IL

I'm not sure if it was Missy _____ or Karen _____. They both lived in Hinsdale and were "arranged" by my parents. Missy was slim with long hair. Karen was not fat but honestly big-boned with big tits and boisterous. Think of Lainie Kazan in *My Big Fat Greek Wedding*. She let me fondle them.

We were in my 1972 gold Chevy Nova which I bought from my sister. I think we were in a forest preserve near Hinsdale. I had no idea what I was doing. Her father worked for Zenith Electronics, so my family got a great deal on a big portable color tv. It sat on a rolling cart. – Tim

———————∇———————

San Francisco, CA

Being picked up by a blind date who had lied about his age, weight, and body type, and who took me out to a fancy French restaurant on Geary Street where he loudly proclaimed his love for me, calling me his "baby doll," as I shrank under the leering attentions of the staff, who were convinced that I was a rented boy. By the end of the evening, I was so upset with him for lying to me about everything that I went into a screaming litany (long since forgotten) ending with " … and I'M NOT YOUR FUCKING BABY DOLL!" – Allan

———————∇———————

San Francisco, CA

I have a long history of bad dates, so it's difficult to single out just one. Probably San Francisco, 1979. Guy I met in a leather bar. We went to his place, which he kept in pitch black. He refused to take me upstairs to the bedroom. I wound up sleeping in the living room after some pretty lousy, one-way sex. Ironically, I ran into him again six years later just before I was getting ready to leave SF to return to Canada. I didn't realize it was the same guy until we got to his place, and he pulled the same move. I just left. – Sean Martin

———————∇———————

Vienna, VA.

The Barns of Wolf Trap. A guy I was dating (because he drove a Jaguar and had a phone in his car in 1986!) was an opera queen. He was trying, unsuccessfully, to get me to like opera. He thought if he took me to an opera that was sung/shrieked in English (*Postcard from Morocco*) I would enjoy it more. I didn't. – Gregg Shapiro

———————∇———————

Chicago, IL

Asked a girl out to hear Mozart's *Posthorn Concerto* performed by the Chicago Chamber Orchestra. When we got there, and she found out that the concert was free, she got indignant and announced, "I don't go on cheap dates!" and she left. – R. M. Schultz

——————▽——————

Chicago, IL

Well what do you mean by "date"? Like actually going out with someone, it might be the blind date where the guy used the word "n———r" about ten times in the first ten minutes, before I just got up and walked away. OR if you're including trick, the time I threw up on a guy while going down on him – his spunk was that foul. I apologized profusely and he said, "That's okay, it's happened before." – Rick Karlin

——————▽——————

Salt Lake City, UT

I've had really, really, bad sex. I've had bad dates where I've walked out. The worst sex I've had was with a dear, dear friend of mine. He was this big bear and we were friends forever and I finally decided to go home with him. The minute we got in bed I started laughing hysterically. I couldn't stop. – David Hardy

——————▽——————

Palm Springs, CA

It was about a year ago. We met at Starbucks and by the time we'd finished chatting for forty-five minutes or so, he had already tried to convince me to move in with him. We were going to fall in love, and we would never be apart again. It was horrible. As we were walking to our cars, he grabbed on to me and I finally just said to him, "You seem like a very sweet guy but this isn't my thing at all. I'm sorry but I won't be at your house tonight and I won't be there tomorrow morning. I won't be going to Idyllwild with you for the weekend and ... No! No! No!" I've probably had other bad dates along the way, but in recent history, that was the worst. – Tim Parrot

What's the worst date you ever went on?

—————▽—————

Boston, MA

The worst date was when I went to a bar and picked someone up and brought them home to my place. Neither one of us could decide whether they wanted to be the top or the bottom. Both of us got very frustrated and overheated and said goodbye. His name was Manny. – Roy Alton Wald

—————▽—————

Chicago, IL

Oh my goodness, how to pick just one. It might be a tie between the time I went to dinner with a nice man and spent the whole time complaining about a homophobic uncle, and the lunch at Ann Sather, where my date grabbed the knife out of my hand because the way I was buttering my roll drove him mad. – David

—————▽—————

Chicago, IL

Was out at dinner and my ex was at the same restaurant and he decided to come over to chat. – Ruben Cruz

—————▽—————

Chicago, IL

I met a guy off Gay.com many years ago who drove out to meet me in Chicago from the suburbs. When he arrived, he was so dissimilar to his photos I didn't believe it was the same person. We had dinner because I wasn't sure what to do – the whole time he talked about how many men were pining for him and all his gay friends fall in love with him, and was utterly repugnant and arrogant. The cherry on top was when he proudly announced he was a Republican because he thinks poor people are lazy (I'm mixed-race and grew up poor) so I got the check as soon as I could and paid for it just to get out of there. Then I told him he needed to leave because I was not going to do anything with him that night and he insisted that I was secretly in love with him. I just shut the door on him. – James Conley

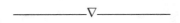

Chicago, IL

Lots of bad dates in my life but the most memorable was a guy I met through a personal I took out in the *Reader*. We met for coffee. He talked about himself a lot. I decided in my head not to tell him anything about myself unless he asked. The only question he asked was if he was as good looking as he described. I told him he was handsome, for what that was worth. He tried hard to get me to like him and I couldn't figure out why. – David Fink

Chicago, IL

It was a guy that I met at the Rocks. He seemed interesting enough and he was definitely a cutie. We made a date to go to dinner at a "fern restaurant" on Broadway called "The Brassery." We had a good meal and flirty conversation. I asked him to come to my place to get high. We smoked, made out and started to get down to business. Suddenly he stands up, points at me like he's holding a pistol, and makes several clicking noises with his tongue. I think to myself "what the fuck?" He does this several more times. I lost my hard-on, and my interest, but I was willing to, at the very least, do him and get off that way. And that seemed to work for a while until once again he started with the pointing and clicking noises. It was too disturbing. He seemed utterly clueless that his unusual behavior was – well, weird. I grabbed my alarm clock and in a panicky voice said, "Oh my gosh, I forgot that I have to be somewhere and I'm late already." He got very angry, told me I was a waste of time, rude, not all that attractive, and could stand to lose some weight. I told him he needed to leave. On his way out the door, I pointed at him as if I was holding a pistol and made a couple of clicking noises with my tongue.

I saw him out at the Rocks several times after that. I would say hello but he would give me an eye roll and sneer. Alrighty then. Whatever. He was by far the worst date, and the worst trick, EVER! – Deschicago

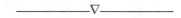

Columbus, OH

My worst date actually started out as one of my best dates. I had met a very handsome, witty guy and had asked him out to dinner. I don't remember the restaurant, but I fondly recall that the evening was lots of fun. We talked about books, our life stories and there was a lot of laughter. As the evening progressed, I really felt that I could fall for this guy. He seemed to be everything I wanted in a man. The perfect date. At the end of the evening, he pulled out a book that he had recently finished: *A Yellow Raft in Blue Water* by Michael Dorris. He urged me to read it and handed me his copy after writing his name and number in it. We ended our date flirtatiously and I was already looking forward to date number two. A few days passed and I rang him to ask about seeing him again. I didn't get an answer, so I left a message for him. A few more days went by and still no call from this sexy man. I left a second message and I'm sure that there was bewilderment in my voice as I explained that at the very least that I had hoped he would call me back so that I could return his book. It wasn't until a few weeks later that I bumped into an old friend who happened to know my date as well. I told him about what had transpired and how confused I was, since I knew that he had enjoyed himself on that date. My friend paused and then told me that the guy had committed suicide a few weeks ago. I was just gutted. I never bothered to try and figure out how soon after our date that this tragedy occurred. It was all I could do not to question our brief time together and what I might have done had I known. I did learn some time later that my date had been HIV+. Could this have been some sort of driving force that led to his death? It is all speculative and I will never know. I still have the book. – Brett Shingledecker

Los Angeles, CA

The worst dates are when people lie about their appearance. You meet someone online, they send you a picture of them that's 10 years old and 40 pounds lighter. Then you meet them! I met this really sweet man a year ago. He could tell that I was stunned when I saw him walk in the cafe. He said and I quote, "I know my face looks swollen because I've been to the dentist." I asked when, and he said, "Seven years ago!" – Jason Stuart

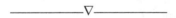

North Carolina

In college after I came out, I met a guy at a bar and we seemed to hit it off. He lived in another city, so I drove up to meet him (at his suggestion). He chose the restaurant and asked to be sat in a more private spot. I asked him if he was embarrassed to be seen with me and he said he just wanted privacy. As the evening went on, he revealed he wasn't "out" and his parents didn't know. He came from money and said they would disown him if they found out. He was very rude to the wait staff and snapped at the manager when they asked how everything was. By the end of the evening I was already convinced it would go no further. He asked me to get a hotel room and stay the night (not offering to go half in) so he could be with me. I told him I needed to get back to school as I had to be up early the next day. He got upset and said he never should have agreed to meet me and that I wasn't worth the effort. He ended up driving away angry. – Bill

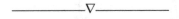

Coronado Island, CA

The worst date that I went on was with an ex (we had broken up a short time before). She was drunk and high before we went out on the date. We ended up in her room in the barracks on Coronado Island. – Pat Cummings

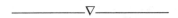

San Francisco, CA

The first date after losing my husband. I had thoroughly explained the situation to this gentleman. Yet he thought I was ready to hop in the sack after dinner! – Daniel Goss

San Diego, CA

Well, it's rather difficult to select just one because there were so many. One that comes to mind was in San Diego, around 1979. I was already full on cross dressing and well on my way to wanting a sex change as it was referred to back then, but really struggled to keep trying to fit into a straight lifestyle and wasn't doing very well at it. I met this very hot woman where I worked as a checker and night stock clerk at Safeway; a really good, well paying, union job back then. She was a customer who came into the store frequently and we sort of became friends and I was very attracted to her.

One day I asked her out and she agreed. I was stunned because I had a very low self-esteem of myself and felt incredible shame and quilt over my secret life as I had begun calling it. Other times on dates I kept that secret part about my life just that, a secret, but this time was determined to come out to her and tell all about myself and my love for all things feminine; my dresses, make-up, wigs, lingerie, and just wanted her to help me make that big jump to becoming s total woman for good.

It was a total disaster. Starting off with some wine and a strong joint we enjoyed getting high together and then I opened up. She totally couldn't handle it and flew off the handle screaming at me that she thought I was a man, not some freak. I was totally devastated and sat in my car crying after being told to leave her house. I felt so rejected and believed her that I was a freak. – Denise Chanterelle Dubois

———————∇———————

Chicago, IL

I met this hot black dude from Haiti on a Saturday morning at the Original Pancake House on Bellevue back in the mid-'80s. As I was leaving, I went to his table exchanged info and spoke, later to meet up that night at Melrose Diner. When I arrived, this hot butch dude was in a full-length fur coat, fur hat and enough makeup to notice. A total bait-n-switch to me and it ended after we had a Coke. – Malone Sizelove

———————∇———————

Texas

In the fall of 1984, I was 20 years old and working my way through school at a record store that sold classical music. Not only that, I had also just broken up with one of my co-workers, a 30-year-old guy named Larry.

A few weeks after the big fight that convinced me we were through, another one of my co-workers, a 35-year-old named Allan, asked me to go out to dinner with him. So I did.

Allan was a nice enough guy, but I thought he was pretty boring and super pretentious. And I didn't find him very attractive. I thought he resembled a cross between Art Garfunkel and one of those sugar skulls you find at Mexican Day of the Dead celebrations.

But I went on a date with him anyway for two reasons: 1) he offered to pay, and 2) I wanted to make Larry jealous.

What Allan didn't know was that Larry had the hots for him. I knew Larry had the hots for Allan because that's just the kind of thing Larry would scream at me to make ME jealous during shouting matches at the store. Did I mention that although the romance had fizzled, Larry and I were still working at the same store? Because we were still working at the same store.

So Allan and I went out for a sushi dinner at a very nice restaurant (much nicer than what I could typically afford as an impoverished university student). The sushi was very good, but Allan talked about himself the whole evening. He was obviously trying to impress me with his world travels (at the time, I had never left the US) and his law degree (it's true he was a lawyer, but he worked in the record store because he hated practicing law and was experiencing an early onset midlife crisis). I smiled, laughed at his jokes, and acted interested. When you're a twink, not much is required from you by way of keeping up your end of the conversation.

After dinner, Allan suggested having a night cap at some nearby bar, but I pretty much knew what was on his mind (getting to third base), so as soon as dinner was over, I gave him some spiel about having to get up early the next day for a class and said good night without even giving him a hug.

As far as disastrous dates go, I suppose that was pretty tame, but it did have the desired effect. I had not mentioned our date to Larry, knowing that word would eventually get around in our small store. Sure enough, the following weekend, Allan casually mentioned our date to Larry, and Larry was beside himself. He angrily demanded to know what happened on our date, but I gave him bland, circuitous answers which only fanned the flames of his anger even more. To my relief, Allan never asked me out again. But he and Larry did eventually hook up. They dated semi-seriously for about a month before that romance fizzled as well. Apparently, Allan bored Larry just as much as he had bored me. – Edward Thomas-Herrera

Chicago, IL

A couple of them, all in Chicago. One was with a guy at a small Hispanic diner at the corner of Clark and Lawrence. He kept trying to be witty (in English) with the waitress who barely spoke any English. The other was a cop who I met at a restaurant downtown. He kept rubbing my crotch with his foot under the table. After some conversation, turns out he was married (to a woman) but played around. In both cases, I never saw them again. – Bernard

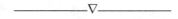

Chicago, IL

Prior to 1989, I was a raging alcoholic and rarely dated. If I did date, the "worst" date would have been me. – Leo Schwartz

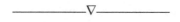

Minnesota, MN

A guy that would only have sex in his car ... in a parking lot ... in the dead of winter ... outside a convent. – Mark Abramson

———————∇———————

Chicago, IL

She seemed like a nice person. I picked her up for a date and throughout the evening she turned into five different people, seems she was a double Gemini. I could not get her home fast enough. – Marge Summit

———————∇———————

Chicago, IL

I never dated a lot. I would get to know someone and kind of slide into it. I didn't trust anyone and felt scared of rejection. I do remember that I had a really great date and at the end, when he was leaving, after he dropped me off, he turned to me and said, "I really like you, but if I see you on the street and I am with my friends, I probably won't say hi. You understand," and then he drove off leaving me stunned. – Honey West

———————∇———————

Chicago, IL

Lately, I've actually been having some luck meeting people to date through sites like Grindr and Scruff. I had been texting back and forth with one guy for a while and we decided to meet. I went to his apartment in Lakeview. We were going to walk his dog to the Starbucks in Wrigleyville in Chicago and get to know each other, face to face, for a bit. First off, I was more upset that his poor dog, a lab mix, was probably 20 to 30lbs overweight than the fact that his profile picture was at least 10 to 15 years old. It actually took me a moment to officially determine that he was the same guy in the photo. But honestly, I truly get that putting yourself out there is hard ... and if you have to fudge a bit at first to feel better ... well ... Anyhow, we set off and I soon learned that he was really interested in architecture ... which might have been fun, if I would have been able to understand anything he said. He would start a sentence – "Oh, I wonder why they used terracotta there ... " But then he would turn his head away from me and mutter the rest of his thought in this weird rambling whisper. I couldn't comprehend a thing that he was saying. We got our iced coffees and let his dog run (as much as she could) and he finally asked me about what kind of writing I did. I told him I was a freelance journalist and that I also wrote about genre films and the personalities involved with them for my site called Big Gay Horror Fan. He gasped, loudly, and his left hand flew to his chest, clutching his pearls style. "Horror," he shrieked. "No, no, no, no! Like slashers? I can't do that. Thrillers – maybe. I love that one with Meryl Streep on the boat in the river years ago ... but horror. No, no, no, no!" When I finally could get a word in, I let him know what I found culturally significant and important about the genre ... but, perhaps not surprisingly, it was definitely our first and last date. – Brian Kirst

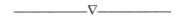

WHAT'S THE BEST DRAG SHOW YOU EVER SAW?

Milwaukee, WI

Pridefest, Milwaukee, a performer in a straitjacket climbing a tent pole to *Crazy* by Patsy Cline. – Douglas

———————∇———————

St. Louis, MO

Sometime around 1992 I got my family and friends of my mom to get her over to the bar I worked at, Magnolia's in St. Louis. There was a nice cabaret setup upstairs. It was her birthday, and the main performer Petrina Marie and the regulars put on a really great show in her honor. A packed room made it more fun, and I videotaped it. Sad thing was after it was all over, I had to work – I cleaned the entire complex through to about 10 AM. And back in 1984 and '85 I was the DJ for a cabaret show at a lesbian bar, Genesis II. It was male drag queens, and a female that did Janis Joplin performances. Never a dull moment. – Todd Jaeger

———————∇———————

Dallas, TX

In the spring/summer of 1991 I worked at the Village Station in Dallas as a bar back. Some nights I worked in the show lounge upstairs in the Rose Room, so I saw a lot of great performances. But the best was a drag queen called Amazing Grace. She did comedy on Monday nights. Grace was the funniest performer ever. She had her alter ego, "Kelly Kelly," who was supposed to be a rich white girl from Highland Park (ritzy area of Dallas), and she would also perform to a lot of TV show themes. I think *Wonder Woman* and *Sanford and Son* were my favorites. She invented lyrics to the *Sanford and Son* theme, which I wish I remembered. From the stage, she would order drinks from the bar and we would mess with her by adding a bunch of olive juice or something to it. She'd drink it onstage but never once fell out of character. She would just work it into the act. Grace was an amazing performer and a really sweet man. His real name was Corwin Hawkins, and he eventually made his acting debut in the Keenan Ivory Wayans film *A Low Down Dirty Shame*. Unfortunately, Corwin died in 1994 of AIDS complications. – Brent

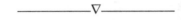

Chicago, IL

I don't remember the "best" drag show I ever saw because of the vague definition of "best" in this context. I really like all drag shows; the ones where you can't determine if the performer is in drag as much as the ones where the person in drag is dressed to the nines in ballgown and six-inch spike heels with make-up better applied than Charlie's Angels – and a full beard! Delightfully campy!

But I particularly liked the Baton Show Lounge on North Clark (which is relocating to N. Broadway in Uptown due to escalating rents in its present location) because of the Motown Revue I saw there in about 2007. – Paxton Anthony Murphy

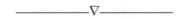

Chicago, IL

I prefer a female impersonator who can actually perform the music rather than merely lip-sync. I remember a short-lived bar on Oak Street in Chicago which I think was called La Cage, where the "girls" performed the songs. A couple were terrific! – Tom Chiola

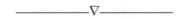

San Francisco, CA

I've seen quite a few. I was involved in the San Francisco Court System for a while which was all drag. I was in a couple of their productions as the eye candy. You wouldn't believe it now but it's true. I worked for Empress XIII and she put on a bunch of drag shows, some of the Empress Balls that they used to do for the coronation. I also saw the drag show at Finocchio's, that was a good polished drag show, but my favorites were the Empress Coronation Balls. – Steve

———————▽———————

Ottawa, Canada

I was judging Mr. Ottawa Leather in November of 2000. I was the current American Leatherman, and they had what I thought at the time was one of the most incredible drag performances, and now I cannot remember her name, but she did a spot-on Bette Midler as Dixie, and I think that was her drag name. I did not see a lot of drag shows but certainly saw plenty of drag performers over the years. Some other favorites would be the Kinsey Sicks who I saw the first time at MAL in Washington DC, I don't recall the first year they performed there when I saw them. Maybe 1999, or 2000. Also, at MAL the first time I saw Varla Jean Merman, and then saw him out of drag, I was really blown away. I have also been fortunate to have worked with Roy Haylock aka Bianca del Rio in New Orleans before Drag Race so those are a few that stand out to me. – Dean Ogren

———————▽———————

Washington, DC

I was a drag performer for quite a while, around 15 years. I had the opportunity to see so many amazing shows and be a part of them. I traveled the county with Club Casanova and Mo B. Dick. I partook in the International Drag King Community Extravaganza (IDKE) as well as the Great Big in DC every year. It's hard to choose between those two conferences and shows, as they were both showcases of the best drag performances on stage. The second to last Great Big in DC had a certain electricity to it though. The Kinging community had expanded and this amazing growth had been transferred onto the stage. The acts were phenomenal – *Kill Bill*, *Chicago*, *Flashdance*, spoken word, opera, and so much more that weekend. – Cody Las Vegas

———————▽———————

San Francisco, CA

Charles Pierce. I was sneaking into the Gilded Cage when I was 18 years old. In those days bar age was 21. Charles Pierce had two giant moments in his career that were punctuated by falling ill to hepatitis. He had a really rough course. He became famous, at least among those of us who followed him, for the differences between before and after the hep. Before he did the younger characters, Liza Minelli, I don't remember if he did Cher ... he probably did. Then afterwards he focused on the older characters, Bette Davis, Tallulah Bankhead. His conversations between Bette and Tallulah were fabulous and hysterically funny. – Bill Barrick

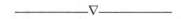

Fire Island, NY

Only because she was a legend, I would consider this the best. When I was going out to Fire Island in the late 1970s, Divine would perform. She'd hang out at the same resort as I did, at the pool, out of drag. She was amazing. She was Divine. That, to me, had been the best. – Randy Warren

Cincinnati, OH

Not sure it was the best, but I was at the point at which I realized drag was a legitimate artform: 1991 in Cincinnati, OH. The Dock used to have these big drag productions on Sunday nights. This one particular night, it was Drag Hollywood Squares. They had constructed a three-tier set with nine drag queens each dressed as a different celebrity (even a "Paul Lynde" in the center square) and a drag host. Two people were pulled on stage from the audience to play the game for prizes. The impressions were spot on. I don't remember the drag performer's name, but she wasn't just doing a Bette Davis impression, she was Bette Davis. – Misha Davenport

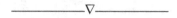

Chicago, IL

The art form of drag is such an amazing amalgamation of talent, color, texture, sound, performance – how to ever choose one performance over another, I cannot. I do recall a drag talent show, however, that was especially fun at the bar Sidetrack here in Chicago. My friend's co-worker

Steven dressed up as *Wonder Woman* – or something like *Wonder Woman* – and lip synched *Holding Out For A Hero* by Bonnie Tyler. The song, which I'm sure you've heard, has a throbbing bassline and sharp percussive Tom Tom drums and fast snare drum rolls. Steven got up on the bar and strutted all the way down, walking to the beat, throwing up his half-cape behind him as if caught in the wind and flipping open his eyes so that his mega-long false eyelashes whipped up. He'd hold each one of these poses to accentuate the percussive hits of the song. It was one of the best performances, drag or not, that I think I've ever seen live. – Matt

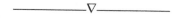

New York, NY

I've seen hundreds. But hands down, Lady Bunny in *24-Carrot Lady* sometime in the early '90s at the venerable gay cabaret, the Duplex. Bunny sarcastically (?) doing B-level show tunes, cabaret dross and songs from HR Pufn'stuf was hysterical enough, but the connecting Greyhound bus "soundtrack" of her leaving her childhood home of Chattanooga and then bringing the lights down so she could pickpocket the first row? Genius. – Steve Lafreniere

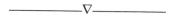

San Francisco, CA

I haven't been to the kind of show that I think of when I hear the phrase "drag show." I've seen more drag at square dance conventions than anywhere else. And it's intentionally bad drag, which is sometimes very, very good.

In 1996 at the San Francisco convention called "Stars, Thars and Cable Cars," Lois Carmen D'Nominator (Mike Blizzard of Chicago) and T*A*M*I Whynot (Bob Young, then of New York) lip synched to Ethel Merman singing *Gee, it's Great to be Here* and did some things so funny that I started having trouble breathing through my laughter, and the room started to spin a little (no, it wasn't an earthquake). – Rick

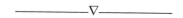

Washington, DC

In 1979 at the first March on Washington for Lesbian and Gay Rights, out on the grass before the march started, I saw The United Fruit Company

doing street (grass?) theater. They played a preacher and church ladies, and I remember this bit:
Preacher: "The Bible – I say, the Bible encourages sodomy!"
Church Lady: "And I'm living proof, Lord!"
Preacher: "It says in the Bible – it says – it says, 'go DOWN, Moses!'"
Church Ladies: "Hallelujah!"
– Rick

—————∇—————

Norfolk, VA

It was at the College Cue Club, I cannot remember the Drag Queen's name but the number she did started with her in a coffin and other queens paying their respects. Then once they had all filed by, then she sat up in the coffin and broke out into a rousing lipsync of *And I'm Telling You* from *Dreamgirls*, hopped from the coffin, furiously emoting all over the place, and ending in a finale sliding clear across the stage on her knees! – Bud Thomas

—————∇—————

Madison, WI

2004. My roommate and good friend at the time, Steve, had always wanted to drag, but was too nervous and self-conscious about it. He also had some hang-ups about masculinity, and as much as he admired drag queens, couldn't bring himself to try it. I encouraged, or rather, adamantly insisted that he try it, and he did, privately in our apartment at first. Through his connections he scored a gig in a local drag show. Like most Madison queens we had to go south to Chicago to get him outfitted. Steve didn't have any gay cultural reference points, was oblivious to drag history, and didn't necessarily have the queen attitude, but he looked beautiful in drag and could actually sing as well. When he got up on stage at Club 5 to sing (not lip sync) to a Burt Bacharach song (literally the only music he knew), it was glorious and he was positively elated. I've been to better drag shows all over the country, but seeing my friend finally break free and come into his own while performing in drag for the first time was truly unforgettable. – Shane K.

—————∇—————

Miami Beach, FL
Tampa, FL

I've been to many drag shows including the Miss Florida Pageant at the Fontainebleau Hotel. The best, however, would have to be Roxanne Russell singing *My Way* while removing his drag sitting at a lighted vanity. It was a beautiful performance. A close next would be Billie Boots in Tampa, FL. – Tom

—————▽—————

East St. Louis, IL

Top of the (Red) Bull, a small bar in East St. Louis. A wonderful, tiny place where everyone knew everyone else, including the performers, by name. Two twin brothers, Don and Ron, starred, one as Donna Drag and the other as Lana Kuntz. There may have been more professional ones later, but the Bull was a great good time. – Anonymous

—————▽—————

San Francisco, CA

I was a member of the Angels of Light in San Francisco. And before that I saw the Cockettes regularly. I also worked as the bouncer for Cabaret/After Dark dance club in SF. So I saw Sylvester regularly, Craig Russell. Sylvester, of course, was in a class all his own. Divine, Tihara, Hibiscus. I can't remember them all. – Bo Young

—————▽—————

Las Vegas, NV

1990-ish. It was one of the first drag shows I had ever seen. Up 'till that point I had only seen the local girls that I knew as boys. The Vegas show just wowed me. I sat there with my mouth open. These men were flawless and their recreations of the celebrities they were performing were spot on. – Jim Hensley

—————▽—————

Greensboro, NC

It was at a Triad Pride event and was hosted by a (now gone) Club by the name of Warehouse 29. It headlined some of my favorite local talent at the time, including Miss Triad Pride, Paisley Parque, as well as Fuschia Rage. The thing that made this interesting was that there was also a volleyball game for charity where the drag queens would be facing off against the "trannyz" (a local transsexual volleyball team) for charity. It was the most fun I ever had. – Christian Bane

San Francisco, CA
Milwaukee, WI

Not an actual show, but I was in San Francisco and walking down the street was a Queen in Divine drag. She had the makeup, hair and clothing down to a T, down to the high forehead and the arched eyebrows. I rushed up to her and gushed, and she was positively gracious and kind.

Another time, I went with a female friend and the 9 year old daughter of another friend to Milwaukee Pridefest. It was fun to walk past the protesters who thought we were a couple and taking our daughter to Pride. But then we had to explain the haters to the child. But in the middle of trying to explain it, she saw some tall, beautiful drag Queens and said, "They look like Barbie!" She was entranced. I enjoyed the show even more seeing them through her eyes. – Anne

New York, NY

SO MANY, but the first one that leaps out is seeing John Kelly do Dagmar Onassis late at night at the Pyramid. It was beautiful and funny, it was sad, about death? Maybe Dagmar was lip-synching Violetta? But it was transformational for me, laughing and crying at the same time. I'm also ... you know, any time Kiki and Herb performed, although that's probably not really a drag show, but it set the bar for the kind of fearlessness that thrills me. I remember thinking that watching Logan Hardcore do an afternoon pool show in Cherry Grove a few years back – in BAKING heat, in drag, running around the pool in 7" heels, huffing poppers and climbing the facade of the hotel to do a number on the roof. Thrilling, terrifying, brave, and funny as hell. It also makes me remember seeing Ethyl Eichelberger in the PBS broadcast of *The Comedy of Errors* from Lincoln Center. Not a drag show, but the combined smarts, lunacy, outrageousness and truthfulness hooked me. – David Zinn

———————▽———————

Chicago, IL

I was working at the Baton/Shante (Alexandria Billings) was on stage. I was watching her and dropped a tray of drinks down someone's back and all over their mink coat. I was fired that night. – Joseph G

———————▽———————

Chicago, IL

The Chicago Kings at Circuit in the late '90s. They also did shows at Martyrs. I loved the energy and enthusiasm of those shows. There was still a lesbian scene in Chicago and it was great to see so many women together having a good time. – Chicago T

———————▽———————

Cardiff, Wales, UK

Minski's Cabaret. They have drag shows every weekend and I've been a few times. On this one occasion they went all out with the costumes – lots of feathers and glitter and not much else. The main act was the most amazing queen ever, I'm certain she sang live and she was so funny I almost peed myself more than once. I can't remember her name, because it was probably about thirty years ago, but I'll never forget how she belted out Shirley Bassey numbers and strode around on heels that would have broken my leg before I left the house. She'd pause in singing whenever she spotted anyone of interest to her in the audience and throw one liners out. I was scared to go to the toilet (probably didn't help with the almost peeing myself). – Nephy Hart

———————▽———————

Sydney, Australia

1996 Newtown (suburb of Sydney, AUS). Saw a tribute to ABBA where the movie *Priscillia, Queen of the Desert* was filmed. They re-enacted the film, with outrageous outfits. – Robert

—————————∇—————————

Washington, DC

In the fall of 2004. I forget what year but it doesn't really matter. I went to Miss Adams Morgan Contest, a huge drag gala extravaganza. Several thousand people (no exaggeration) attend each October around Halloween to watch the contestants lip-sync to songs. – Jeff

—————————∇—————————

Los Angeles, CA

I produced a play in Hollywood, CA. It was called *Pageant: The Musical*. It ran for five months and was a joy at every performance! – Dave Russo

—————————∇—————————

Key West, FL

A nightclub called Aqua. Faith Michaels and her wonderful ladies. – Michael Burke

—————————∇—————————

Atlanta, GA

The best drag was the Armorettes in Atlanta. Mary Edith Pitts performing *Eternal Flame* with sparklers coming out of her ass is an image I'll never forget. – Daniel

—————————∇—————————

Chicago, IL

Nina West's "Heels of Horror." That queen filled an evening with song, dance, and so many pop culture references, I couldn't keep track. I wish I could remember more of it. – Jordan

—————————∇—————————

San Francisco, CA

The Miss Haight-Ashbury Beauty Pageant at the Great American Music Hall in 1987. Each contestant had to do an evening wear, swimsuit, talent, and question-answering event, and the best was Miss Coin Wash, Cobalt Blueberg, an African American glamazon who announced that she would sing "a folk song of her people," which was Toto's *Africa,* while she made a giant martini for the judges – just one, in a giant martini glass. When she won, because of course she did, she accepted her crown while singing *I Did It My Way* in pig-latin. – Alec Holland

$$\nabla$$

Chicago, IL

My favorite drag performance was one number at the old Uptown Underground cabaret. A drag performer and two women dressed up like '40s WACs lip-synched and boogie-woogied to the old Andrews Sisters song *Boogie-Woogie Bugle Boy from Company B.* I loved seeing the quintessential song of the '40s – you know, when men were men, goddammit! – being done in drag. Plus, the hip young audience – probably their *great-grandparents* lived during the '40s – clapped and hooted and hollered and shook their shoulders. In one drag number, several different universes coalesced. – Bill

$$\nabla$$

Dallas, TX
Chicago, IL

Around 1984. I saw the legendary Charles Pierce in concert for an AIDS charity fundraiser. He rocked the house with his Bette Davis, Joan Crawford (and Collins) impersonations. My favorite joke of his, why sex with a woman is like a ride at Disneyland? It's hard to get on, it doesn't last very long and when it's all over, you just want to throw up.

Another time, in Chicago (circa 1994), my friend, Bill Salek, who was the cashier at the Brown Elephant, asked me if I wanted to be a judge for a drag show fundraiser for HBHC [Howard Brown Health Clinic]. It was at Buddie's bar on Clark Street and Bill had choreographed an homage to Barbra Streisand from *Funny Girl (His Love Makes Me Beautiful),* replete with bridal gowns and Ziegfeld chorus girls.

Of course, you couldn't live in Chicago's gay community and not remember Ginger Grant (RIP) performing *Just a Friendly Little Cat* at the

Baton Show Lounge. – David Clayton

—————————▽—————————

Chicago, IL

The best drag show I ever saw had to be the first time I stepped into the Bistro in Chicago and witnessed the Bearded Lady, Tommy Noble et al swirling, twirling, dancing and lip syncing to the fabulous disco tunes of the day. It was the mid-'70s, I was young, everything was fresh, new and wonderful to my eyes! I have since seen countless drag performances as well as occasionally participated in drag myself, but there is nothing like the first time! – Paul Mikos

—————————▽—————————

Tampa, FL

An AIDS Benefit in Tampa, FL circa 1989. The opening set was a graveyard. Four beautiful, shirtless men carried a coffin on stage to the Funeral March. They propped the coffin up against a grave when the music changed. The coffin swung open and a queen named "Rene" burst out singing *And I Am Telling You I'm Not Going*. She was dressed in a gown with a large sequined red ribbon bedazzled across the front. – Eric Andrews-Katz

—————————▽—————————

San Francisco, CA

Any show by the Kinsey Sicks, America's first Dragapella Quartet. – Allan

—————————▽—————————

Chicago, IL

Hmm. That's a tough one. I think every drag show I've ever seen is the best ever, but I do have a special place in my heart for Gurlene and Gurlette, with whom I did a couple shows with at a small club called Lower Links in Chicago in the early 1990s. These shows were lowbrow but high falutin' and the most enthusiastic audience ever. – Terence Smith

———————∇———————

Knoxville, TN

At a gay bar in Knoxville, Tennessee. It was about 2005 and the show included Drag Kings and Queens. The music included very few show tunes but instead some new wave and rock. The attire seemed more natural and not all put on and glitzy. The crowd was a mix of supportive gays, straights, men and women. I truly loved it! – Paul Harris

———————∇———————

West Palm Beach, FL

West Palm Beach, probably 1993. It was a bar attached to one of the many gay motels down there, and I think it's been torn down. But Florida drag queens know how to put on one very serious show. – Sean Martin

———————∇———————

Chicago, IL

Night of 100 Drag Queens at Sidetrack in Chicago, a medley of James Bond theme songs. – Rick Karlin

———————∇———————

Provincetown, MA

It was Craig Russell at the time his movie came out. He was a performer from Canada. I can't think of the name of the movie. He had a really good show. The same year I had also seen Charles Pierce, again in Provincetown. – Roy Alton Wald.

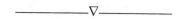

Portland, OR

It was in a bar called Dahl and Penny's, it had a large front bar and then a back bar with tables, small cocktail tables, and a stage. They put on regular performances there, some by the Court and some were just hangers on. It was always a lot of fun and they didn't take themselves too seriously. They always did a terrific job. That was in the late 1970s, early 1980s. – Tim Parrott

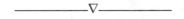

Las Vegas, NV

Boylesque. There was this fat, white, drag queen. She came out and did her number, some song about having a baby. *I'm Having His Baby* or something like that. At the end she turns to walk off stage and this black baby drops out from between her legs. How the fuck she kept that thing in that long I don't know. That was hilarious. – David Hardy

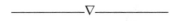

South Bend, IN.

It would have to be at a sad little place in Indiana called "The Seahorse Cabaret," in South Bend. I went there with a group of friends from New Buffalo, Michigan. After several cocktails, the show began. An older entertainer came onstage with daisy duke cutoffs, a wife beater t-shirt, and stiletto heels. Not the prettiest, or most professional looking drag I had ever seen, but this seasoned pro looked as if she had a few more performances tucked between her thighs. She lip-synched to the Two Non-Blonds song *What's Going On?* She twirled. She flailed her arms wildly. She flipped her wig back and forth. There was applause and cheers, then she stopped suddenly and grabbed her ass. "Son of a bitch! Fuck me! This fucking implant!" she screamed. Two guys came from off-stage, knelt down and began examining her butt. "Is this part of her act?" we were asking each other. You could clearly see that the implant in her left butt cheek had shifted down during her routine and was now slumped down her left leg. It was unsettling to see. The music stopped, the stage lights went dark, and she was led off stage as she cupped the sagging silicone in her hands. The show continued with other performers. Later, she returned on-stage in a different costume. "Oh my god, I'm totally embarrassed," she said as she covered her face with her hands. "Can you all ever forgive me, or should I say, can you all ever forgive my plastic surgeon?" There was loud laughter and applause. I think everyone in that bar stood up and went up to the stage, shook her hand or gave her a hug, and gave her money. She was in tears, and placing her hand over her heart, repeatedly said, "thank you." It was spontaneous and special. Driving back to New Buffalo, we all agreed it was the best drag performance we had ever seen. – Deschicago

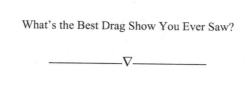

Chicago, IL

No "drag show" really stands out to me – they all seem pretty close to the same. The person I really enjoyed and respected was Memory Lane. She hung out at lots of the same places I frequented – Bistro, the Rage, Paradise and, of course, my memory is pretty shot from all the fun that was constantly had in the '80s. She was upbeat, very pleasant, sociable, non-discriminatory (to women) and genuinely nice. T.L. Noble always cracked me up – I don't know if he was really a "Drag Queen" but was sure fun! – Anonymous

Chicago, IL

I saw Chicago artist Doug Stapleton perform as Gurlene Hussey at N.A.M.E. Gallery (with Beth Tanner) in December of 1996. This was a year or so after his performance partner Randy Eslinger (Gurlene's sister, Gurlette Hussey) died of AIDS, continuing the spirit of the trailer trashy Gurlene and Gurlette Hussy shows with an undercurrent that felt deeply poetic and achingly beautiful. The performance made me realize that drag shows had potential to explore the human condition at much deeper and profound levels, and that's why it was the best. – Anonymous

Chicago, IL

It's not a traditional drag show per se, but Jinkx Monsoon's "The Ginger Snapped" cabaret show was phenomenal, touching, funny, and so beautifully crafted. – James Conley

Detroit, MI

I don't know if I would say it was the best drag show, but it was the funniest. This very large bear of a man came out in a floor length formal, wig, full makeup and started his show to Nancy Sinatra's *These Boots Were Made for Walking.* When she got to the chorus, she hiked her formal up and she was wearing combat boots. I almost wet my pants. – Guy Sands

—————▽—————

Mykonos, Greece

In 1987 I went to Mykonos. My travel companion never showed up at the airport, so I went alone. I met some great people there and one of them is still one of my closest friends. He and I went to an outdoor drag show. At one point, a drag queen simulated expressing milk from her breast at the packed crowd and people moved really quickly to avoid the liquid touching them. – David Fink

—————▽—————

Chicago, IL

That had to be the Jewel Box Review. I saw them at the bar on Cottage Grove Ave. way back when. Me and the lead singer, Stormy, chatted for a long time. – Marge Summit

—————▽—————

Chicago, IL

The Cycle Sluts, a genderfuck comedy troupe from (I believe) San Francisco. In 1976 they appeared at the Vic Theater in Chicago, presented by the Broadway Ltd., a gay disco. – Bill Williams

—————▽—————

Atlanta, GA

The Sweet Gum Head and the "Return" of Rachel Wells. Children can look up Miss Wells. A true icon. The "Gum Head" was billed as "The Showplace Of The South." The entertainers were phenomenal ... Heather Fontaine, Dina Jacobs, Hot Chocolate, Lisa King, Lady Shawn, Miss Chablis ... etc. – Daniel Goss

—————▽—————

New York, NY

Ian MacKinnon and Travis Wood, as well as Bill Mayer and Alan Ishi, all produce grand drag shows in Los Angeles right now. But I must admit that the best drag show I ever saw was in 1966 in New York, first at the La Mama Experimental Theatre Club and then at the Caffe Cino. It was an actor named Charles Stanley as Jean Harlow in playwright H.M. Koutoukas' *Tidy Passions*. You may see Jim Gossage's photo of Charles performing this at the Cino while Koutoukas watches at https://caffecino.wordpress.com/1949/09/12/a-magical-cino-moment/ – Robert Patrick

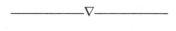

Milwaukee, WI

The best drag show that I saw was the first one that I saw when I was 18 years old (1971). It was held in the Holiday Inn on Wisconsin Avenue. My brother's apartment mate, Dale, was one of the drag queens in the show. Many of the people in the show were friends of my brother. So I knew them socially. It was a whole new thing for me to see them on stage. – Pat Cummings

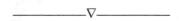

Chicago, IL
Malaysia

The best one was in Chicago's Baton Show Lounge. I was most impressed with the performer who impersonated Diana Ross. Another surprising one was in Malaysia where the performers sang in their own voice and tell jokes and stories. – Chen Ooi

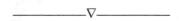

New York, NY

Without question, the unmistakably garish and cringe-inspiring Dina Martina in September 2012 at the Laurie Beechman Theater in New York City. After croaking her way through a rendition of the Propellerheads' *History Repeating*, she announced, "I nailed it! I nailed it to a cross!" and belched. Between her glitter-green wig and her oversized lips, the color of Walgreen's Merlot, I was smitten. – Robert W. Fieseler

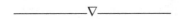

Chicago, IL

Just this past Sunday at brunch at KitKat Lounge in Chicago – Madame X!!
She was unbelievable – she actually sang all of the songs by Lady Gaga,
Amy Winehouse and a few others! Incredible! – Kit Welch

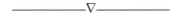

New Orleans, LA

The absolute best drag show was the My-O-My club in New Orleans for
female impersonators. Their talent was only surpassed by their beauty. One
of the happiest moments was when one came over to our table and
borrowed my silk chiffon duster and paraded around the floor. In New
Orleans, I was always in places that were frequented by tourists. – Janan
Lindley

Chicago, IL

Monica Monroe at the Baton doing the operatic number from *The Fifth
Element*. It was high art. – Mitchell Fain

New York, NY

I was only able to see the dress rehearsal as the actual show was cancelled
because of infighting within the Gay Activists Alliance (GAA) membership.
I headed a committee at GAA called Fundraising and Pleasure and after the
success of the first Christopher Street Liberation March we started planning
the next fundraising event. It would be held at St. Peter's Church in
Chelsea. It was to be a dance happening, a flower child circus. Joshua Light
from the Fillmore East had agreed to do the light show and there were a
number of theatrical happenings planned to sporadically occur during the
event. One performer, Natasha, had been crowned Miss Black Universe a
couple of weeks before. For Natasha's act, a muscular dancer dressed in a
leather jock strap towed a rope onto the center of the dance floor. At the
end of the rope was Natasha in prize drag, would strip out of costume,

revealing that he was a man and then would shoot off a gun and paper flowers would drop from the rafters. The ultimate transvestite, flower child, anti-war trip.

I knew, good theater raises peoples thinking and emotions, but I was not prepared for the fury this concept raised amongst the members of GAA. Some of the women said it would be offensive to them, others found it offensive to African Americans, others thought it reinforced stereotypes. I thought they were all being ridiculous and showing their own inner racism, sexism and homophobia. The dance went on as otherwise planned but Natasha's' act was not allowed to take place. – Philip Raia

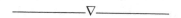

Evansville, IN

The best drag show I've ever seen happened around Christmastime 2014 in my hometown of Evansville, Indiana, at the only gay bar in town, which is called Someplace Else. When you enter this bar, the main dance floor is always empty. You have to go through the door in the corner, which takes you up a narrow staircase to the upstairs bar with low ceilings and a tiny stage. That room is always packed. She took the stage in a short red Santa skirt with the classic white fur trim and hat. She must've been 80 years old, and looked exactly like my memaw. Brenda Lee's *Rockin' Around the Christmas Tree* came on and Miss Jackie P. Lee kicked her bare little Elaine Stritch legs and took dollar bills with a huge smile. She was living. As I panicked with excitement in the front row, Jackie quit lip-syncing mid-song, sat down next to me and said in a gravelly smoker's voice, "My god, this is exhausting." She got back up and did two more numbers. – Devlyn Camp

New York, NY
Chicago, IL

As someone who has written a book on drag – *Drag: Combing Through the Big Wigs of Show Business* (Rizzoli, 2019) – I've seen a lot of drag during my lifetime. I've always been a drag hag.

I used to run into RuPaul and Lady Bunny clubbing in the East Village of the late 1980s. I went to at least a half dozen Wigstock festivals and have the T-shirts to prove it. I've seen live performances by such bygone legends as Divine, Sylvester, Leigh Bowery, Charles Pierce, Dean Johnson, the queens of *Paris is Burning*, even Milton Berle in drag.

I've been to more gigs by Lypsinka, Charles Busch, Varla Jean

Merman, Joey Arias, and Dina Martina, than I can shake a lipstick at. I knew Hedda Lettuce before she was green and Bianca Del Rio when she was still nice! So picking one drag show as the best one ever is tough.

I *can* still quote Divine's beyond-filthy "Denver omelet" joke from the time I saw her at La Cage in Chicago, so that's definitely up there. And the 1994 show at Town Hall called "Charles Busch's Dressing Up" to celebrate the 25th anniversary of Stonewall was astounding. That's where I saw Berle in a dress. Mr. Pierce was tasked with getting him off the stage that night and it wasn't easy. Milton didn't want to leave. Even Bea Arthur was there – so all manner of drag was represented.

But the one drag show – if it can be called a drag show – I attended that actually affords me bragging rights is the Love Ball. That was the fashion industry AIDS benefit at Roseland that the party-giver deluxe Susanne Bartsch and Annie Flanders of *Details* magazine staged that first shed mainstream light on the drag balls of Harlem. It was there on that night in May 1989 that we all got to see "voguing" up close for the very first time. Madonna, it should be noted, didn't record *Vogue* until six months later.

Everybody who was anybody in the New York City fashion/club demimonde was there that night. Kate Pierson of the B-52s was a model. Anna Wintour held court at her table. David Byrne, confused by the proceedings according a *New York Times* report, rubbed elbows with Willie Ninja. It was all that and a bag of hair clips.

I recently saw footage from that night in a documentary and, my god, it brought back memories. Back then, the Love Ball was just one more fabulous night among so many fabulous nights, but now I can't believe I was in that room, striking a pose with the cool kids. – Frank DeCaro

Paducah, KY

I've been to so many drag shows, but I remember my favorite one was at the bar Hearts in Paducah, Kentucky, where I saw my best friend Jayne Payne, the Queen of Hearts. I helped her get ready and she did songs from my favorite movie, *The Rose*. – Jeffery Meskenas

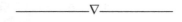

Chicago, IL

Marge Summit took me to see Chilli Pepper open for the Weather Girls at the Vic Theatre. Hands down Chilli has some of the best legs in the business. We would then go to the Baton on Sunday nights and see Chilli perform and I was in love. I have heard from more than one woman to say the same about Chilli. The Baton has the best of the best. I do love me some Ginger Grant and *Harper Valley PTA*. – Terry Gaskins

————————∇————————

WHEN WAS THE FIRST TIME YOU REALIZED YOU WERE "DIFFERENT?"

Chicago, IL

I was 5, the very single dad who lived next door. The man was widowed just days after his son was born. His mom arrived from Poland to care for the child. But the Dad had a habit of stripping off his suit from about the corner of our block. In warm weather he would be shirtless and furry by the front door. For lawn mowing all summer he wore only a bright red speedo. I would go out to our yard and sit at the fence and stare openly. While I was clearly attracted and often offered to help, he would always politely refuse and toss my frisbee or ball for me. As a result, I have been attracted to older furry men with blue or green eyes my entire life. Add in an accent and I'm a pushover every single time – Mike Martinez

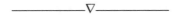

Detroit, MI

Probably by the fifth grade. I remember one kid – a late in the term transfer in from some other state. I remember his name, Jack Givens. I thought he was neat. That was the extent of it. He moved away almost as quickly as he arrived.

By the eighth grade, one of the girls in our neighborhood would hang around with some high school guys. I stalked them at a long distance (not her per se). I don't think I lusted over them, strictly speaking, but I did obsess about them. I never met them.

I didn't have sex (with anyone) until I was 32. One friend said of people he knew in their 20s that they were wasting the best years of their lives. Well, I didn't even get started before the best years were history. I've been behind schedule for the rest of my life. Maybe that's why I didn't get AIDS (though I did get scabies, Hep B (three days), herpes, and rectal gonorrhea over time – the last time being 1981). – Anonymous

———————▽———————

St. Louis, MO

Age 5, at least. Back in the late 1960s I managed to see some "hippie era" magazines like *Evergreen Review* and was drawn to the mod clothing ads which sometimes had shirtless or even naked men with beards and/or moustaches. One issue's cover had the famous naked photo of Allen Ginsberg and his partner, and I was fascinated. Not truly understanding sexuality, it had me wondering why I was always then looking for photos of, hopefully, shirtless men with facial hair and hairy chests. – Todd Jaeger

———————▽———————

Texas

I felt different from a very young age. One memory that stands out is 3rd grade. My best friend in school was a very effeminate boy who had no other friends. One day riding the bus to or from school, some boys in the seats in front of us turned around and started calling us fags. At 8 years old, I didn't know what that meant but I knew that it wasn't something you wanted to be called. My friend looked them straight in the eye and said, "I know we are!" I looked at him in bewilderment and he said, "Trust me." That same school year he got in trouble for kissing me in class. – Brent

———————▽———————

Brigham City, UT

When I was a kid, I used to beat off a lot and nobody seemed to be as interested in it as I was. I was 12 or 13 and realizing that I liked the boys better than the girls. Although, I had to play along like everybody else. I grew up in a small town with about 5,000 people. There was one other person I found out was gay later. We actually spent a night in bed together not realizing the other was gay. – Steve

———————▽———————

131

Chicago, IL

Grade school. I liked to perform and had a crush on Mr. Bowles, my fifth grade teacher at Little Flower Grade School. – Tom Chiola

——————▽——————

Huntington Beach, CA

I just noticed in the playground I played more with the girls than with the boys. That was at a Catholic school that I went to. It made it really interesting to try and figure it all out. – Great Big D

——————▽——————

Illinois
Lafayette, IN

I think I always knew. I used to say, "When I grow up to be a boy" all the time. My sisters and mom would correct me and tell me about getting my period one day and everything that goes with that. I refused to believe it. My sisters would introduce me to their friends, and I would kiss their hands and bow to them. I have no idea where that came from.

Although I was assigned female at birth, I always knew I was male. I never had fantasies where I was female. In my mind's eye, I was always in a tux and male at my idealized wedding. I distinctly remember sitting backwards on the toilet to pee the male way for quite a few years when I was young. Even as I was getting my period and being gifted with large breasts (why is it always what you don't want that you get in abundance?) I was still being a male.

Transitioning was not a thought at that time or even when I came out as a lesbian in college. The representation of trans individuals had not been positive. My exposure to trans people were through mainstream media that made a joke of them or killed them. The lack of positive representation and the general abhorrence I saw about trans people kept me in the trans closet a lot longer.

It wasn't until I started doing drag in Lafayette, IN, then Chicago, IL, and being comfortable in my drag that I truly began to live as myself. Everything clicked into place. I could see the man I was supposed to be, and be praised for it, onstage and in the community. The drag community was a bit hesitant at first but eventually I was able to find my fellow transmen onstage as well. I thank IDKE and the Great Big for expanding my drag community beyond the small minded and tokening producers in Chicago.

I came out three times. First as lesbian, then as a drag king, then as a transman. I think that deserves more than a toaster. – Cody Las Vegas

———————▽———————

New York, NY

When I was 11 years old. We would get the *New York Post* and the *Daily News*, and I remember flipping through and – vividly, I'll never forget this – the personal ads at the back of the paper. For escorts. There was a guy half naked. I thought to myself, I'm feeling something I shouldn't be feeling. There was definitely an attraction to seeing this guy in the personal ads, an escort. – Randy Warren

———————▽———————

Chicago, IL

My father and I played catch – threw a ball. I didn't enjoy it; and I knew that I was supposed to enjoy it, and I felt bad for not enjoying it. – Rick

———————▽———————

USA

1976 at my aunt's house for a very awkward Christmas party (it was my dad's sister; my parents divorced in 1974 and this might have been our first Christmas with his side of the family since the divorce). My older cousins were watching reruns of *The Wild West* and I found the show pretty boring until Robert Conrad appeared in tight pants and shirtless. I felt hot and confused. I was seeing something that no one else in the room seemed to be noticing. – Misha Davenport

———————▽———————

USA

I remember a dream when I was four or five, wherein I was trapped in a house fire and saved by a Tom of Finland-like fireman, with an open coat and furry chest. Imagine my surprise when as a teenager I saw a Tom of Finland drawing of said firefighter. But "realized I was different?" A neighborhood boy hit me when I tried to kiss his forehead. Probably six or seven. – Steve Lafreniere

——————▽——————

Wisconsin

From my very first moments. – Neil Cooper

——————▽——————

Chicago, IL

When I was a child, but it wasn't about sexual orientation. My difference was rooted in class – growing up working class in a school district that was upper middle class made me feel like an outsider. – Anonymous

——————▽——————

Lima, Peru

I'm not sure; my life's mindset constantly oscillates between "I'm unique" and "I'm just like everyone else." Right now, it's a mix of both. But I take it you mean sexual orientation/gender identity, so uhhhh ... Probably my teen years, around when I was 14 or 15, I realized most if not all my friends were queer. I felt "strangely" comfortable with them, and only realized I was also like them when I started having a crush on who would become my first girlfriend. Even then, I still didn't quite feel "different," since I fit in so well within my friend group. I knew we were a minority, but the first time it really struck me was when one of my close friends was kissed by another of my friends (both girls) and she told her parents, and they reacted badly, and the whole school found out about it, and I tried to get close to her to talk (at the moment I was in a school for girls, and the only one in the whole school with a pixie cut) and one of her (asshole) friends got between us and wouldn't let me get close to her, saying I had to, at least, keep two meters away. That was just shocking, it completely burst my bubble. I walked away because I didn't want trouble, but then I cried about it to my mom, and weeks later she said something during an argument along the lines of "Why do you dress like that? That's why people tell you to stay two meters away from them!" Dick move, mom. – Robb

——————▽——————

Chicago, IL

In the fifth grade I realized I was different. A neighbor and classmate, and I, would do homework together at a small desk in his basement while his mother gave piano lessons upstairs. He would reach over and hold my dick through my pants while we did our fifth-grade homework. I never had the nerve to reach back and touch him. I loved it when he touched me. I loved it when he held his hand in my crotch for hours while we did our homework together. – Bob

—————▽—————

Spryfield or Dartmouth, Nova Scotia, Canada

Oh, kindergarten, I'm sure. Not "different" in that sense (that wouldn't come until I was 20 or so), but I was a left-handed kid (and resisted all efforts to make me be right-handed, firmly) who could already read and write (and sign my name in cursive). I was a very serious kid, and pre-teen, and teenager. Only in my 30s did I start to even remotely try fitting in. I knew it was largely futile until then. Try telling a teacher in Grade Four who asked your religion that the answer is "none." She asked what my parents were. I said, "I don't know. I'm not my parents." – Tim Murphy

—————▽—————

Madison, WI

Like many LGBTQ people, I always felt different. I do remember a very early conversation with my mom, I think I was about 5 or 6 years old. I asked her "When I grow up, will I be a boy or a girl?" She said it was a silly question, but I remember pressing on and asking her, "What if I don't like boy things? What if I'd rather be a girl?" She said the questions were ridiculous, so I stopped, but I definitely knew early on that I was different from other boys, I just didn't know exactly what it meant. – Shane K.

—————▽—————

Wyoming

Public Camping site. I was probably about 10 years old. I went to the public bathroom/shower and saw a man just step out of the shower. He was maybe 30 years old, well built, and covered in thick dark hair. I stood there and stared for what seemed like hours till the man said, "Hey kid, what you

135

staring at?" At that point I turned and ran out. Completely forgetting I went in to use the bathroom. Forty-five years later, I still have visions of that man. WOOF! – Jim Hensley

—————————▽—————————

Indiana

Apparently, when I was about four I asked a playmate to cuddle with me. I really don't remember doing that, but I remember the scolding I got when my mom overheard. Another time when I was a little older a school friend came over and we were supposed to change into play clothes. She had issues about changing in front of our dog because he was a boy dog. But I saw her nipples and they were darker than mine and I was entranced. But something told me not to stare or ask to touch them. But I didn't forget them. – Anne

—————————▽—————————

Kenmore, NY

Fell in love with the cub master's son – Glen

—————————▽—————————

Portland, ME

I learned what gay meant from Mary Tyler Moore. I had always known I was attracted to boys since I was around age five and started to meet other kids my own age (in nursery school, I really, really wanted to be friends and play with another boy named Jimmy). And I had those feelings as I grew into a teenager, though by then I knew my feelings were different – but I didn't have a word for it. Anyway, one Saturday evening in the mid-'70s, my mother and I were watching the *Mary Tyler Moore* show. I was probably about 15 years old or so. In the show, Mary was dating a man she really liked, but at the end of the show he told Mary they couldn't go further because "I'm gay." I didn't know what that meant, so I asked my mother. My mother paused for a moment, and then said simply, "That means he likes men instead of women." So then I had a word for being different: *gay*. – Jeff

—————————▽—————————

Hickory, NC

My family was somewhat poor but managed to do some things when they had the extra money. One time, we went to a wrestling show and for some reason, I couldn't help gazing at the wrestlers' packages. Some were so big. I was 11 years old, and later that night when I got to bed, was the first time I ever touched myself "down there" as well. – Christian Bane

———————▽———————

Utica, NY

In 1960, I was starting kindergarten at Columbus Elementary School in Utica, NY. I was just shy of my 5th birthday. I never had any sense that I belonged and always felt socially self-conscious for reasons I did not understand. – Dave Russo

———————▽———————

St. Louis, MO

When I was five in grade school and every time I saw one guy in class I went into a day dream of kissing him. Had a hat he gave me, and I just loved the smell of it and was extremely protective of it. He moved to another city the next year, and I was in shock for several weeks. – Robert

———————▽———————

Iowa

I guess looking back it would have to be around 1st grade I knew I had same sex attraction. I wouldn't accept it until I was 28 years old, unfortunately, due to my homophobic upbringing. – Anonymous

———————▽———————

Australia

In high school, maybe 1974. I was mesmerized by another girl in class. – Susan H

———————▽———————

Palo Alto, CA

Always. By which I mean I think I've never felt NOT different? My first memory (4? 5?) is tied up with my desire for men (long story but short version is figuring out that if I fell on some playground equipment, the very friendly (and it was California so he worked out in swim trunks) attractive man who worked out on the fringe of our play area would come pick me up to comfort me. So I fell, and he did pick me up and hold me. I've always, I think, started with the idea that I wasn't like other kids. I feel like my process of discovery was realizing that I was more LIKE other people than I thought, rather than discovering my difference, if that makes sense. – David Zinn

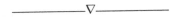

Mobile, AL

I was very young, preschool, when realized I wasn't athletic like my other brothers. – Rain Perez

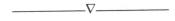

Perth, Australia

I realised I was different probably when I was 9 or 10. That's when I started getting called names at school. I didn't understand what the names meant, except to know they were mean and nasty. Nor could I understand why people were being so mean. I was the same person I had always been. I was kind and friendly to everyone. Only a few years later in high school, when the boys started dating the girls did I realise why people had been so horrible to me. It was a real "Ahhhhh" moment. – Mansfield

—————▽—————

Chicago, IL

I was about 12, and we were on a boy scout camping trip. There was lots of semi-nudity as is usual on those trips. Lots of swimming in underwear or nude, so little left to the imagination. One of the slightly older guys came out of the water in tighty-whities, and you could see the outline of his magnificent credentials. They were larger than anyone else's, and he was clearly unconcerned that they were so visible. I was riveted by the view, and all I wanted to do was stare, even though I had to pretend I wasn't. I knew right then that this was really what I wanted, even though it took me another 15 years before I acted on it. As my late partner was fond of saying, "Somebody missed a lot of fun." Understatement of the century. – Ripley

———————▽———————

Wheeling, IL

Sometime in my elementary school years. Summer break. A lanky next-door neighbor wore a revealing swimsuit. I was quite turned on but had no clue what to do with those yearnings. Alas. – Michael Burke

———————▽———————

San Francisco, CA

Waiting to board a train in SF carrying me to college in Missouri – stopped at a book store to get reading material and stumbled on the gay section. I realized that I was getting turned on by images in a picture book. I didn't buy it, of course, but I thought about it from there on! – Brian

———————▽———————

Chicago, IL

Since I could form coherent thought, I've been drawn to the differences that set us apart as humans. At a young age, I wanted something about myself to stand out from the rest of everyone. I was fascinated by cartoons and movies depicting people with extraordinary abilities and still am, honestly. In some of my more formative years, I became obsessed with the *Sailor Moon* universe. I loved to watch the characters in that show defend the world all in the name of love, and justice. That should have been a big hint for me that I was gay, but denial is powerful. – Jordan

———————▽———————

Chicago, IL

A great-uncle's barn took a stroke of lightning and burned to the ground. After his family built a new one, but before they put any livestock or hay in it, they held a barn dance to celebrate. I was eight years old and my brother nine. One of our cousins introduced us to a neighbor of theirs who was in his late teens. He was so friendly he danced with us, swinging us about in his strong arms as if we were his girlfriends. We and the onlookers laughed, as people said in those days, until we thought we'd die. I, though, realized dancing with that man made me feel as if I'd already gone to heaven. I wasn't like my blasé, I'll-play-this-silly-game, brother. I was different. – Ron Fritsch

————————▽————————

Wales, UK

I've always known I'm different to everyone else because I'm autistic, but as far as being LGBT is concerned, I figure it was about 1972 when I was 8. I hit puberty very early and I remember sobbing for days because I had boobs and periods and I couldn't be a boy anymore. I honestly believe that if I knew then what I know now I'd have been trans. As it was, I lived in a remote and very conservative valley at a time when we only had two channels on the TV and no mobile phones. By the time I started to become aware of the big world outside I was already married. I got married at 18 because that's what people did, and it was never a big romance. From day one sex was an issue and basically it was something I did because that's what people did. Bear in mind that my mother was 40 when she had me and grew up in the '30s and '40s. The marriage eventually ended because of my dislike of sex. He found someone who enjoyed it a lot more.

I then entered a period when I experimented more with BDSM and with women. I had a few short relationships with women, but I didn't enjoy sex any more with them. I got my kicks out of domination not sex.

I then met and eventually married my second husband who was far more progressive and understood my feelings. We had sex because I wanted to make him feel good even though I wasn't enjoying it any more. I have never had a vaginal orgasm and I can probably count on fingers and toes how many orgasms I've had period. I put away all my BDSM things because my husband was strictly vanilla. This is when the whole gender issue arose again. I didn't feel that I wanted to transition and I still don't, but I recognise there is a huge part of me that is far more masculine than feminine. I have never worn dresses if I could help it and my inner dialogues have always been male. I even had a name I would call myself when no-one else was there (as an autistic person I often referred to myself in the third person both internally and out loud. Even now I carry on an internal dialogue basically narrating my own life. In this dialogue I am Ash and male)

After the end of my second marriage in 2006, I discovered that there is a thing called asexuality and it fitted me like a second skin. Now, I feel at home as a non-binary asexual and I really wish I could have realized that decades ago. – Nephy Hart

—————∇—————

Chicago, IL

I was in the eighth grade, living in a suburb of Chicago, Bellwood. I had a friend who I rode bikes with. One summer, he wanted to drive around looking for shirtless men mowing their lawn. He wanted to circle back to a specific block because he wanted to get a second look at a certain man. He just exclaimed, "I just love men!" I looked at him, then at the guy mowing the lawn, and realized I loved men too. Maybe love is too strong a word, but I recognized my feelings were the same as his and those feelings were different than my older brother's and everyone else around me. – Peter

—————∇—————

Chicago, IL

Circa 1958. My earliest memory of being different was when I was perhaps four years old, watching an old *Tarzan* movie in the 1950s. Feeling a tingling in my thighs. Johnny Weismuller made me gay.

Later, in high school, being teased (and bullied) for carrying my books like a girl, in front of my chest, instead of under my arm and at my sides, like the boys did. – David Clayton

—————∇—————

Chicago, IL

I should have realized it in junior high. At the end of every day, when kids were lining up to get on our busses, some young school assistant (late teens?) was there; I never saw him at any other time. Unlike the male teachers and admins, who always wore baggy polyester dress slacks, this kid wore tight jeans. TIGHT jeans. TIGHT. Every day while waiting in the hall for my bus to arrive, I entertained myself meditating on his prominent Levi-Strauss bulge. This was long before I even heard the word "queer," so I never talked about this fascination with anyone – till now. But I wonder how many Future Faggots of America stood with me in that bus line shyly peeking at the biggest crotch we had ever seen. – Bill

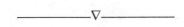

Florida

Between the ages of 3-7. I started having visions of the Great God Pan. At the age of 7 Pan appeared and said, "You will follow Me the rest of your life." I readily agreed. Nobody wanted to know about my dreams at all. – Eric Andrews-Katz

Chicago, IL

I wish I would have gotten this question when I was younger. Being gay is so part of who I am now and has been for so long I don't really remember feeling different. As a kid I slept/played around with a few of my friends, so we were all kinda "doing it" and experimenting. We didn't talk about it, so I guess we knew it was different. Most moved on and it was childhood exploration but, for me, being gay is who I am. – Mike Uetrecht

Illinois

Late '70s/early '80s. My life has been dictated by my differences. I had a different skin color/hair type than most of my family. I enjoyed playing with the same toys as my sisters, but they were girls and I was not. I come from generations of people who were socially awkward and, coincidentally, did not fit in or have many friends or attend parties and such.

As far as being sexually/romantically different, I cannot pinpoint an exact moment of epiphany, but I will say that I seriously began to resent the endless birthday/Christmas gifts from uncles and boyfriends of aunts which were carefully calculated to make me into more of a "boy," or at least the version they wanted me to be. I can't tell you how many football-related items were shoved down my throat as a kid. I had my eye on the Ken-doll-shaped packages under the Christmas tree. – Kirk Williamson

Ohio

As a little boy, maybe seven or eight years old. My aunt had a summer home on a lake in Ohio and I was there for the week. It must have been around the 4th of July because there was a big celebration on the beach with lots of activities for the kids. I was in some game with other boys in the water. I don't recall what it was, but it was competitive and things got rough. I hated the roughness, but all the other little boys seemed to having such fun. I just wanted to be alone with a book, or maybe with my cousin, Cathy, and her Barbie dolls. – Rick R. Reed

———————∇———————

Detroit, MI

I think that would have to be the first time I tried on a pair of my mother's shoes. Let's see ... I was about 12, so that would be 1970. Mom had some of her shoes stored in our basement and I was home alone for some reason or another, and noodling around, I came across them. I HAD to put them on, and put them on I did. A bit wobbly at first, but I quickly got the hang of it. Afterwards, I wondered if any of my friends had done that, indeed if my own father had. I decided that they had not, and therefore I was different. And special. – Terence Smith

———————∇———————

Lincolnwood, IL

I was 5 years old. I want to be like my imaginary friend Bob. He lived in the 5th board from the front door in the entry hall of the house. Bob was a boy and I wanted to be like my friend Bob. I did not do girl at all! I would rip the cloths off dolls I was given, then take the heads off. I wanted to play with my brother's old toys. He had an Erector Set in the basement, I would go down and play with that. It was a battle with my mother on what I would wear. I hated dresses. I had one dress they could get me into for when we had to dress up. It was blue and had a white elephant belt. Otherwise it was pants, t-shirts and gym shoes. I played with Gumby and Pokey, my father's tools – the gender appropriate toys of the '70's ... nope not going to happen. Fuck Barbie, I wanted a race track. Etch-A-Sketch, Lite Brite, were the toys of my youth. When puberty hit, I was a very unhappy camper. Menstrual cycles and breasts were breaking this tomboy's heart. It would take finding the leather community to start my journey. Chuck Renslow helped make me the man I am today. I am forever grateful to Chuck and Harry Shattuck. They allowed the SLUTS to take over the pit in the Eagle on Thursday nights. I was learning that gender is fluid and not set. I became a butch leather dyke where in play I was a leather man. The '90s and 2000s a lot of butch dykes started to transition to men. The

143

internet joined people and information together. We now had language, and information we did not previously have. – Jake Cohn

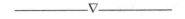

Davis, CA

That's a tough call. When we were 5 years old my best friend Steve Brady mooned me out his bedroom window and I knew I loved that sight of his butt. Of course, I didn't know I was gay and never heard the word. When the TV show *Daniel Boone* aired when I was about 9, I knew I was in love with his son, Israel, but of course could tell no one. Also, while 9 and visiting NYC, my 12 year old brother called me a queer. I don't think either of us knew what it meant but I knew it was different and it was definitely fitting for both of us.

From about 8-10 years old I used to play with plastic army men. I had one that was my favorite because he was laying on his stomach aiming a rifle and I adored his plastic butt. I still have that army man buried away somewhere. – Paul Harris

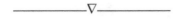

Chicago, IL

When I tried touching a girl's breasts in high school and felt absolutely no sexual longing whatsoever. – Allan Hurst

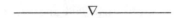

Northlake, IL

The first time I realized I was different was in the 4th grade in 1966. It was a Monday morning at St. John Vianney school in the suburbs of Chicago. Sister Camille was asking the class to share something they had done over the weekend. I stood up and told of a very interesting documentary I watched with my mother on PBS about homosexuality. I thought nothing about that was shocking or wrong, it was a fascinating subject and I was an innocent, curious sponge. Well ... Sister Camille quickly stopped me short and said that what I had to share was very interesting indeed, but we would talk about it privately after class. Which we did. She was very kind and gentle with me and explained that not everyone at the age of 9 was as informed as me, and that I was special, but needed to be more careful about what I shared with others as some people would not understand and would treat me poorly. How right she was! – Paul Mikos

───────────▽───────────

Montgomery, AL

Middle School. I had a really good friend (girl) who was black. My mom freaked out when she saw the sweet note she left in a yearbook, then looked her picture up in the yearbook – being raised in the South made having a black "girlfriend" difficult! Especially since I was realizing that I really wanted to be with other guys! – T

───────────▽───────────

Montreal, Canada

1958. I was watching a Steve Reeves movie – seriously – and I knew I was reacting to it in a way I probably shouldn't have. – Sean Martin

───────────▽───────────

Chicago, IL

When I was about 8, my cousin John explained to me that there were homosexuals. I think he wanted to shock and disgust me, but I confounded him when I asked if some people didn't have sex with both men and women. He was disgusted and reprehended me, "No one would do that!" He was wrong. – R. M. Schultz

───────────▽───────────

Los Angeles, CA

I was probably six. I was going to the beach with my neighbors and the mom said, "Well you and Bobby go and get your swimsuits on. So, Bobby stripped naked in front of me and I was thinking, "Oh I feel so good. I feel so happy." This was way pre-puberty but I remember thinking, "I love looking at him naked like that." I knew, instinctively, to keep my mouth shut about that too. Through grade school I was always trying to peek at people's pants and stuff like that." – Curt Miller

───────────▽───────────

Chicago, IL

Watching a TV show with a clown that jumped on a trampoline and his clothes flew off with each jump. I found it exciting and knew I shouldn't have. I was 4 or 5 years old. – Rick Karlin

————————▽————————

Detroit, MI

I believe it was in high school when I developed a huge crush on a friend from scouts. I fought it for a long time, even getting married and gathering my wonderful daughters, but eventually it ended. Shortly after I met Donald, and we have been together happily for 33 years. – Guy Sands

————————▽————————

Indianapolis, IN

At age three or four I was having dreams and I would be walking out into the woods and I'd see this lady laying down in the grass. From some direction this man was walking up to her and as he came down on top of her, I ended up being her. So he was coming down on top of me. That's the first recollection I have of being a gay person, without knowing what gay was. – David Hardy

————————▽————————

Portland, OR

At a very young age. I have one vivid memory. I was two or three years old. We lived out in the country and my folks managed a large ranch that had walnut trees and filbert trees. The owner scheduled a guy to come in and dust the trees with pesticide, probably DDT at the time. To kill all the bugs. He landed his helicopter in one of the pastures. As he came walking toward the house, my mom and I were outside. He was tall and lean and wearing very tight jeans, cowboy boots, a big white Stetson hat and a tight western shirt. It was a spring day. As he walked toward us, my eyes got bigger and bigger. Finally, when he got close to us, I ran over, wrapped my arms around his legs and wouldn't let go. He's trying to shake me off. My mom was saying, "get off that man." – Tim Parrott

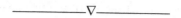

Michigan

I was that boy who was macking on girls in 3rd grade on the monkey bars and had built quite a collection of straight porn with a couple of friends in a tree house (my first experience with socialism: the collective, pooling our valuable resources and sharing them). I would go down to the drugstore and find *MAD* or *Cracked* and I would nest a *Playboy* in the middle, looking like I was checking out the funny stuff in *Mad* when I was ogling the hoobity-boobities. Then one day, leaning in toward the *Playboy*, my hand brushed the thing next to it – *PlayGIRL*. The experience was almost entirely physical – it was as if somebody had been giving me salad and telling me it was a steak, when here, clearly, was the steak. From then on, there was no doubt in my mind. I know there are many men who denied the feeling of difference, or perhaps didn't know what they wanted. I always knew what I wanted, regarding just about everything. I am not saying that I'm superior because of this, or smarter, or, most importantly, happier. In fact, knowing what I wanted has often stood in the way of happiness. But knowing what I want has certainly provided me with a steering rudder for my life. – Alec Holland

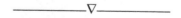

USA

When I was a kid. Just growing up not having the same interests as other boys. Just being interested in what other guys looked like. It wasn't a sexual thing. I just thought men were more interesting. Especially if they had facial hair. Dad always grew a beard every summer. I was disappointed when he shaved it off all the time. – Roy Alton Wald

Chicago, IL

I was born in Chicago but my mom and I moved to the cornfields of Illinois when I was about 10. That was the first time I realized I was different. I'm mixed race and I was the only brown kid in school, I spoke English and Spanish fluently and the school thought people who spoke Spanish were learning disabled so they tested me. I grew up low-income but also in the city many people don't own property but rent, in this town nobody rented anything and there were no apartments, only homes for the rich, and trailers for the poor. I didn't fit in any category and no one knew what to do with me and made that very apparent. – James Conley

—————————▽—————————

Hammond, IN

1980, listening to the Baptists in Hammond, IN, doing their Sunday school brainwashing thing about heaven and hell and how all gay people were going to burn forever ... I knew it was me they were talking about. It made me feel ultra-special! – Ruben Cruz

—————————▽—————————

Chicago, IL

I never knew I was different until classmates, teachers and adults started letting me know I was, and they did so in mostly cruel and abusive ways. I had no healthy point of reference for all the rejection and frankly, neither did they. – Anonymous

—————————▽—————————

Chicago, IL

I think everyone is different. I thought most guys had same gender attraction and that it didn't mean anything. It wasn't until long after my early sexual experiences that I identified as gay. It helped that *Penthouse* always had a letter with a gay experience making it seem pretty normal to me. – David Fink

—————————▽—————————

Chicago, IL

I can't identify a particular moment, but I began to realize I was different when I was around 10. I became aware that I reacted differently to certain things than my friends did or than my parents expected me to. For example: comic book images of superheroes like Robin (Batman's boy companion) and The Human Torch turned me on. I was similarly aroused by pictures from Bible stories (Jacob wrestling with the angel), Greek mythology (Zeus and Ganymede), and Shakespeare (Rockwell Kent's famous woodcut illustrations of the Bard's complete works – lots of men in tights). My self-protective instincts told me I shouldn't share that with my friends or family. – Bill Williams

————————∇————————

Atlanta, GA

I must have been 4 or 5. I knew that I was attracted to my truck driving uncle. Of course, I didn't know what "it" was but I knew that I was drawn to him. – Daniel Goss

————————∇————————

Chicago, IL
Boston, MA

That's hard to say. I didn't think of myself as gay in high school or college, I felt more asexual than gay. Though there was one conversation I had when in high school with a football player (who in retrospect I realize was coming on to me) that made me feel different, in a special way. I still recall it. He was flattering me and I didn't understand it. But after the conversation was over (nothing ever happened), he got in his car and drove off, waving to me as he left. It was very simple, but the attention (I was a sophomore, he was a senior) gave me a warm feeling, not sexual, just special in a way other things (like academic achievement didn't). The first time that I really accepted being different was in Boston. I was 23. I had picked up a copy of *Penthouse* and was going to the hotel where I was staying to jack off. It wasn't working ... and somewhere a light went off and I realized I'd been focusing on the guys in these photos and not the women. It was shortly after that that I went to a gay bar in Chicago. – Bernard

————————∇————————

Texas

There were three boys in my family and I was the middle child. Three years after my older brother had his First Communion, I had mine. Two years later, my younger brother would have his. Three years after my older brother joined the Boy Scouts, my parents made me join. Two years later, my younger brother joined. Three years after my older brother got braces, I got mine. And so on and so forth. Every ritual, every milestone of growing up male would be first experienced by my older brother, then repeated three years later with me, then two years after that with my younger brother. There were no variations to this cycle. None. When my older brother took an interest in girls, I figured it was only a matter of time before I would too. So I waited. And waited. And waited. When my younger brother started taking an interest in girls, I realized the pattern had been broken. – Edward Thomas-Herrera

————▽————

New Orleans, LA

I was 12 and argued with my mother about getting my hair cut short. She said no but I got it cut anyway. I met her at the bus stop and she refused to walk on the same side of the street with me. I didn't understand what this could mean at the time but obviously she suspected something. – Janan Lindley

————▽————

Chicago, IL

I was a happy child until about 5 and when we played house in kindergarten, I went to play the mom and a little girl said, "You can't play the mom you're a boy." I started that day to lie and hide about who I was. – Honey West

————▽————

Chicago, IL

The first time I was called a "fag" in 5th grade. When I asked my father what that was, I thought, yeah ... that is me and what I'd like to do and with whom. – Malone Sizelove

————▽————

Chicago, IL

Since I was a boy, I remembered I was more interested in men. I had a crush on my handsome English schoolteacher who drove a red convertible sports car and was very friendly to me. That was a defining moment for me. Even though before then I played around with a schoolmate a couple of times which I looked upon as something fun to do. When I started to have a crush on my teacher, it confirmed that I was different. – Chen Ooi

—————▽—————

Grand Prairie, TX
Belle Buckle, TN
Niles, CA

It wasn't sexual difference I was made aware of. In grade school in Grand Prairie, Texas, in junior high school in Belle Buckle, Tennessee, and in high school in Niles, California, I was beaten up for "carrying too many books" and "making everybody else look bad." I had already realized I was gay and what that meant from the books they beat me up for carrying. – Robert Patrick

—————▽—————

Puerto Rico

That's a tricky question. I don't remember having that feeling. I knew I was attracted to boys since I was five, but in Puerto Rico that didn't make me "different" – men experiment sexually with men more commonly than in the US. I thought "gay" meant being effeminate, I didn't think it meant being sexually attracted to men. It was not really until high school or college that I figured out that "gay" included sex! – Melo

—————▽—————

Naperville, IL

I was a second grader in the Chicago suburb of Naperville, IL, and it was the first and only spring I'd decided to sign up for little league. Our team was the Orioles, and we had a star my age named Colin. He was tall and elf-eared and cut like an ax, and I still like saying his name. Colin was a starting pitcher and a power hitter who took forever with his rituals in the batter's box, tipping his hat and tapping his cleats with the bat, before crushing homer after homer.

I, like the rest of his teammates, morphed into a rabid fan, and I often forgot the game when I played it, forgot my position, forgot the score, because the only thing I cared about was Colin the All-Star. Colin could get emotional on his "off days," when he didn't measure up to his ideas of being Superboy. He sometimes cried in anger, and coaches pretended not to notice. It was startling to see such frustration pour forth from a

151

glimmering being.

I became something of a cheering section for Colin as he pitched his tough games. By that, I mean I screamed, "Come on Colin, another strike!" ... "We did it once, we can do it again," etc. from the second base line or the outfield or wherever my poor coach put me – no doubt to the embarrassment of my father – when it became clear I would no longer field a ground ball or take anything from a pitcher but a walk. I had a new job.

Colin told me he liked my cheers, and he encouraged me to keep it up throughout rest of the season. Thus, did I become more cheerleader than player in my duration with the Orioles, which made me (my friends explained) an oddity. Colin advanced to little league "majors" the next year, a real step up, and I didn't sign up for more baseball. It just didn't feel right. I couldn't imagine cheering for some other guy. – Robert W. Fieseler

———————▽———————

Chicago, IL

It had to be the time I went to the show with a girl I met in high school, her name was Pat. She lived near the stockyards back then, so I picked her up and we went to the show on 63rd St. After the show I stopped in to meet her mom and then the hail came down. She said, "You can't drive home in this hail." So I stayed over, and that was that. After that night I knew I was gay. But it made sense, because in grade school I had a mad crush on my art teacher, Ms. Banks. – Marge Summit

———————▽———————

Central Illinois

Growing up I never really thought I was different. My mom gave me terrible Tupperware bowl haircuts; bought me my first G.I. Joe doll and I ran around barefoot and shirtless until I was 4 or 5. I read comic books, collected Hot Wheels and played Cowboys and Indians. I had all the *Planet of the Ape* dolls who drove around in a Barbie camper. (I never owned a Barbie as a child).

As I got a little older it was Friday night roller-skating and cotton candy for the ride home.

Posters of Shaun Cassidy plastered the walls of my bedroom along with that iconic poster of Farrah Fawcett. It was when a friend of the family called me a dyke when I was about 10 or 11 that that label was put on me. I did not even know what it meant. I was just a kid in a small town trying to be a kid. By then I was being called other things like fat or ugly or poor or some other awful thing. Dyke was just another ugly thing that now was being used in my own house. I hate that word until today. As a teen I found new wave and men in make-up and *Purple Rain*. All kinds of different. My kind of different. – Terry Gaskins

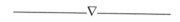

Rhode Island

Standing in my backyard against the fence that bordered the Carr family. Peggy Carr, who dressed like Angie Dickinson (as *Police Woman* undercover as a 1970s hooker), said to the other women lounging at her above ground pool that, "Millie's (my mother) kids were born backwards; the boys should have been girls and the girl should have been a boy." I went from being an outgoing, popular kid to a self-conscious scaredy-cat. It took me years to get back to embracing my different-ness. – Mitchell Fain

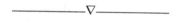

Kentucky

The first time I realized I was different was in the 1970s. My mom sent me to a therapist who gave me a book to read with a chapter called "Homosexuality." I thought, "Wow, this is me." – Jeffery Meskenas

New York, NY

From a very young age I always knew that I was different. My mom always claimed that was because I was born backwards. Contrary to most deliveries where the baby's head comes out first my buttocks appeared first and my feet were by my ears. As a youngster I was always encouraging show and tell, primarily with my male friends. When I was about eight years old, I received a serious lecture from my dad who was very concerned having heard reports from my Mom about stories from some of my buddies' parents. My dad was on a Navy leave and asked me to get in the car with him so he could explain to me that my behavior was not acceptable. When I was 12, I went into a Roman Catholic Seminary and after one year, I left to spread my own wings. It wasn't until I was about 17 years old that I finally embraced and accepted that I was different. After returning home late one night after an encounter with a male that I'd been dating, I was confronted by my parents and the next morning attempted suicide. Finding myself in a hospital bed with my stomach being pumped finally gave me the courage to embrace and accept my differences. – Philip Raia

New York, NY

Looking back at my liberal, somewhat privileged upbringing, I never thought of myself as a gay man. I thought of myself as being a young man with an open mindset when it came to dating. I thought of myself as bisexual. I dated women first, and then added men at 23. I guess I never thought of myself as different this way. It was New York, and it was the '70s and bisexual activity was all around us. I slept with whom I wanted, although the sexual encounters with men were becoming more of the regular near 1980, when I was 23. Moved to Chicago in 1981, and everything changed. I worked at Loading Zone. In 1985 I met a man who was a combination of both my favorite female traits, and my favorite male traits. This changed my thoughts from sleeping with woman again. Different, I don't know. Maybe, maybe not. – Ralph Lampkin

New Jersey

As a kid, I was always doing my own thing – drawing Goldie Hawn's *Laugh-In* body art on my G.I. Joe in permanent marker, playing laundress with a Suzy Homemaker washing machine hooked up to the bathtub facet, chatting on a fake princess phone with my imaginary friend, Cathy – like any boy really. But then I went off to school and there were plenty of kids who were only too happy to point out that everything I liked, they didn't. My obsession with *Batman* was acceptable, until I told them I wanted to be Batgirl. But I did! As for my purple two-wheeler, they said, "That's a faggot bicycle."

The teachers always loved me – I was a really good student, except for Phys Ed – but many of my classmates thought I was weird. And you know what? I was, at least compared to them. I really did live in my own world, my own pop-culture fantasyland. Now, I can say, thank heaven for being the odd one out. It has served me well. But at the time, I wasn't happy being so, well, noticeably different.

I had friends to be sure. But each of my pals was a fellow misfit – smart, funny, and queer, in all senses of the word – and together we were anything but popular. We were bound together by our oppressors. We didn't know we were gay, but they did, and they never let us forget it.

I really do think that a person doesn't realize he's different until someone brands you "the other." That guy or girl never points out how different you are because they want to make you feel good about your individuality. They're doing it to bring you down, because they know you have more fun every day than they do, and they can't stand that. It's hideous what they can do. A fellow can spend a lifetime trying to gain back the self-esteem those kids so nonchalantly destroyed on a New Jersey playground in 1969. — Frank DeCaro

———————∇———————

WHERE WAS THE WILDEST PLACE YOU EVER HAD SEX?

USA

Wild? Not really but it was the loading dock at work, with the UPS guy. – Douglas

——————▽——————

Long Beach, CA

This depends on the definition of wildest. A party in a Long Beach oceanfront condo. Blowing a guy in the rear master bedroom. My boyfriend of the time, David _____ walked in. I rolled off the far side of the bed attempting, unsuccessfully, to hide. He took me into the bathroom, found a tube of KY and raped me. – Tim Cagney

——————▽——————

Chicago, IL

With my late fiancé. He was looking for a house closer to where I lived, and we had been attending open houses all over. One Sunday afternoon we wound up in the guest bath when an argument broke out downstairs. We locked ourselves in and promptly had impromptu sex on the vanity, counter, and side of the tub. It was exhilarating. Upon leaving he told the realtor, "I decided not to make an offer, the guest bath has an odd smell." – Mike Martinez

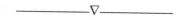

Chicago, IL
Washington DC
New York, NY

That's probably a judgment in the eye of the reader. I'd answer that in categories.

First, upstairs and downstairs at the Gold Coast, downstairs at the Redoubt, in the backyard of the first Touche on Lincoln, the backyard of Manhandler, and years later at the basement of the Eagle.

Second, in the parking lot across from the Gold Coast, behind a hot-dog (no symbolism there) stand. We came home and he wanted me to piss on him. I drank three beers but couldn't piss. He claimed he was the son of the senior member of the medical practice at Rush where I had my internist. The name matched, so I don't think he was making up the story.

Third, in a variety of alleys and backyards (of unknown people) in various parts of town.

Fourth, in the back storage area of a movie theater in DC. One night, there were a few dozen of us. I climaxed four times in two hours. The only time that ever happened. Also had paid quickies with touring video performers, two or three times. They were duds, partly because I was a dud.

Fifth, in movie theaters in mid-town Manhattan (both free and paid). I don't remember any of their cinema names.

Never in parks, beaches, streets, public toilets (I'm not counting the Newberry as public), etc. (I never spent more than a few minutes – total – at the Rocks. For me, it was always the abandoned Nike missile site).

I sometimes wonder if doing so many of those sorts of things are the reason I've reached age 77 and never had a relationship (beyond a one or two-weekend stand). – Anonymous

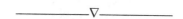

Palm Desert, CA
San Francisco, CA

I'd like to say it was in the late-'90s in Palm Desert, California, in the middle of a street (with little lighting)... BUT, for a more epic experience, in 2000 when I was in Sacramento and San Francisco for a porn shoot for a flick that turned out to be *Rural Erections* (from Altomar, released in 2001). While there, the director took me to a place in San Francisco that once a month had a pansexual get-together. It was only $10 to enter, you put your clothes in a paper bag and the attendant told you a number you had to remember. The place had three floors and a courtyard (this place has been used in NUMEROUS porn shoots, straight and gay). After about 10 minutes I felt comfortable being naked around a couple hundred naked men AND women. At one point, I was asked to lie back on the carpet while a guy wanted to focus on my balls, while about five other guys surrounded me and touched me. I get tantric full body orgasms from being touched, and I was definitely blissing out. At one point a guy was concerned and looked at my friend the director, who told him I was fine, not on any drugs nor anything, that I just felt things so deeply. After a lengthy time of this, my friend felt I needed a break. While gathering my senses, two gals standing nearby said to me, "That was so sweet" with smiles that showed they really enjoyed watching my experience. – Todd Jaeger

————————∇————————

Chicago, IL

The wildest place I had sex was probably on the pool table at Manhole, sometime during the '90s. It was one of their wild underwear party nights. – Brent

————————∇————————

Northbrook, IL

A Sybaris. Ok probably most people would not think this was the wildest place as it is known to be a romantic getaway for couples to have intimate times. But when you sneak people in through the gate to your cottage, for a gay men's birthday party it turns it into a bit more of a wild time. We had I think 5 of us there for my birthday, I don't recall what year it was, but we had to keep going out and picking up others to bring them in as the rules are strict as to no parties other than those booked in with memberships. We had a pool room, and hot tub, the whole thing was crazy. – Dean Ogren

————————∇————————

Berlin, Germany

"Lab-oratory" in Berlin has theme parties in a large warehouse space. We attended a "sports" party where you strip upon entry, put your clothes in a checked bag and wear your favorite sports gear. There was a large bar in the center of the space with various nooks and crannies where you could do just about anything. Slings upstairs, bathtubs for those into piss and scat in the back, catacombs-like dark spaces to get lost in. It was great to be able to take a break and have a drink before diving back into the complete decadence. – Tom

—————∇—————

Chicago, IL to Lafayette, IN

In a red Chevy S-10 stick shift truck on Lake Shore Drive leaving Chicago, headed back to Indiana. Needless to say, the truckers loved us on the interstate. My partner at the time was quite talented, which is why I mention the stick shift. That's all I'm going to say about that. – Cody Las Vegas

—————∇—————

San Francisco, CA
Rammstein, Germany

Buena Vista Park. I got bent over a downed tree and screwed. That was probably the wildest place ... no wait, I'm sorry, the forests of Germany when I was active duty at the station at Rammstein. I had a patient who was Air Force Reserve and he was only there for a couple of weeks, so there was some sense of safety. He came in with a cold and one thing led to another and we were screwing in the snow in the forest off base in Rammstein, Germany. – Bill Barrick

—————∇—————

New York, NY
San Francisco, CA

I've had a lot of wild sex places experiences. I would have to say the trucks in New York. I had no fear. We'd go up and walk into these dark ... couldn't see a thing, and you'd go in and fuck and do everything in the dark. You didn't know if there was a serial killer on the loose. I would do this all the time. However, moving out to San Francisco I got into the leather scene and the Eagle. I got invited to a sex party at a warehouse and there was fisting everywhere and all sorts of things, but I got into all this stuff. It was scary at first. – Randy Warren

—————∇—————

Chicago, IL

On a golf course. – Jack Delaney

———————▽———————

Chicago, IL

Back of the bus. – Marc

———————▽———————

Provincetown, MA

I had driven across the United States. I was in college, I hadn't come out at all. I was with a straight friend and we got separated on purpose. I went to a gay bar and had sex in the bar. Just a blow-job. I don't even think I was 20. – Randy

———————▽———————

Signal Hill, CA

Outdoors at the top of Signal Hill right against an oil well drilling rig. – Great Big D

———————▽———————

USA

The restroom of the Cheesecake Factory. The stalls have a floor to ceiling door that locks and it was roomier than my first studio apartment. I have no regrets. – Misha Davenport

———————▽———————

Chicago, IL

It depends what you call wild but during the late '90s I dated the owner of a funky clothing store on Halsted St. here in Chicago. We were in the shop after closing one night and the lights were largely turned out. We kissed and I could feel a rack of faux-fur clothing brush up against my arm. Clothing at the store was steamed and fussed over daily so I was aware that it would be faux-pas to ruffle anything on the racks. To my delightful surprise, my boyfriend took both hands and pushed me right into the rack causing me to bring the entire display of fur, neoprene, and bright shiny prints down to the ground; it was a soft and colorful landing. I do hope they were able to get everything back to sale worthy condition the next day. – Matt

————————▽————————

Georgia

Oh, the Straight To Hell question. Besides back rooms and bushes? Probably an aisle at a 7-11 in rural Georgia. – Steve Lafreniere

————————▽————————

Chicago, IL

In an abandoned building in New Town/Lakeview in May 1987. Pre-gentrification, the area was pretty seedy, and there were boarded up buildings here and there. Guys would sneak into them for quickie sex. That particular afternoon, I met a cute Blatino guy at Belmont Rocks, and we decided to have an "adventure" in a derelict two flat on Buckingham Street near Broadway. I let him tie me to the first floor stair bannister and fuck the cheese and crackers out of me. It was spooky sex there in the half-light and eerie quiet, with hanging pipes, holes in the walls, and broken glass all over the floor. His name was Diego. Unfortunately, I never saw him again. – Corey Black

————————▽————————

Chicago, IL

Before Hebrew lessons to prepare for my Bar Mitzvah, another Bar Mitzvah student and I would trade hand jobs in the synagogue bathroom. – Bob

————————▽————————

Virginia Beach, VA

It was somewhere around 1981-'82 I had sex in the Atlantic Ocean on a crowded summer day somewhere near the 23 Street area of the beach. This

161

was, at the time, the gay section of the beach but just happened to be almost in the center of the tourist area of the "Redneck Riviera." – Bud Thomas

———————▽———————

Chicago, IL

Outside in a construction site. – Giovanni

———————▽———————

Wisconsin

In a corn field. – Anonymous

———————▽———————

Chicago, IL

Many work places. A retail store I worked at while we were open. Also, at the Pleasure Chest in Chicago with someone who worked behind the counter. – Eric Kuznof

———————▽———————

Chicago, IL

2015. It was very late on a hot summer night along Clark street in Andersonville. I was walking home, but meandering, not quite ready to go home yet, but knowing full well that cruising in the age of apps was usually futile. I saw a guy in the distance walking towards me, and as he got closer I was struck by how handsome he was. Our eyes locked, and just before he passed me, his hand subtly grazed over his crotch. I immediately turned around to see him looking right at me. We both stopped, walked up to each other and exchanged quick "hellos." Not wanting to waste time, I motioned him to follow me. We walked a bit in silence, along the cemetery walls, and turned a corner. I passed St. Boniface Catholic Cemetery constantly, and there's a small section where the wall and fence gives way to a small opening. Months prior I had made a mental note that if I ever needed to enter the cemetery after hours, this was a way in (I didn't know why I would ever need to do that, but the note was taken regardless). After a clearing of nearby street traffic and the area was empty, I led him up the wall and through the small iron fence opening. He was hesitant at first but I said, "It's ok," as if I had done this before. Once inside, we scurried into the darkness, with just enough moonlight and ambient city light to guide us. Among the safety of gravestones and trees, we started making out, and eventually removed our shirts and dropped our pants to our ankles and started blowing each other. After about 10 minutes of intense cocksucking, he moaned "fuck me." I bent him over a nearby tombstone and started fucking him. The teenage goth in me would've been proud. No one was around, so we weren't afraid to be noisy, and he certainly was. When we were done we joked about the ridiculousness of the situation, and thanked the dead and the undead for use of their space. Thankfully, we were both free from Catholic guilt, so we left with smiles. – Shane K.

——————▽——————

Peru

The ruins of Machu Picchu are certainly right up there. – Bo Young

——————▽——————

Joliet, IL

One of the High Schools – after the school was closed for the day. I was friends with the night watchman. He would invite guys to come after 10 pm and we would have sex parties. Pretty much everywhere in the school was some kind of sexual encounter, yes even the teachers' lounge and on stage in the auditorium. – Jim Hensley

——————▽——————

Indiana

Snuck into a construction site and fucked on/against a bulldozer. – Anne

——————▽——————

Cherokee, NC

There's a chairlift that takes you up the side of a mountain, so you can see all of Cherokee up high. There's also a little nature trail with different herbs and natural remedies on the trail that the tribe used to use at the top. A lot of people go for the view but few go for the trail. It had dusted a light coating of snow the night before, and we went to the top, laid out a blanket right off the trail and had some of the best sex I've ever had. I caught a cold, but it was totally worth it. – Christian Bane

—————∇—————

Aptos, CA

Rest stop with a bunch of guys like a chemical formula of electron bonds – Glen

—————∇—————

Chicago, IL

Besides the bath houses ... guess it would have to be in the park. What is now the Peggy Notebaert Nature Museum. – Joseph G

—————∇—————

Big Sur, CA

We did it in the middle of the road in the back woods. 1972 – Dale Williams

—————∇—————

Interstate-270, Maryland.

(Depends on what you mean by "sex"). In the winter of 1995 my occasional fuck-buddy boyfriend Frank and I were driving back to DC from a day ski trip to Whitetail ski resort in Pennsylvania. Frank was driving and after we got onto the main highway, I had an idea to play with him. So I reached over and unzipped his pants and pulled his dick out, and got him hard. Then I took off my seatbelt (so wild and dangerous!) and leaned over and sucked his dick and jerked him off as he drove. He was moaning and tensing and shooting his load, and since we were going about 70 miles an hour in heavy traffic, I kept reminding him (ordering him) to keep his eyes on the road and a tight grip on the steering wheel. We didn't crash. – Jeff

—————∇—————

Burbank, CA

In a star's trailer on Warner Brothers Studio lot. His makeup man was just outside the trailer and we were on a very short break between takes. – Dave Russo

————————∇————————

Wisconsin

Off a country road somewhere in Wisconsin. Inside a parked car. In the midst of cornfields. Middle of the day ... I do so love the Midwest. – Michael Burke

————————∇————————

Venice, Italy

I think that's all relative! But I'd say in a palazzo on the Grand Canal in Venice. Just oral. – Daniel

————————∇————————

Chicago, IL
Munich, Germany

I don't know if it was all that wild. I had a friend in Chicago who had been trying to get in bed with me for years, and I was visiting him. He took me to my first gay porn movie, and afterward we had sex in the alcove of the library. But the wildest place I ever saw sex was the Eagle in Munich, Germany. We were visiting for Oktoberfest, and went to the Eagle, which was packed. At one point I needed to pee, and Owen pointed me at the rest room, knowing what I would see. It was a large room with a standard trough-like pissoir at the back, and maybe fifteen lines of guys standing and waiting to get to the front. Owen let me stand in one of the lines (I'm sure laughing the whole time) until I got close enough to the front to realize that these guys were waiting to get up to one of the men who was kneeling. So, the world's most efficient blow job lineup. I went to find the real bathroom. Later, we ended up in a group of Americans, and one guy came up patting his quite red lips, giggling. "I just blew twelve guys," he said, rather out of breath. – Ripley

————————∇————————

London, UK

The royal apartments behind Buckingham Palace. Met a very distinguished guy at the Hoist while living in London 1999? We had sex at the bar, and then he offered to take me home when bar closed 4AM. Black Bentley pulled up, and on the way, he suggested I come over to his place where he would provide breakfast. Had more sex and then woke up to a butler standing over me with a silver tray asking me if everything was all right. Guy I met was a 35 year old Viscount who had residency in the royal apartments due to family owning the tariffs on nut trace via the West Indies. Dated for 4 months, but wanted me to marry him, and I just felt difference in backgrounds would never work. He didn't work, he was a full time philanthropist, I was a working class manager at a bank. – Robert

Wales, UK

In a pine forest. Also one of my biggest regrets. It seems like a good idea and it smelled awesome but it took hours to get the pine needles out of my buttocks. (Try filling your underwear with pine needles then sitting on them in a car for half an hour). – Nephy Hart

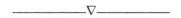

Chicago, IL

On the way home from a Megadeth concert in Chicago and me and this other guy were from southern part of the state at the time when after scoring some K2 in Peoria at an old record store we got high and really horny. So we pulled over in this cemetery in the middle of nowhere and did it in the car. It was actually a really dark period of my life. – Anonymous

Perth, Australia

I have had sex in lots of wild places. I was at a nude beach and noticed a boat pull up several metres off shore. The two men on board were naked, so, braving sharks and jellyfish, I swam out to the boat and had some fun. I have had lots of sex on beaches. I was working in an adult bookshop and had sex on the premises. I locked the front door, put the "Back in 5

Minutes" sign up and got off with a guy who had the largest, fattest cock I have ever seen. I have played around under tables in restaurants, at the back of cinemas etc. – Mansfield

———————∇———————

Saugatuck, MI

The privately-owned dunes in Saugatuck, Michigan, north of Oval Beach, countless summer afternoons. High, nude, waiting on my towel for the right guy (or guys) to come along. And when it happened, making sure everybody who wanted to could see. – Anonymous

———————∇———————

Chicago, IL

In the summer of 1997. In a booth in a sake bar with an office services salesman who had beautiful long hair, great tattoos, and also drove a Porsche. – Fester

———————∇———————

San Francisco, CA

On the altar in the cathedral of the Russian Orthodox Church in Exile in the Sunset District of San Francisco. As with hot tubs, it sounds better than it is – lots of candles create a furnace-like heat and they drip a lot, there's not a lot of soft places, and after Gyorgy the priest was done, he had this whole I-feel-guilty thing we had to work through. – Alec Holland

———————∇———————

Tennessee

I wish I could say that it was with the brooding Spanish boy I met at the big, queer hippie commune I visited in the mountains of Tennessee but alas, that would be glorious fiction. In truth, I met up with a boy at around 3AM outside of my apartment. It was midsummer and we sat in the grass in the adjacent park with a few beers and chatted/drank just enough to break the ice. Soon enough, I was on top of him, trying to open his shirt in the dim light. In the middle of it all, we see the glare of a flashlight and my first thought was that we had been discovered by the police and I quickly covered myself. We were lucky; A group of drunk college students with a flashlight walked by us, oblivious. When we realized that we had not been found out, we retreated toward the river bank down the hill and finished what we started, and it was glorious to be in nature at our most primal. He kissed like he savored it. – Jordan

―――――∇―――――

Atlanta, GA

On the car hood on a rural road outside of my hometown. Under the DJ booth of Backstreet in Atlanta, Georgia. – Mike Uetrecht

―――――∇―――――

Orlando, FL

In the underground passages underneath Disney World. It's a gay man's rite of passage (in Florida) to have sex with a Disney employee, in the maze of underground hallways that criss-cross Disney World. We accidentally came across two other couples. – Eric Andrews-Katz

―――――∇―――――

Chicago, IL

I was at a bachelor party for someone I hung out with and in sports together during high school. I was in my early 20s and still in the closet. We weren't getting along at the time and I was sick of his homophobia (and fighting my own). His best man, a very attractive and sort of All-American looking guy, brought in a stripper and the beer started flowing freely, to say the least. I was standing at the keg waiting to get more beer when he, the best man, got in line for a refill too. I noticed he was wearing cologne. He obviously knew he was going to be around a lot of drunk men and a stripper, who was he trying to attract? I often find straight men wearing a nice cologne irresistible, so I started talking with him. He said he wanted to show me something in the living room. After that, he wanted to show me something in the kitchen. Then he wanted to show me something in the linen closet with wooden louvre doors. That's when I knew he wanted to have sex. Everyone at the party was so drunk, they didn't even notice it. In fact, we made two more trips to the linen closet that night. Years later, I went to a reunion that my married friend (still homophobic) also attended. I asked him about his best man. He too got married. I asked him if his bachelor party was as wild and he said, "Yeah, we were all pretty drunk!" I still feel somewhat guilty for having sex with this best man at his bachelor party, but in way, it's funny how opportunities are sometimes found in places where you'd least expect. – Anonymous

———————▽———————

Tyler, TX

1975. In a cemetery with my boyfriend, J.P. On a balmy summer afternoon, eating fresh peaches and licking the juice off each other's bodies and finding fun places to hide the peach pits. Later, in 1980, I joined the mile-high club with a Jordanian flight attendant on a 14-hour flight from New York to Amman. – David Clayton

———————▽———————

Palm Springs, CA

2011. I blew a guy right in the middle of the busy bathroom at Hunter's. When a line started to form, I regained my composure and rejoined my press group at the main bar. – Kirk Williamson

———————▽———————

Evanston, IL

Early 1980s, with a Northwestern student, underneath the L tracks in Evanston. Several trains whizzed by overhead, squealing, sparking, and rumbling, while we trysted. – Rick R. Reed

———————▽———————

San Francisco, CA

Around 1980 I took the Greyhound bus from Davis to San Francisco 80 miles away. While on Castro Street I met this handsome lad from San Jose named George Hamilton. He was with his friend and former lover. None of us had any place to go but they had a car so they drove to the Palace of Fine Arts/Exploratorium in San Francisco. It's a beautiful setting featuring many statuesque buildings and formations. His friend waited in the car and George and I looked for a place to play around. We saw a 10-foot tall enclosed circular pillar-lined decorative building. We were able to climb to the top and to our sheer surprise there was an abandoned sleeping bag in the saucer shaped roof. I then proceeded to have beautiful sex under the stars with George. Whenever I see the Palace featured in movies or TV I think of that night. – Paul Harris

———————▽———————

Chicago, IL

The absolute wildest place I've had sex? Nothing tops me behind the wheel of a 1980 Chevrolet Sting-Ray, (t-top, black outside, red inside), on Lake Shore Drive, doing a hair over 90mph, while getting a blowjob. And blasting the Rolling Stones. (Police? Not to worry. I was with a white boy. His boyfriend's car, I might add). To this day, the sound of all that horse power at my feet makes me hot. – Terence Smith

———————▽———————

Palos Verdes, CA

Oh, this by far is my favorite story:
    I got my first car at 16, just in time for warm weather. I had heard of Sacred Cove in Palos Verdes, California. It was then a legal nude beach in an almost perfect circle of a cove. The straight people sat on the east side and the gay men sat on the west side. I was female at the time, but I certainly felt more comfortable sitting on the gay side of the beach naked. There were far fewer gold star gays in 1978 then there are now. Individual gay boys and men would come over and ask if they could put their towel next to mine and visit. After a half hour of visiting and smoking pot that made me horny, I would size up the gentleman next to me and decide if I wanted to have sex with them. I was on the pill and never worried about pregnancy or STDs in those years before we realized that HIV was among us.
    We would go out and sit in the tide pools on the reef and touch each other in foreplay and then move along around the bend to the rocky outcroppings and fuck. I guestamate that during those two seasons of fun, I had somewhere between 150 and 200 men that I had sex with. It was always pseudo-doggie style because it was too rocky to lay down. I had my favorite rock to plant my arms on when I was getting banged from behind. One day I felt that I was being watched while one of my regulars, John, was fucking me. This 60-something man had his cock out and was masturbating while he watched John and I fuck. It was the best orgasm that I ever had. That was the day that I learned that I was an exhibitionist. I went to Sacred

Cove 2 or 3 times a week, sometimes more often, from April to October during 1978 and 1979. I would arrive around 10 am and not leave until the sun was setting. My skin from head to toe was chocolate brown from long days in the sun. It was my own private outdoor bathhouse. I was 16 and 17 then. It afforded me the luxury of having underage sex with men who would never know the evil mean girls that ruled my high school and would have shouted "SLUT!" if they had heard that I had even been fucked by one guy. When I heard during 1994 that two church ladies had successfully petitioned to have Sacred Cove made a clothing-mandatory area, I was sad that others would never know the fun I had. In today's climate full of random violence, I realize that I was very fortunate as a 16 and 17 year old girl that I hadn't been raped, kidnapped or killed on one of my sojourns to Sacred Cove. – Regalos Urban (Born cisgender female during 1962. Transitioned to male at 26 during 1988)

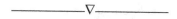

Montgomery, AL

The most memorable sexual experience for me was when my first husband and I had sex with four other guys. It was just in one of the guys' apartment at college. Nothing special about the place but the experience was quite memorable! At that time in my life I felt that I would always be wild and free – multiple sex partners. Have been monogamous for the last 28 years (with my second husband for 6 years and my third husband for the last 22 years)." – T

Chicago, IL

Wow … let's see. Was it in Forest Home Cemetery by the grave of Emma Goldman when I was in High School? Or perhaps the back alley behind the Cell Block when I snuck behind a dumpster to pee and a guy from the bar asked if he could "take it?" I accommodated. Or maybe it was a drunken encounter in a freezing cold, vacant apartment on 2nd floor of a building at Clark and Belmont after I picked a guy up on the street after leaving Berlin? Or the time I cruised a guy on the bus downtown and followed him into a bathroom on the 15th floor of a building on Jewelers Row? Possibly an impromptu orgy with two other guys also named Paul in an elevator at Newberry Plaza? Oh … there's more … dunno … you be the judge." – Paul Mikos

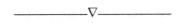

San Diego, CA

Summer of 1975 in a van parked on Harbor Island in San Diego with a local police officer who was a close friend and we spent three hours and never got together again. I later found out he was married to a woman who threatened to make him lose his job if he ever saw me again, they're not married anymore, and he's been with his husband for about 15 years. – Art Healey

Chicago, CA

On the staircase inside Marshall Field's Men's Store, which was largely unused, and was well known as a place to take tricks one picked up in the men's room there. The mezzanine men's room at Water Tower Place was also extremely sexually active in the mid-to-late 1970s." – Allan

Portland, OR

There are two freeway rest areas south of Portland and they were notoriously cruisy. And I went out one night cruising for truckers. I almost exclusively went looking for truckers. By the end of the night I'd done nineteen men. That was including a threeway with a male trucker and his female driver. I wasn't that long out of being divorced so I still knew what that thing was in the slit. I couldn't resist this big blond Adonis who wanted to fuck me while I ate his partner. – Tim Parrott

Washington DC

It was a play space. It was a place for straight and gay people who were experimenting. I was going with this guy that was showing me different leather and bondage scenes. He liked tying me up, so we used this scaffolding and he had ropes coming down off the scaffolding. He bound me up so that the rope supported me. I was no longer on the ground. My legs were tied back and up. He tied my dick up and he was swinging me back and forth. It was a lot of fun. They also do suspension there too. The first time I went there he set up a suspension gathering and there were several men who got suspended. I wasn't brave enough to do that. I was hooked but it was more for a pull scene, where I was pulling and he was pulling. I was pulling away from him and he was pulling me. Just tugging on it." – Roy Alton Wald

————————▽————————

Santa Monica, CA

What comes to mind is in the back of a van parked in front of an X-rated movie theatre on Santa Monica beach. – Anonymous woman

————————▽————————

Detroit, MI

I think that the wildest place I have ever had sex would be on the hood of my car. Don and I went up to see his folks and decided to take a ride. We turned into a lane which ended in an open field. We got out and were sitting on the hood of the car. I unzipped my shorts, and Don pulled them down and went down on me. Then we switched. It was, shall we say, invigorating. – Guy Sands

————————▽————————

Berkeley, CA

I was at the Steamworks in Berkeley and they have a platform way in the back where people walk up and they give blowjobs and they do glory holes. I saw two men having really wild sex and there was a really hot muscle man on the bottom with his dick stuck down through the platform. So I crawled under the platform and gave him a blowjob while everyone else was on top. – David Hardy

————————▽————————

Vancouver, Canada

1988. An abandoned school where a friend wanted to make a commercial for a leather store there. Four of us stuck around after everyone else was gone, and it was a very wild wrestling/sex party. Freezing ass cold, but no one cared. – Sean Martin

———▽———

Chicago, IL

In the balcony of the Vic Theater with my husband. – Gregg Shapiro

———▽———

Chicago, IL
Melrose Park, IL

The balcony of the Vic Theater, Chicago. Runner up (only because it was an incomplete session) on the Tilt-A-Whirl at Kiddieland in Melrose Park, IL. – Rick Karlin

———▽———

Chicago, IL

There's a cat-walk under the Wacker Avenue Bridge. We could see the people on the boats, but they didn't see us. – R. M. Schultz

———▽———

Baltimore, MD

Edgar Allen Poe's grave. I was going downtown Baltimore on a bus. And this very hot guy, a construction worker, had a huge package. He got off the bus and I followed him, and we went into a graveyard and he blew me on Edgar Allen Poe's grave. – John Condon

———▽———

Chicago, IL

In one of Marshall Field's "Trend House" interior design rooms on the 7th floor. The wild deed took place in a tastefully appointed bedroom showroom while furniture shoppers were wondering in, out, and about. Nobody saw us. I don't think anybody saw us. I wonder if anybody saw us? – Deschicago

———————∇———————

Athens, OH

I suppose the wildest place I had sex was a glory hole situation in the washroom at the student union building of Ohio University in Athens. I sucked and sucked and sucked, and the guy finally came, while other guys were waiting to use the stalls. The next day, the hole was boarded up. – David

———————∇———————

Chicago, IL

It was Gay Pride Day and my then boyfriend and I had to use the bathroom really bad. There was a church we found with a one person toilet so we both went in together. Being a little drunk and horny, we both started making out and soon after started banging like rabbits. Never got caught. – Ruben Cruz

———————∇———————

Columbus, OH

My "date" and I left the bar in his pickup truck. He stopped at the 7/11 to pick up a 6-pack for him and a cellophaned rose for me (how romantic!). He took me to an abandoned house where his hunting dog, Wilma, howled and bayed from the kitchen the entire time we were at it on (what was left of the) family room floor. I'm pretty sure he had probably just been released from jail. – Brett Shingledecker

———————∇———————

Chicago, IL

The front stairs of the Shedd Aquarium in Chicago, at 4pm on the 4th of July. The aquarium closed early and I was dating an exhibitionist so we screwed on the stairs while tourists were just out of sight in the gardens. – James Conley

———————∇———————

Southern California

The wildest place that I had sex was on the front hood of an El Camino, on the side of a highway, in the mountains of southern California. Anne, my lover at the time, and I went out for a drive in the mountains. She got a wild look in her eyes and pulled off of the road. She asked me if I was adventurous. I was – the rest is herstory. – Pat Cummings

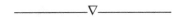

Memphis, TN

I'd say the time I picked up a truck driver in his semi and we pulled over on the interstate and I did him in the back. I was living in Memphis at the time and still recall how exciting it was. – Daniel Goss

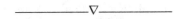

North Carolina

Hard to narrow down, but ONE would be outside on my parents' deck in the back of our house while my parents were asleep in their bedroom less than twenty feet away. – Bill

Minneapolis, MN

One weekend I went to see Michael perform in a Sondheim review put on by the college theater department. By this time, I was gay enough to know Stephen Sondheim. I loved seeing Michael sing and dance on stage. He was stunning. What gay man hasn't watched a handsome guy performing on stage or in a film and fantasized about being able to meet him, kiss him, and take him to bed? I sat in the audience, surrounded by strangers who didn't know my secret, spellbound by his voice and his face. I had never felt so much in love and I had never felt so sad about it.

Afterward, when he'd said his good-byes to the rest of the cast, he and I walked through the snow back to his apartment. It was the week of their winter carnival, so we came upon elaborate snow sculptures all across the campus, one of them a life-size igloo. We crawled inside and started making out, deep French kissing, groping hands unbuttoning the flies of our Levis, taking turns going down on each other until we started to laugh. We had a nice warm bed a couple of blocks away. – Mark Abramson

———————∇———————

Kassel, Germany

Among stack of tires, outside, after hours at a car repair shop, with a guy that worked there (we met in gay bar about 4 blocks from the shop). The other "wild" place was inside a statue of Hercules: in Kassel, Germany, there is a statue of Hercules on a ridge overlooking a former imperial palace. You can climb up into the statue and look out the eyes. The last set of stairs are very narrow. A young guy was coming down as I was going up, we had to squeeze past each other (usually people wait, so it's one way traffic but he opted not to, makes me think he'd done this before) ... as we squeezed past he gave me a look – we both paused and laughed because we were so close – and then just started making out. It happened that quickly. Fortunately, it was an overcast day and there were few tourists. – Bernard

———————∇———————

Chicago, IL

In the back seat of a cab. I was outside Glee Club/Crobar and a hot guy I'd noticed in the bar was also waiting for a cab to pull forward. I asked him where he was going. Near my place so I said, "Wanna share a cab?" ... hoping to get this guy in my bed. In the back of the cab he was feeling up my crotch and then unzipping my pants. He took my cock out and laid his head on my lap sucking it sideways. The cab driver said, "Is he gonna be sick!?" I said, "No, he's just tired from a long-distance flight." I had a happy ending just as I neared my stop and into the night he went. – Malone Sizelove

———————∇———————

Cincinnati, OH

I only feel comfortable sharing this story because it involves my husband, Ryan. We didn't have sex, per se, but we blew each other on the industrial rooftop of a downtown Cincinnati nightclub called Alchemize in the rain. Earlier that night, I'd watched Ryan, my little queer punkboy, emit a cloud of beer-mist from his lips onto the face of a rival in the mosh pit. Club lights backlit the cloud as he did it, and I fucking cheered. I'd never dated someone this ill-mannered before, and I had to reward him sexually. We ran upstairs to the club's empty VIP section and found an extension ladder in a storage room, which pointed us through a skylight to the roof. As I fell to my knees, it started pouring rain, and we stripped. At some point, people from a neighboring building shouted words of encouragement, and Ryan gave them the finger. Reader, I married him. – Robert W. Fieseler

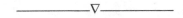

England, UK

In a church in 1982. I was living in England with my lover, Emlyn Williams. He had a country house in a small village. One weekday we went for a walk and arrived at the local Anglican church. It was empty. We had sex. I was terrified that the parson or his wife (who lived in a small house nearby) would walk in, but Emlyn didn't seem concerned. Afterwards, we went back home – and then Emlyn realized he had left his glasses on the church pew. So, I had to go back and ask Mrs. Parson to let me into the church to retrieve the glasses. It was all very *Vicar of Dibley*. – Bill Williams

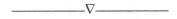

Zacatecas, Mexico

In the indigenous ruins outside the city of Zacatecas, Mexico. Just a blowjob, but hey! That still counts as sex, in my book. – Melo

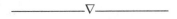

New York, NY

Living and working in New York City during the height of Free Love, that's a hard question to answer. Was it in the Rambles in Central Park, was it the Soldiers' and Sailors' Memorial Monument in Riverside Park, was it on the abandoned piers along the Hudson River, was it in public restrooms, movie theaters, was it in the bathhouses or the backrooms at the after hour clubs? Given the complexity of this question let me play it safe by telling you about an encounter in NY's Meat Packing district. At night, near the West Side Highway in the Village, truckers would park their vehicles in small lots with loading platforms, awaiting the market's opening at sunrise. After attending David Bowie's Carnegie Hall debut concert, I left dressed in leather and feeling horny. Wandering around the Village I decided to check out the trucks. I stood under a lamppost crotch grabbing myself viewing all the ongoing activity. To my surprise, suddenly I became the center of attraction as I was being approached by a number of the men. A hot looking hippie, dressed in denim, began to come at me brushing the others away. He stood in front of me and our eyes locked as he dropped to his knees. A number of the others began to masturbate while watching us. Suddenly my hippie buddy, who I had earlier seen at the concert, stood up and said you're coming home with me. That was 45 years ago, we've been together ever since and thanks to marriage equality I can call him my husband. – Philip Raia

—————∇—————

New York, NY

On a balcony overlooking Fifth Avenue in New York City. – T.C. Burfield

—————∇—————

TELL ME ABOUT THE FIRST TIME YOU CROSS-DRESSED?

Chicago, IL

High School Senior skit. The first and only time I ever cross-dressed. I simply have the wrong shoulders for fine gowns. – Mike Martinez

—————————▽—————————

Detroit, MI

First and only. I tried on mother's beachwear bra in our bathroom (1952?). I have no recollection of why I did that, nor of my reactions. Never did it again. Getting rid of that much paper was a problem. – Anonymous

—————————▽—————————

St. Louis, MO

Probably around 1994, and it was required! While an employee of the bar Magnolia's, each year we had to take part in the bar's annual "Hookers' Ball." It was a big drag show that also included employees in drag. I donned my plastic dance pants (I was a dance minor in college), a leather harness and a motorcycle helmet, and lip-synced to Two Nice Girls' rendition of *Speed Racer* and a gay version of *Leader of The Pack* from the Joan Collins' Fan Club (Julian Clary). Later in the show I wore my mom's old fuzzy green bathrobe and a horrid blond wig, lip-syncing to Gloria Balsam's song *Fluffy*. Both performances went quite well. I've never been into drag nor interested in cross-dressing, so that was the only time I ever did that. – Todd Jaeger

————————▽————————

Chicago, IL

The one and only time I cross-dressed was Halloween, 1994. I was going out with a couple of friends to a Halloween party being thrown by my boyfriend at the time. I borrowed a wig from a girl I worked with, and one of my friends did my makeup. I squeezed into a little black dress I found at a thrift shop, and wore combat boots, a necklace I had gotten a few years before, and a large top hat. My boyfriend was not happy I was in drag and didn't want anyone at the party (who were mostly his college friends) to know we were dating, even though all his friends loved it and were taking pictures with me. We got into an argument and I left the party with my friends. We spent the rest of the evening at the Aloha Bikini Bar on Halsted (where Cellblock is now). – Brent

————————▽————————

Woodstock, IL

Opera House. I was performing in *Mame* as Older Patrick, but they also needed my voice on stage for the rest of the show. As it would not be good to have older Patrick appear before the second act, they had to do quite a bit to cover up my looks. So for the opening scene, I crossed the stage as a flasher in a trench coat in front of the curtain, then quickly was back behind the curtain where a dress was thrown on me as I took off the trench coat my pants were pulled off, I had the nylons on under the pants, and a skull cap beaded cap was put on my head and I was the "color" of her party where Patrick first meets Mame. The number is *It's Today*. The dress was a modified original movie costume that had been picked up from an auction of a big movie studio by the costume designer. Well, final dress rehearsal the alterations were not done yet, so I was a bit exposed in the backside. It was fun for just that number. – Dean Ogren

————————▽————————

Everywhere

Pretty sure I've been doing that my whole life. I am the youngest of six with four sisters and one brother. I remember shopping for new clothes with my mom and sisters. I used to beg for the jeans, t-shirts, and button downs I saw in the boys' section. My mom and sisters would bargain with me about clothes. If I got the 4 or 5 feminine tops and nice pants, then I could have one of the rough and tumble t-shirts. So many bargains struck and so many threadbare boy clothes in my life. And so many feminine tops not worn and gifted to charity. – Cody Las Vegas

———————▽———————

San Francisco, CA

I have to admit that I have. It was Halloween, Randy and I went together as flappers. I was a matronly flapper. I still have the dress. I can't get into it anymore. Walking down that hill in those heels was terrible. We walked down to the Castro and then to a party. Those were the days when we had big Halloween parties in the Castro. – Steve

———————▽———————

Chicago, IL

Halloween party when I was probably in second grade. My oldest sister had taken dance classes and there was a box full of her old costumes in our attic. There was a two-piece yellow midriff outfit with fringe that moved so well and fit me like a glove. And I won the costume contest with my dance skills and bitchin' wig. – Tom Chiola

———————▽———————

San Francisco, CA

The only time I cross-dressed. I was drunk. It was Halloween. My friend Sonny had left some cleaning with me and she was livid because I got stains on it. I put on a dress and went to the Twin Peaks, sat on a stool for a little while. I've never been comfortable in drag. Or the concept of drag. That's the only time I ever did. – Bill Barrick

———————▽———————

New York, NY

I think it was when the New York City Gay Men's Chorus would do these Halloween events as a charity thing. Each year was a theme and one year it was prohibition and I had a boyfriend who was a hair stylist. At the time I had quite a bit of hair. I didn't need a wig. I was a flapper. I just absolutely adored it. I had so much fun. I had a dress designed just for me. – Randy Warren

—————∇—————

Chicago, IL

I did it for Dragocious, which was a benefit to raise money for the Rodde Center, a precursor to the Center on Halsted. – Jack Delaney

—————∇—————

USA

On Halloween in a Women's Studies Class. We had had a previous class on how oppressive fashion was and I made an off the cuff remark that it applied to both genders as men can't wear dresses. The professor told me I was free to wear a dress to class on Halloween. I borrowed clothes from two of my friends in the class. They also did my makeup. They weren't lipstick lesbians, but, bless, 'em, they did their best. I ended up looking like everyone's drunk aunt. Someday, I'll be a pretty girl, mama. Someday. – Misha Davenport

—————∇—————

Cambridge, MA

In 1979 or 1980 a bunch of people from Lesbian and Gay Folk Dancing in Harvard Yard got together for a quilting bee – one woman's sister was getting married. It was a friendly, pleasant gathering. We sewed, we talked. At one point someone opened a trunk to pull out lots of ladies' accessories. Everyone tried on something. I put on a little blue pillbox hat with a tiny blue veil; I thought it would be fun, but instead I felt very strange and took it off quickly. I wonder now if it threatened my very uncertain sense of self. I wonder if I have a stronger sense of self now. – Rick

—————∇—————

USA

In Jr. High and High School, I was obsessed with Samantha Fox. So much so that when I was a high school junior, I thought I could not only dress in drag but also lip sync and perform AS Samantha Fox in a drag contest at our Metro-West gay bar, Club West. I bought a used wig from a drag queen, had clothing help from a friend who was very good at sewing, and took every opportunity to show everyone my dance moves and interpretation of *Naughty Girls Need Love Too*, always asking for constructive criticism. Do I need to tell you that while I bravely went through with my performance in the little upstairs dance area of the club, no, I did not win. I still have the earrings that I fashioned from a dog chain and thrift store clip-on's. – Matt

———————▽———————

Louisiana

My mom was a photographer and there's a shot of me around six years old, in a long gown and a 1940s hat with a veil over my face. – Steve Lafreniere

———————▽———————

Indianapolis, IN

I was about thirteen. I did it a few times, and decided I liked bondage better. – Corey Black

———————▽———————

Lima, Peru

Oh boy, probably since I was a kid, 4-5 years old, I used to wear both my mom's and my dad's shoes for fun, and when we played house in kindergarten I was always the husband (I was in an all-girls school, so yeah). It's funny when I look back on it, back then I didn't think we could be "wife-and-wife." I didn't even consider it. It was pretty heteronormative. – Robb

———————▽———————

Madison, WI

1986-7. I was about 6 or 7 years old the first time I cross dressed and it was simply a means to an end. I used to go to a neighbor's house to play with two brothers who were around my age, Alex and Daniel. In their basement we used to play "Indiana Jones." I had never seen an Indiana Jones movie but according to Alex, if you were the "girl" you could just sit there and wait to be rescued, and not partake in any of the fighting. So, I put on a skirt, a beautiful necklace (Mardi Gras beads), and a ratty wig that they kept in a costume box, and I just sat on a beanbag, leafing through old National Geographic magazines while Alex and Daniel wrestled and beat each other up. I never really liked them, and playing the girl was the perfect way to get out of interacting with them. – Shane K

———————∇———————

Virginia Beach, VA

The first time was around the age of 4. My mom dressed me in drag with boobs, eyelashes and all for Halloween – and yes there are pictures. – Bud Thomas

———————∇———————

Chicago, IL

Aside from being dressed as a flapper in a pillowcase and doing the Charleston in a Cub Scout skit, the first time for real was in 1977 when 25 friends put on a Musicale to celebrate the Queen's 25th anniversary on the British throne. My starring role was as Sally Bowles. An audience of 250, all by invitation. I did it for several Halloweens in subsequent years, as a gender fuck with a Marilyn Monroe wig and my full beard. I also had my necessary glasses to see who was looking back. – Anonymous

———————∇———————

Chicago, IL

September of 2009 or 2010. I swore I would never ever do this, but it was to impress my new boyfriend (now my husband). It was a large group of us doing a drag bar crawl. This was the first, and only time, I ever did it. – Frederick

———————∇———————

Ottawa, Ontario, Canada

Probably Hallowe'en, 1982 or 1983. Cross-dressing is not really a thing for me. I prefer to express my gender through actions and words, not so much clothing. I was forever being told boys didn't wear pink, and I said, "It seems we do." – Tim Murphy

—————————∇—————————

Chicago, IL

I was on Berlin's Gay Pride float, the theme was Liza Minnelli's wedding to David Gest and I was Diana Ross. – Eric Kuznof

—————————∇—————————

San Francisco, CA

Halloween, 1973? The headdress was a papier-mâché toilet with a fist rising out of it clutching lavender and pink ostrich plumes. The dress was a red, satin, mermaid tail, form-fitting "Marilyn" dress (hers was pink) not unlike what she wore in *Gentleman Prefer Blondes*. The headdress was made for the Angels of Light show *Paris Sites Under the Bourgeois Sea* at the San Francisco Opera House. I don't like being in drag, believe it or not. Make-up makes my skin crawl. And I'm not much of a fan of drag in general. I don't mind others enjoying it. It's just not for me. – Bo Young

—————————∇—————————

Joliet, IL

Well the first time I don't remember. There is a picture of me at about a year old standing on the sofa, my mother dressed me in a frilly little dress with a bonnet and booties with lacy socks. The next time I was maybe 17. I was scary looking, bad blonde wig, terrible make-up and an awful red dress. There is one picture from that night and when I compare it to the last time I cross dressed there was an enormous difference. – Jim Hensley

—————————∇—————————

Milwaukee, WI

I'm not really a cross dresser but one time I did get all dykey, my hair slicked back, jeans and a cutoff flannel shirt and a jean vest and bunch of keys hanging off my belt loop. I have no idea why I did that, but I was just in a mood to do something different. Anyway, I was at a rock band at a straight bar and this little femmy chick kept flirting with me. I kept kissing her in the women's room and feeling her up and of course she ditched me at the end of the evening which was just as well, I was aware she was just a tourist. She was wearing makeup and high heels and looked like the total high maintenance package which is not my thing at all. But it was fun. Especially under her boyfriend's nose. – Anne

———————∇———————

Washington, DC

I forget what year, but it doesn't really matter – I went to Miss Adams Morgan Contest, a huge drag gala extravaganza. I had never worn drag so my friends who organized our trip (by limousine!!) also helped me choose an outfit from their vast basement racks of drag clothes. I wore a gold lame sheath dress, elbow-length white gloves, and soft, black wedge shoes. I also put on a little lipstick, and pulled on a thick blonde wig which, with my beard made me look rather like Barry Gibb in a dress. Also, I didn't carry an evening clutch so I just stuffed some money under my nuts in my bikini brief. I was later really glad I wore the soft wedges which were really comfortable, since the other guys who wore conventional stiletto pumps had really painful feet before too long. – Jeff

———————∇———————

Chicago, IL

I ran away from home at 16. I ran from Belmont and Cicero to Belmont and Broadway to the Golden Nugget where I met all the drag prostitutes. I was trying to work the street as a boy, but several queens told me I'd make much more money if I "dressed." So, I did, and I made more money. That was the first time. I later auditioned at Berlin for Drag Race, was hired by Tim and became a Drag Superstar, at least for my time. – Joseph G

———————∇———————

Chicago, IL

I always liked to dress in men's suits as part of dress up or while playing house. I ALWAYS played the dad, used any opportunity I had to wear a suit. I loved ties and would study Robert Brady on the *Brady Bunch* to learn how to tie one. I think it was acceptable because I was a girl. In high school I cross dressed as a cowboy for Halloween. – Chicago T

————▽————

DeKalb, IL

A college Halloween dance at Northern Illinois University. My friend Janice went as a pregnant bride in a formal white gown and train. I dressed as her rather dowdy Mother, who was trying to marry her off. – Michel Burke

————▽————

Mobile, AL

Halloween was working at a restaurant in downtown Mobile and the guys there got me all dressed up. I was a beautiful girl, my boss tried to pick me up. – Rain Perez

————▽————

Bainbridge Island, WA

11 years old!!!! A bunch of us theater kids went to ROCKY HORROR one weekend night when we were having a sleepover at the cool family's house. I was the youngest, I'm pretty sure, and we all dressed up. I ended up in a white (!) flapper dress with a blue belt. I'm sure I had makeup on but don't remember what. Also, ZERO idea what I did about shoes. But god what a fun night. – David Zinn

————▽————

Indiana

I performed in a high school charity called *Big Man on Campus* as Delores de Espada in a blatant effort to win over the Puerto Rican population at my school. While I had them in the bag, I didn't even place in the competition. – Daniel

————▽————

Dallas, TX

Charity drag show in Dallas in 2008. Dressed as Sharon Carpenter with a giant blow up globe, a bag of hamburgers and an air sick bag, singing *Up on the World Looking Down on Creation.* – Robert

───────────▽───────────

San Francisco, CA

OK, I've only done this once and it was for a production of *George M!* – they couldn't find anyone to play the woman who manages the boarding house where the family was staying. I suggested that, because the show is about vaudeville and those shows often used drag, perhaps I could play the role. – Brian

───────────▽───────────

Chicago, IL

The first time I did drag not as Zander Mander was for a benefit show. I used water balloons for boobs. I won best tits of the night. Everyone loved how they bounced. – Zander Mander

───────────▽───────────

Clarks Summit, PA

At Baptist Bible College. One of the dudes who hated me (and there were many, although at the time I didn't understand why) convinced me to wear a dress and wig that he had borrowed from somebody. I wore it to a bonfire and got called out by the college president. He told me to "go take that off!" I ratted on the dude that convinced me, but never heard anything after that. – Fester

───────────▽───────────

Perth, Australia

Apart from sneaking into Mum's wardrobe when she wasn't at home, and also into her make up, I think I was in my early 20s. I really loved what make-up could do. I wasn't so much into wearing women's clothing, although I did dress up in drag a few times. I had a friend who loved dressing in drag and he actually looked like a real girl when he did it. I was more like Boy George – the make-up and weird clothes. He was the real drag queen. – Mansfield

Chicago, IL

My high school held annual junior and senior class plays. The school was so small, everybody in the class had a role in the production. In my senior year, the class and the director chose to put on a farce called *Grandpa's Twin Sister*. The actor who played grandpa also had to play his twin sister. From the outset, I insisted I'd much rather die than appear on a stage wearing a woman's clothes. My classmates and the director, on the other hand, insisted only I could do it. And I was so go-along-get-along in those days, the Fifties no less, I gave in. Imagine my surprise when the rural crowd that came to see the show loved it. "That guy on TV couldn't've done it any better!" they told me. That guy on TV" was, of course, Milton Berle. – Ron Fritsch

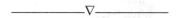

Chicago, IL
Dallas, TX

1957. The FIRST time was when I was about 3 years old. I came from an Irish Catholic working-class family from the Roseland neighborhood on Chicago's south side. My mom had seven kids and a basement full of laundry to do. My parents hired an old black woman named Hattie Jane Parker to help with the laundry and ironing. She was wonderful. I used to go into my sister's closet and put on her petticoats and dance around the kitchen. I can still hear Hattie's toothless cackle as she clapped her hands and encouraged me to be the best little sissy in the world.

Years later, living in Dallas in the mid-'80s, my friend Troy and I shared a studio apartment right off Cedar Springs. Troy was pure-bred Texas trailer trash and really knew his way around a Bernina. He whipped up something fancy in blue lame for me and he was all dolled up in a black and red lace outfit inspired by one of Robert Palmer's backup musicians. We headed to a lesbian bar on the Harry Hines Expressway. Those gals thought we were fabulous. – David Clayton

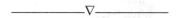

Chicago, IL

I was 3 years old. My oldest cousin was 5 and we were very close friends. She had a trunk filled with child-sized costume pieces and most of them were pink and glittery. It was 1989, after all. She got to be the princess because she was the oldest, and I think I was her lady in waiting, though I didn't have the term for it yet. This was all ok until my mom let me bring home a dress that my cousin owned and that's where the same began. I had no concept of clothes that were for one gender or another; I just thought it was pretty. I just wanted to wear the dress because it looked nice and my cousin liked it so much. My memory of it all is foggy but I distinctly remember the dress hanging on the knob of my bedroom door, my father sternly telling me "No" while I, through tears continually asked him, "Why?" I was not satisfied by the simple answer that boys don't wear those. My parents must have felt badly, because I soon after got my own chest of costume pieces but the pink glitter was painfully absent and replaced with "boy" things. It took all the time for me to tie a knot to make the shiny, red Superman cape a shiny, red dress. I learned to survive on scraps that way, in the privacy of my own imagination. It would not be until I was 27 years old before I would give myself permission to embrace my stifled, starved femininity again, in addition to the hairy, bearded body I proudly own. – Jordan

----------▽----------

Minneapolis, MN

Only recently have I dared to climb into a dress. There's not enough makeup in the world and even after a night of preparation I looked like a sorority house mom. I'm much more interested in naming drag queens than being one. You can call me Militia. Militia Gander. – Alec Holland

----------▽----------

Beloit, WI

1997. In college I was part of the campus gay group, which at that time was called the Alliance. We had a yearly tradition of doing a "drag wedding," where a gay man in drag wed a lesbian in boy-drag. I married my good friend, Kate. My wedding dress was a sea-foam green nightgown I picked up at the local Salvation Army. I had a dorm room overlooking the quad, so I had my friend Jeremy blast the Pixies' *Here Comes Your Man* from my window as I walked down the aisle. Kate and I were proclaimed "wusband" and "hife," though neither of us were ever sure which was which. Fittingly, I suppose. – Kirk Williamson

----------▽----------

Chicago, IL

My first cross-dressing was for Halloween 1979 or 1980. My friend Raul was Ali Baba and I was the church lady. – Scott Strum

—————▽—————

Chicago, IL

Five or six, putting on a wig I discovered in my parents' basement. I put it on and my parents laughed. A couple more years passed, I used to dance with my mom's silk scarfs to Petula Clark's *Downtown* by myself – but no one saw. – David Plambeck

—————▽—————

Chicago, IL

I spent the first 40 years of my life in another gender, that's cross dressing enough for me. – Jake Cohn

—————▽—————

Detroit, MI

Ah, that would have to be the "Wear Something Silver" tour that brought LaBelle to Detroit's Masonic Temple in early 1975. It was the first time I wore full face. I swear, everybody who came to that show wore silver. Girl, we threw DOWN. The audience almost upstaged the show we came to see. The exuberance in the LaBelle song *What Can I Do for You* was real and palpable. – Terence Smith

—————▽—————

Davis, CA

Hmmm, I probably tried putting on one of my mom's girdles when I was about 16. It felt nice on my naked body but that was the extent of it. About 8 years later after I was out, a group of us used to have "Cross Dress Sunday" at our apartment in Davis, CA. Even some straight guys participated. It only lasted for about a month or two but one time I was in full drag and went to the local eatery named Sambos (now probably a Denny's) and when I walked in a young man immediately recognized me and yelled out, "Hi Paul!" I guess my drag was pretty damn poor. My next

192

dilemma was what bathroom I was supposed to use. I didn't stay at Sambo's long. – Paul Harris

—————▽—————

Chicago, IL

The only time I cross-dressed was at Halloween when I was a kid, one of my last trick-or-treat outings. I wore one of my mother's old dresses – a navy dotted Swiss – a blond wig and a mask. I remember people saying, "Here's some candy, little girl," and then staggering a bit when my somewhat deep voice (for a kid) said "Thank you." Ha! Froggy's voice coming out of Darla's mouth. I enjoyed shocking people, but I haven't cross-dressed since then.

But if you want to hear about my explorations in leather, you can buy me a Templeton on the rocks – preferably at Touché. – Bill

—————▽—————

Long Beach, CA

My father passed when I was 8 and my mother passed when I was 16. I am an only child. I was supposed to go and live with another Jewish family until I turned 18 and would be betrothed in an arranged marriage. "Fuck that!" I thought. Thank HaShem that we didn't have cell phones during the 1970's. It was a lot easier to avoid people if they couldn't track you down. I went to live with a female friend from high school and her family. I got a job at a record store. When I got my first check, I negotiated monthly payments on a neighbor's used car. When I got my second check two weeks later, I took it and other money I had saved, went to Sears and bought 3 pairs of Levis 501s shrink-to-fit jeans, a Levis Trucker jacket, and tan carpenter boots with white wedge soles. I stood looking at a package of tighty whiteys and decided to pass on buying and wearing them because I would get caught in them in the locker room before and after gym class. Then I went to a barber and had my waist length, curly hair, cut off and styled like a man. I was free. I was raised as a Sefardi Orthodox Jew in clothes that were decidedly female and covered me from knee cap to elbow with high necks and hair worn under a scarf from the time that I got my first period.

The problem was that I lived with a Portuguese family and the father told me that I had to move out because everyone was thinking that I was in a lesbian relationship with his daughter because of my short hair and attire. I moved into my car for 3 months over the summer. At night, I parked in "the Ripples parking lot." It was a parking lot meant to service the Long Beach Olympic Pool but at the far end across the street was a gay bar that looked like an airport control tower, called Ripples. I would park under a mercury vapor light that turned everything pink and the public restrooms were open back then 24/7/365. They had two cold shower stalls to choose from. I wasn't anxious. I wasn't afraid. I was excited about life and knew this chapter would end and another would begin. When school started, I moved in with Michael and continued to dress as my authentic self. But lesbians were always hitting on me. I never got used to that. I'm strictly dickly. – Regalos Urban (Born cisgender female during 1962. Transitioned to male at 26 during 1988)

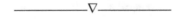

Saginaw, MI

This one is easy. It was Halloween, and Don and I rented Dolly Parton wigs, wore beautiful feathered masks and made dresses out of red table bunting. We had false nails on. Then we went to the gay bar in Saginaw, MI. I was sitting at the end of the very long bar. We had decided not to speak so people would not know who we were. Anyway, this cute number sat down next to me. I pulled out a cigarette, lit it, and noticed I had also lit one of the nails on fire as well. I never broke stride and merely stuck my flaming finger in my drink to put it out. The guy started laughing so hard that he blew his drink out of his nose. True story folks. – Guy Sands

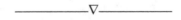

Chicago, IL

Once, four women friends wanted to go as the Spice Girls for Halloween and they recruited me to be Baby Spice. When we walked past the transvestites in front of the YMCA they heckled me, "You better sweeten that walk, honey!" – R. M. Schultz

Chicago, IL

The first and only time. I made a 40th birthday video for my dear friend Jay. – Gregg Shapiro

San Francisco, CA

I went to the I-Beam's Halloween Party one year dressed as Margaret Dumont to a friend's Groucho Marx. It took four of us to get me made up. I shaved off my facial hair, wore a wig and makeup, undergarments, the full megillah. We had to settle for pink ballet slippers spray painted black, because we couldn't find any shoes that fit. My friends swore that the drag was totally convincing, though I didn't believe them – until I got thrown out of the men's room. Alas, no pictures survive of that night. – Allan

—————▽—————

Northlake, IL

The first time I cross dressed I was probably 11 years old and, over the summer, my lifelong BFF Roy wanted to film a rehash of *Gone with the Wind* he called "The Story of Whispering Oaks" in his huge backyard, our Tara, complete with weeping willows, apple trees and a giant poplar tree, which was the tallest tree in town. His brother Mark made a lovely white gown for me out of bed sheets complete with an enormous ruffled hoop skirt, a stiff blond mannequin's wig we found at a junk shop, and a paper Japanese parasol. I was Sheila, and fabulous! – Paul Mikos

—————▽—————

Chicago, IL

Other than costume parties for a fund-raiser I did at North End bar in Chicago, but I had to go to a CGMC [Chicago Gay Men's Chorus] concert at the Chicago Theater first, so I had to go to the theater in full drag. – Rick Karlin

—————▽—————

Indianapolis, IN

I used to dress up as a girl and look damn good. My father dressed up as a woman once and he looked really good too. I dressed up in my mom's clothes all the time, high heels and everything, down in the basement. My brother and I both did. I was about five or six. – David Hardy

—————▽—————

Chicago, IL

Probably when I was a kid. I tried on one of my mom's dresses and high heels in secret and pretended to win an Oscar in the living room. – James Conley

───────▽───────

Hammond, IN

1980, my aunt's closet, my feet were small enough to fit in all her shoes and skirts. – Ruben Cruz

───────▽───────

Chicago, IL

I created a video for my partner's 35th birthday that featured his family, co-workers, friends from our bowling league (at the old Marigold Alley), and other friends. I did a 5-minute skit where I dressed as a blond Valley Girl-ish cheerleader with big tits. "Give me an H. Give me an A. Give me a .... " I knew that it would make my partner squeal with delight because it was so out of character for me. Dressing as a female was not something I was ever interested in doing or anything I wanted to do in front of anyone, but that silly video has been seen by a lot of people. Ugh. I'm not a pretty drag and it freaks me the hell out just how much I resemble my mother. – Deschicago

───────▽───────

Chicago, IL

I wanted to be a cowgirl for Halloween one day, but I don't think I went through with it. My wardrobe supervisor (aka Mom) proposed an alternative costume. In grad school, we used to do a weekly "live soap opera," and I played the head of surgery at Metro General Hospital. My role consisted of finishing my speech by coming around to the front of the counter to reveal my fishnet stockings and stiletto heels. I also played Francis Flute in a production of *A Midsummer Night's Dream*; in the mechanicals' play, Franny plays Thisby (in our production, my dress was kind of a burlap sack – very glam). – David

Tell Me About the First Time You Cross-Dressed

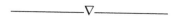

New Orleans, LA

My bisexual sister and her lesbian posse decided to host a game show theme party down in New Orleans where we all lived at the time. The woman hosting the party that evening was Bob Barker. I was Carol Merrill. I mean, who among us hasn't practiced the gentle hand swoops and beckoning fingers that was the mesmerizing glamour of daytime TV? I shopped the thrift stores for a pair of high heels and a lovely jewel-tone shamrock green silk dress. I found the perfect bouncy wig. Finishing touches included nude pantyhose and a lovely coral lip. The party was great fun & we all had a big time that night. The following week, Hurricane Katrina devastated The Big Easy and I took this as a sign from God that maybe I wasn't meant to do drag. – Brett Shingledecker

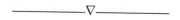

Chicago, IL

The only time was for a croquet party hosted by a softball teammate. The team got drunk at Market Days and bought dresses we wore to the party without telling the host in advance. None of us wore wigs or makeup. Just guys in dresses. – David Fink

Chicago, IL

As a sophomore in college, my least favorite class at the Theatre School at DePaul (in Chicago) was my makeup class. I especially hated putting the thick base that was required for most assignments on my face. For me, it was like that feeling you get when your feet get accidentally trapped between your sheets and your blankets and you can't move. Torture! In my day-to-day life, I've always kind of liked to throw on my horror movie t-shirts and jeans and just get out the door in the morning, as well. My fashion sense is nonexistent. A younger cast member, in a show I recently did, used to holler at me for wearing white socks. I, honestly, couldn't understand why that was a fashion no-no. But I did begin to put on black socks all the time because he would lift up my pant legs, back stage, and check. So … no, I've never crossed-dressed. I appreciate the art and the precision of process as a whole, but (as a personal project), I think all that time and preparation would just make me antsy and stressed. – Brian Kirst

Atlanta, GA

I think I was 17 and having gone to the Sweet Gum Head I was drawn to trying drag. I got a job at Chez Cabaret in Atlanta. My Streisand was a killer! – Daniel Goss

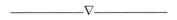

Chicago, IL

It was in the mid-'80s on NYE in Chicago. A bitter cold night. My friend dressed me up for fun and I had the time of my life. I was anonymous and pretty and got lots of attention. That shy, scared person got to be someone else for the night. I went to a bar that we frequented, and it is one of the most impactful nights of my life. – Honey West

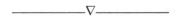

Chicago, IL

I can only recall cross-dressing once. I was 12 and it was Halloween. My mother dressed me up in some of her clothes. She invited a neighbor over to see my Halloween costume. My mother had done such a convincing job, I still recall the shocked look on the neighbor's face who I'm sure was expecting something silly. Because of that shocked look, I opted for a different Halloween outfit. – Bernard

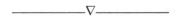

Indiana
Chicago, IL

I've done little drag-like experiments as long as I can remember, like painting my nails before a Boy Scout meeting or dressing up to lip-sync to Disney princess songs in front of my camera in my bedroom. I was a kid in Indiana. The first time I did it seriously was for a production of Lanford Wilson's *Balm in Gilead* in college. I was 18 and studying theatre at Columbia in Chicago. I played Franny, a transgender sex worker. We actually cut my hair shorter so I had this Mia Farrow look. I wore a red bustier, black lace robe, and fishnets down to little red pumps. This play takes place in a café with a lot of characters, and I remember running around stage in my pumps, shouting at scene partners with the wind whipping my robe around me. In one scene, I was lifted up onto a table by this hunky guy and we were alone on stage, laying on the table making out. I felt beautiful. I later heard that a student who wrote a paper about the play said I walked in heels like I was born in them. Still one of the best compliments I've ever received. – Devlyn Camp

———————∇———————

Rhode Island

In private: My "spinster" Great Aunt Dottie was glamorous. She had leopard print peignoirs and marabou feathered bedroom slippers and boldly colored costume jewelry (including clip-on earrings) ... so ... How could I resist??? She caught me once; she winked at me, and as she backed out of her room, said, "Don't make a mess!" I worship her still.

In public: In 9th grade I insisted on going Trick-or Treating as a "prostitute." I looked amazing!! Lol. I brought a Polaroid to school the next day. A rather butch female classmate named Meg said sneeringly, "What? Do you want to be a girl?" I very quickly replied, "No. Why? Do you?" I maintain that this was the proudest moment of my gay life. – Mitchell Fain

———————∇———————

Milwaukee, WI

Full on cross-dressing for me began in 1965 when I was twelve and a babysitter for a 6-year old boy. He never caught on till the very end as I was very careful. The mother, Bonnie, a very attractive woman in her 30s, divorced, loved to play the field with a slew of boyfriends, so I got a lot of babysitting gigs with her. She trusted me and wanted a boy babysitter, so I fit the bill; little did she know!

The kid, Brian, loved me as I played games with him, let him stay up to watch the big RCA color television that Bonnie had, (and which amazed me!), and I let Brian eat whatever he wanted. I always knew Bonnie would be out late, always spent the night there, and always knew that Brian would eventually get tired and hit the sack without fail. It was a simple game of attrition and waiting him out.

That was my moment. As soon as Brian was out cold, I'd start going thru Bonnie's hot clothes; mini-skirts, cute tops, go-go boots, hot lingerie, tons of make-up, perfumes, even cool wigs. It was a 60's Mod Squad set-up and I relished every moment of getting dressed slowly and deliberately. This was the first time in my life where I had the chance to practice in a relaxed setting and was able to hone my skill in the art of being a woman. After getting all made-up I'd look at myself in Bonnie's full length, 3-plex mirror and marvel at how much a woman I was and how beautiful I was. In fact, I looked so much like my older sister, whose clothes I had experimented with when given the chance, it was uncanny.

I would often switch out outfits and shoes going from boots to heels for a different look; even experimenting with different make-up/wigs, and would often then open a can of coke, make some popcorn, and watch some TV, before finally calling it a night and taking everything off, putting it all away, and sadly, lastly, removing the make-up and wig till the next time. – Denise Chaneterelle Dubois

————————▽————————

New Jersey

You know how Patsy Stone on *Absolutely Fabulous* says, "You can never have enough hats, gloves, and shoes"? Well, she's not whistling disco.

Growing up in the Sixties and Seventies, I LIVED for my mother's accessories. It was a good accessory time. I loved to play with her faux Pucci-print silk scarves, her over-the-elbow opera gloves, her pointy-toed mules, and her mink stole. I didn't slip into her dresses – I didn't dare. Well, not until she brought home a red halter dress. That, I couldn't resist. I put it on, popped one of her wigs on my head – it was the Sixties and everybody's mother had a wig or two in the closet – and made my mother take pictures of me in the living room. I looked fabulous and when those pictures came back from the drug store, I told people she was my sister.

Many years later, long after ingénue roles were out of my grip, I played a Jewish mother in a web series called *Spooners*. "Goldie" was not as pretty as that little girl in the halter dress, but for an old broad in a pink velour running suit, she was pretty cute and that bitch got every one of her laughs. – Frank DeCaro

————————▽————————

Chicago, IL

The 1st time I ever cross-dressed was in my home as a young child probably around 5 or 6 years old. I started running around in my sister's white First Communion dress. I was prancing around in her bedroom feeling a strong sense of freedom and liberation. She caught me in the act and had a look of bewilderment on her face. Since then I have always felt a sense of shame around cross-dressing. Well that didn't stop me because I'm now approaching 38 and I'm in drag 3 nights a week. I guess you can say it was my destiny. – Natasha Douglas aka Joey Kiening

—————∇—————

Carbondale, IL

The first time I cross-dressed was at the *Rocky Horror Picture Show* in 1976/'77. It was in Carbondale and it ended up on TV because of a local church protesting it. We were eating dinner and it came on the 5:00 News. There I was, in sort of drag. – Jeffery Meskenas

—————∇—————

HAVE YOU EVER MET ANY GAY OR GAY-FRIENDLY CELEBRITIES?

USA

Having worked in a book store and a theatre, as well as having been a radio DJ, some of whom I was thrilled to get to hang out with and talk to were Tab Hunter, Kaye Ballard, Chris Xefos of the band King Missile, the Del Rubio Triplets, cartoonist Tim Barela (of *Leonard & Larry* fame, who I have become good friends with), porn icon Ed Wiley (aka Myles Long, whom I also became friends with), photographer John Rand, Brian Dawson (1970s *Playgirl* centerfold and later famous leather daddy), and, of course, authors Rick R. Reed! – Todd Jaeger

———————▽———————

USA

Sophia Loren: I fell to my knees in front of her (arms extended, bowing at the waist: think worship pose). She was on a red carpet. She paused and blew me kisses. Receiving line to talk to her was very long and before I could make it her handlers ended handshaking. She saw me in line though and again blew me kisses. – Bernard

———————▽———————

Chicago, IL

I sat across the aisle from Gore Vidal the day after the 1968 Democratic National Convention. I later learned that every member of the Illinois

Communist Party also attended. We didn't meet. Andrew Sullivan (before he was known) at some political gathering. Do touring porn stars count? – Anonymous

—————▽—————

Chicago, IL

I used to go to the former Crimson Lounge in Hotel Sax on the near north side of Chicago. I went a couple of times when Samantha Ronson spun gigs there while she was dating Lindsay Lohan. While Sam Ronson was working in the DJ mixing booth, Lindsay sat in the VIP section with her entourage usually smoking a cigarette in blatant disregard for Illinois's Clean Indoor Air Act which bans smoking in public places.

One time I was there when they were having an ongoing fight. Lindsay Lohan was wearing Daisy Dukes shorts and a halter top. All I can say is Sam Ronson is a damn good mixer because she didn't miss a beat while carrying on this argument with Lindsay. At one point, Lindsay stomped into the booth, cigarette waving in hand and loudly argued with Sam but because of the loud music track the details could not be heard. Then Lindsay stomped out of the venue, returning 15 minutes later in more appropriate dress code club attire.

So how did I know Sam Ronson? When I passed the DJ booth, I gave a nod and a thumbs up to my fellow queer and received one in return! – Paxton Anthony Murphy

—————▽—————

San Francisco, CA

I met Carol Channing when she appeared with Empress Char. I was backstage and I tripped over her. She's this little short chick. We had a brief moment of me apologizing about tripping over her. In '67 or '68 I met Lainie Kazan. My boyfriend at the time knew some influential people and we were invited up to her hotel suite, the hotel St. Francis, and had cocktails were her and her entourage. – Steve

—————▽—————

Chicago, IL

I have met a few gay or gay-friendly celebrities at book or CD signings. Holly Woodlawn, Rupaul, Sandra Bernhard at Unabridged Books, Greg

Louganis at People Like Us Books, are some examples. My most memorable gay-friendly celebrity was Liza Minnelli at Tower Records on Clark in late 1992. My friend and I stood in a huge line that snaked all throughout the store. When I got to her I was so star-struck I couldn't manage to say anything. She signed my *Results* album and wished me a Merry Christmas. – Brent

_____▽_____

Los Angeles, CA

At the airport. Tim Gunn, he was on my flight from New York to LA. I was going out to go to Las Vegas to meet my good friends for a boys' weekend in Vegas, for a birthday, it was 2011. He was in first and so was I, had used an upgrade and it was fun to see him, and he was very gracious to sign an autograph while we waited at baggage claim. He was in LA for the Oscars that were that weekend. – Dean Ogren

_____▽_____

Chicago, IL
Washington DC
New York City, NY

Aside from meeting and having the honor of being photographed by the illustrious and talented St. Sukie de La Croix, I went on tour with Mo B. Dick, met Leslie Feinberg at a rally in DC, and met Lea DeLaria in Provincetown while I was performing.

Sukie photographed my friend Spike and I for an IML advert for Windy City Times. Ironically the caption was, "IML, not just for the boys." We're both transmen. Sukie had also been to various drag shows as well as community events documenting them for prosperity. He's always been a pleasure and fascinating conversationalist.

I had met Mo B. Dick at a previous drag show when Club Casanova had performed in Chicago the year before. Mo B. Dick was a consummate professional and performer as were my other tour mates. The tour I joined was a hard luck tour. Anything that could go wrong did. One performer was going to stop touring, so I had been asked to tour with the group. I joined in time for a different performer to be deported. That tour group experienced a blown ACL [anterior cruciate ligament], a gall bladder removal, a death in the family of a performer, an ovarian cyst, tonsillitis, a blown tire on the interstate, and a partridge in a pear tree …

I met Leslie, an idol for me, through an ex-girlfriend at a rally in DC against Bush and Cheney. While not often awestruck at celebrities, I couldn't say a word meeting them. I'm sure my mouth hung agape during introductions. I do remember asking why they were chanting, "Dick Cheney was a ho." They were actually chanting, "regime change begins at home."

Lea DeLaria is from my hometown area, Belleville, Illinois, a few towns over from mine. A fact I knew for quite some time, as I was an avid fan of hers through college. The drag troupe was performing in Provincetown that weekend. She caught our show and had some drinks with us. I overdrank and spoke to her the next day while very hung over. She is just as boisterous and loud in real life as she is onstage. My headache didn't appreciate it that morning.

Oh, I also met Neil Patrick Harris, well asked him for an autograph after seeing him in *Hedwig and the Angry Inch*. I told him that he made me a very happy bear and he smiled. – Cody Las Vegas

————▽————

New York, NY

Maurice Sendak. That happened when I worked for an antiquarian children's and contemporary book gallery. The owner was a very good friend of Maurice Sendak, and also Sendak was one of his biggest clients for children's books. We were the only gallery that sold his original drawings of operas, posters, book signings. Sendak would come in and one day the owner called and said he wouldn't be in until later. Then Raymond, his partner, wasn't coming in, and neither was the other guy. There were four of us working there. The owner said, when Maurice comes, show him into my office, I have some books on the coffee table and just show them to him and offer him a Perrier. Which I did. Sendak asked me to sit down next to him. He started putting his hand on my leg and I'm thinking to myself, I'm in my boss's office and I didn't know when he was going to come in. I was really naive. I was probably set-up, but I didn't think about that at the time. I apologized and said, I just can't do this, and walked away. – Randy Warren

————▽————

Palm Springs, CA

Huell Howser at Gold's Gym in Palm Springs. He liked my legs and I liked his voice. – Great Big D

—————————▽—————————

USA

I was a feature reporter at a major metropolitan newspaper for over a decade. Larry Kramer was a delight (opinionated, but thoughtful as he actually seemed to want to hear about what I had to say about things). A *Hairspray* era Harvey Fierstein was prickly (not sure if it was just an off day, but he was rude and curt in all his answers). Thomas Bierdz, a former soap star now painter, sent me a nude pic after our interview. While it might have been on accident on his part, it was certainly more revealing than anything I said about him in print, believe you me. Lynda Carter (TV's *Wonder Woman*) shared a moving story about being humbled meeting all the gay men over the years who told her they got beat up on the playground for trying to perfect the "*Wonder Woman* spin." – Misha Davenport

—————————▽—————————

Paris, France
Chicago, IL

A friend in Paris knew Jimmy Somerville and invited him to dinner there once. Very sweet, but I could hardly penetrate his Glaswegian accent. Marlon Riggs, Henry Geldzahler, GB Jones, Gary Indiana, Dennis Cooper, Bruce LaBruce, Lady Bunny and Vaginal Davis have stayed at my house at various times. Met Madonna on a staircase in NYC, Debbie Harry and Boy George at dinner parties. Loads more in NYC. Also, I've been friends with David Sedaris since 1980s Chicago. – Steve Lafreniere

—————————▽—————————

Madison, WI
Chicago, IL

I met Shirley Manson, the lead singer of the band Garbage, in August of 1999. My friend Monica and I saw her walking down State Street and we followed her into a Bath and Body Works and nervously approached her. She was very gracious and modest. We talked about b-sides, college life, Tori Amos, and lotion scents. She autographed our notebooks. I was so excited to meet her, as Garbage was one of my favorite bands. A few years later I would frequently run into the other Garbage band members at the Rainbow Room, a gay bar near the state capital. They were always gracious and happy to talk to fans. Garbage has always had a huge queer following, and Shirley especially has been an outspoken advocate for LGBTQ rights since the beginning of her career.

In 2007 I met Jake Shears, lead singer of the Scissor Sisters, at the Unabridged Bookstore, where I worked. They were performing at the Riviera Theatre that night. When he approached the counter, I introduced myself and he seemed surprised to be recognized. He said that he thought Unabridged was better than any bookstore in New York City. We talked books, Michael Chabon, shitty dressing rooms, and the first time he played Chicago years prior, where I saw him for the first time. I hadn't gotten a ticket for the current show but he was kind enough to put me on the guest list to get in the show for free. He bought the perfect mixture of literary books and smut and went on his way. The show was, of course, amazing. – Shane K

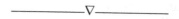

St. Louis, MO

I have met many gay celebrities in my time. One was comedian Fortune Fiemster. I was headlining St. Louis Pride one day and she the next. I was sitting outside the hotel and she walked up and sat down. We had a lovely looooonnnggg conversation. – Zander Mander

Chicago, IL
Joliet, IL

I have met so many people over the years. My top four would be Cher, Liza, Eartha Kitt and Liberace.

Cher and Liza I met at book signings. For Cher I was at the door of the store at 5:50 am to be first in line. The store didn't open until 11 am. It was the grand opening of the Virgin store in Chicago. I could not find her black roses, but I brought roses that were a dark eggplant purple. I went up and gave her the flowers and she signed the items I had for her. I thanked her and started to walk away, and she grabbed me by the arm, stood up and said, "Thank you for the flowers. They are just beautiful," then gave me a hug. I thought I was gonna faint. The woman I had been a fan of since I was 5 years old was hugging me. When I walked away, I had to go sit down for a couple minutes, I was so flustered.

For Ms. Kitt it was opening preview night of *Lady Day and the Emerson Bar and Grill* at the Athenaeum theatre in Chicago. She gave in incredible performance. She was wearing this lovely wrap around white dress. The last few minutes of the first act I noticed that her left hand never left her hip. When she came back for the second act she seemed fine. After the show was over, I walked out the front door where so many people were standing waiting for her to come out. I realized that she would come out the stage door not the front. So I went around the back and waited about 40 minutes for her to exit the building. My companion and I were the only two people there. When she came out, she autographed our programs and we proceed to have a conversation for almost 30 minutes. I asked her about the end of the first act. She told me the clasp on her wrap dress snapped and she was holding her dress closed. She seemed larger than life on stage but when she was standing in front of me, she was quite petite. She was a lovely and gracious person. I met her again several years later doing her night club act at the Wintergarden. My table was against the stage and most of the show she was standing right next to me. I went to greet her after the show and she told me that she thought I looked familiar, she remembered our conversation from years earlier. She gladly autographed a poster I had brought with me from the show where we had first met. I treasure that poster since she is no longer with us.

Liberace on the other hand was a completely different experience. It was maybe 1982 at the Rialto Square theater in Joliet IL. I was working as a runner back stage. He had been on stage, I turned a blind corner and ran right into him as he was dashing off to make a costume change. I was like "Are you okay, Mr. Liberace sir?" He looked at me with that smile and said, "Call me Lee, my friends call me Lee." "I'm sorry Lee I should watch where I am going," I replied. "Well I have to go and change. It takes time to look this fabulous." And just like that, he was gone. I did not see him the rest of the show. After the show was over and all the patrons were gone, I was picking up in the auditorium and a man came up behind me and tapped me on the shoulder. "Are you the guy who ran into Lee backstage earlier?" he asked. My heart sank, I thought for sure I was in some kind of trouble. I replied, "Is he okay?" the man smiled and said, "Oh, yes, he is fine. He is having a party at his hotel tonight and would like you to come. Can I tell him you will be there?" I am sure I must have lit up at that moment. "Of course, I will be there!" I got the address and knew exactly where it was. There was maybe a dozen people there. I mingled for a while and had a really nice conversation with him and Scott. I went home about 1 am. I had had a glorious evening. Every time he came to town I always got invited to his after party.

The night his brother George died, they heard about it backstage just minutes before Liberace went on. They did not tell him it had happened until after the show. He never came back to the theater after that. He was a sweet and funny man. – Jim Hensley

—————▽—————

Milwaukee, WI

I flirted with Chastity Bono (before he was Chaz.) She was Guest of Honor of Milwaukee AIDS Walk that year. We were there at the opening ceremony and she gave her speech and she was sitting in the back of a convertible waiting to be driven away, presumably to the airport, and we smiled at each other and I said, "Come walk with me" and she smiled and said, "I can't" and we smiled and shrugged and went our separate ways. She was totally hot. She fed my fantasies for weeks. – Anne

—————▽—————

Chicago, IL

I got to be a backup dancer for Cyndi Lauper. She is my favorite. I worked for several Harpo Studios producers and had the chance to meet the big O. She loves her gays. – Joseph G

—————▽—————

Lake Tahoe, CA

Rip Taylor at a supermarket at Lake Tahoe. – Dale Williams

—————▽—————

Washington, DC

Yes, a few: In 1997 Steve Kelso, the gay model, was in DC selling and signing calendars of himself, and I bought one and he signed it and gave me a hug. In 1993 I attended an event in the White House Rose Garden and got to shake hands with President Clinton who is reasonably gay-friendly. Sometime in the early 2000s I met gay singer-songwriter Ernie Lijoi. – Jeff

—————▽—————

Perth, Australia

I have met three gay celebrities. I met Boy George at a club in Perth, Western Australia. He was DJing and since I knew the owners of the club very well, I asked, or rather begged, one of them to let me go up and meet him. He went and checked with Boy George and came back to say he had agreed. I was up those steps like lightning. We even smoked a joint together–his not mine. Then I met Elton John. He was doing a concert in Perth and I was working in a CD music shop at the time. He came in with two assistants and proceeded to buy a few hundred dollars' worth of CDs. I actually served him and after I had finished and he had paid, I asked for his autograph and got it. I also met British comedian, Julian Clary, at the same club I met Boy George. –Mansfield

———————▽———————

New York, NY

A few. The coolest were our dear friend Eugene Burger (a master magician from Chicago who died in August 2017) and Derren Brown (Netflix's *The Push, Miracle, Sacrifice*, etc.). Eugene introduced my husband, magician Robert Charles, and I to Derren in New York in June 2017. Robert and I shared a stage in London with Derren at a memorial celebration honoring Eugene in April 2018. – Michael Burke

———————▽———————

California

As a child, I grew up next door to Phyllis Diller, and used to visit her in her kitchen. – Robert

———————▽———————

New York, NY
Champaign, IL

All of these in NYC in 1975/1976/1977. I was a staff pianist at American Ballet Theatre. Worked with some, was merely introduced to most.
Sir Antony Tudor (I stepped on his foot in the elevator – he told me he'd been stepped on by "greater ballerinas."
Baryshnikov – he was in class several times, used my piano as a barre. I also gave him a frozen yogurt on a very hot day. He remembered it over a decade later when I played ABT class at the Kennedy Center in D.C.
Patrick Bissel – before he was famous. He took classes where I worked in Champaign, Illinois. Very nice guy. I was deeply affected by his death.
George Balanchine – introduced by Patricia Wilde. Cynthia Gregory,

210

Patricia Wilde – I was her personal pianist at ABT. Marvelous woman. There are Balanchine ballets that are not performed any longer because the dancers are not now as good as Pat was.
Alexander Minz – on faculty at ABT. Nice guy.
Bob Fosse – another introduction at some party.
Gelsey Kirkland – played a rehearsal for her.
Most of these by introduction at parties: Natalia Makarova, Maurice Bejart, Erik Bruhn, Robert Joffrey, Nureyev, Jerome Robbins, Bill Jones, Arnie Zane, Alvin Ailey, and many others. – Fester

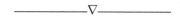

Chicago, IL

The asylum-seeking Rudolph Nureyev, in leather, propositioned me in the Gold Coast when it was on Clark Street just south of Division. *Psycho* star Anthony Perkins, lisping, did the same thing on Central Park West in New York. Asshole that I was in my youth, I declined both of my big chances for a great leap forward in my life. When we're young, it's so damned easy to think we can always do better. – Ron Fritsch

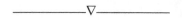

San Francisco, CA

Being a gay writer, I know a lot of famous gay writers, which, of course, is an oxymoron. But at a big library fundraiser years ago, I got plastered with Suze Orman after embarrassing myself by not knowing who she was and, peering at her name tag, pronounced her name, "Sooz", and asked her if she was a children's book writer. She was so relieved not to have a "fan" by her side she grabbed me and we went to a dark bar and laughed and drank and laughed. Then she had to go. Like firemen, I explained to my mortified mother (who IS a fan), financial advisers don't stay long. They never do. – Alec Holland

West Lafayette, IN

In grad school back in the late '70s, Edward Albee came to Purdue to speak at the annual literary awards banquet. He also agreed to talk with a panel of students, and I was lucky enough to be included. At the time, Albee's homosexuality was not something he discussed, so the questions were limited to his plays and theater in general. And, thankfully, no one asked him about the absurd theory that *Who's Afraid of Virginia Woolf* is really about two gay couples. He has always been one of my favorite modern playwrights, so meeting him was an intimidating thrill. Nonetheless, he was charming and gracious for the entire visit. I wish though that he had been able to share his wisdom about being gay with the several closeted grad students, including me. – Bill

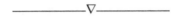

New York City, NY

Late '70s. I used to love stargazing in New York. I remember seeing the great comic clown, Zero Mostel, in a plus-size towel at the Everard Baths. I was walking in Time Square one evening, looked over my shoulder, and there was the First Lady of the American Theatre, Helen Hayes. Returning from an anti-nuke rally at the UN Plaza, I was mesmerized by the blue eyes of the man walking towards me. Paul Newman. I once rode an elevator with Elke Sommer. We had the same dentist. Oh, and I was at an Actors Equity union meeting at one of those midtown Broadway barns. And a tiny, wizzened black woman in her 70s in the back had a question about retirement housing. It was Butterfly McQueen. Everyone at the meeting gave her a standing ovation. – David Clayton

Pittsburgh, PA

2012. I've met my share of gay celebrities, but the one that stands out was the time I met Bruce Vilanch. I was on a press trip to Pittsburgh during their annual Pride In the Streets weekend. One of the organizers took us to a pre-party at his home and there was Bruce, holding court in the backyard. Fortuitously, I had decided to wear my "Bea is for butch" T-shirt, with a picture of Bea Arthur on it. This was my in! I made my way to the front of the line and in our brief conversation, I told him about a certain feature I used to do in Nightspots magazine called "Crotch or Bea Arthur?" in which I would take a photo of someone's crotch and present next to a photo of Bea and the reader had to figure out which was which. Oh, how the lesbians at work HATED this feature, but it got a hearty laugh from Bruce Vilanch. And a laugh from Bruce Vilanch was the most solid endorsement I could ever hope to receive. – Kirk Williamson

Chicago, IL

Lily Tomlin at a Jewish synagogue on the northside of Chicago back when her *Edith Ann* book came out (1994?). I took my 11-year-old son to the reading and signing held there and when we met her, I told her I'd been a fan of hers since I was my son's age. I don't think she was flattered. – Rick R. Reed

———————▽———————

Chicago, IL

You mean other than the two lovelies conducting this interview? Wow. Yes. Too many to count. One of the most amazing ones was meeting David Bowie as he got into his limousine after a performance of *The Elephant Man* behind Chicago's Shubert Theatre. Even more beautiful in person than in a picture. – Terence Smith

———————▽———————

Chicago, IL

Will an author and preforming artist then on *Becoming Caitlyn* count as a celebrity? If so yes! The first time when Kate Bornstein signed *My Gender Work Book* in glitter crayon, then several years later at the University Of Chicago. I tried to take her home with me, after she spoke to the group. I failed. – Jake Cohn

———————▽———————

Davis, CA
Sacramento, CA
Russian River, CA

Vincent Price in Davis about 1980, Harry Britt in Davis around 1978, the original Sisters of Perpetual Indulgence from SF at Davis around 1980. Jerry Brown in Sacramento about 1979. Sgt. Leonard Matlovich at his Steptown Inn Restaurant at the Russian River about 1982. Andrew Sullivan around 1992 in San Diego. Divine's mother near the Parliament House in Orlando around 2002. Okay now I'm grabbing at straws. – Paul Harris

———————▽———————

Los Angeles, CA

Yes, after all, I grew up in Long Beach, California, which had a near daily film and TV shooting schedule. My favorite time was meeting Johnny Mathis around 1978 or 1979. We had been out to the Whiskey A Go-Go and had seen the Runaways perform. We usually went to Pinks or Okie Dog to eat after the bars closed, but we went to Von's Market on Highland in WeHo for some reason. Brian Grillo, who later became the lead singer for Extra Fancy, and I went to high school together and had gone out that night with a couple others. We walked right by Johnny Mathis in the supermarket and Brian said that he wanted to go talk to him, so I joined him. Johnny was friendly and a polite mensch. He asked us about our evening and how old we were. I showed him my genuine California driver's license that said that I was born in 1957. He had a cart with a few items in it and said that it was common "for people like me" to avoid the media and go shopping at that hour, 3 am. I had a rule of thumb from being an Orthodox Jew. It was "Leave celebrities alone. They are people too." I felt that I could empathize with their lack of privacy because I had been stared at so often because of the way my family dressed and had even been approached several times with prying questions. My motto is still, "Just smile and wave" – except for Armistead Maupin. We actually have conversations when we run into each other in the Castro. – Regalos Urban (Born cisgender female during 1962. Transitioned to male at 26 during 1988.)

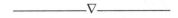

Chicago, IL

I met Wayland Flowers & Madame at Alfie's on Rush Street in Chicago. I don't know if he was famous but was a performer and I think had been on a TV variety/skit show. – Tim Cagney

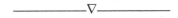

San Jose, CA

I once met and chatted for quite a few minutes with Al Parker at a videotape signing; he turned out to be incredibly sweet and funny and intelligent. I met Cleve Jones of the NAMES project when he spoke at High Tech Gays in San Jose, California. HTG also provided me with the opportunity to meet a number of gay/gay-friendly local politicians, including Susan Hammer (straight but not narrow and ALWAYS impeccably dressed), Ken Yeager, Joseph McNamara (SJPD Chief), Rich Gordon, and Tom Nolan. – Allan

————▽————

San Francisco, CA
Palm Springs, CA

Ian Mckellen when I was in SFGMC [San Francisco Gay Men's Chorus] along with Armistead Maupin, Alan Cumming in SF with SFGMC, Sharon Gless with SFGMC, Carol Channing both with SFGMC and at the local casinos in PS [Palm Springs] area, Florence Henderson with PSGMC, last weekend in LA we met Steven Weber, Adam Schiff and Ted Leiu at the Sexy Liberal Tour with John Fugelsson. – Art Healey

————▽————

San Mateo, CA

Met and nodded across the room to Jim Nabors at a Denny's in San Mateo, where he had gone with his boyfriend after a show at the (now defunct) Circle Star Theatre in San Carlos. – Allan Hurst

————▽————

Montreal, Canada
New York, NY

As a longtime airline employee and former server/bartender in various clubs I have been fortunate enough to meet many gay and gay friendly celebrities. One of the most memorable encounters had to be in Montreal at a stripper bar called the Campus. I was sitting at a booth with friends and heard a very distinctive raspy voice at the table adjacent. It was Harvey Fierstein. We struck up a running banter about the dancing boys, sharing several shots throughout a raucous night. Flash forward a few years to the parkway in front of the Plaza Hotel in NYC where I was assembling with hundreds of other folks for the candlelight vigil for Matthew Sheppard. As I turned to the man next to me to share the flame from his candle, I recognized Harvey. He looked me up and down and croaked in that unmistakable voice, "YOU AGAIN!" and we both burst out laughing. – Paul Mikos

Provincetown, MA

I met Edward Gorey. We were staying there for a week and by chance I saw posters they put up around town for *Crazed Teacups*. It was basically puppets that were animating his stories he'd done. They were pieced together to make a longer story. Lightning effects, a silhouette of a car going up to the house, the cracking of thunder and the puppets. There weren't any people on stage, just puppets. It was really fun. Afterwards I went in line to meet Edward Gorey and shake his hand and have him autograph one of his posters. I loved him. – Roy Alton Wald

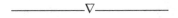

Los Angeles, CA

I actually met a porn star in a gay bar in LA when I was at an NEA convention. His name was Michael something, and I had a couple of videos he was in. Christopher was his last name. He had a cleft in his chin and a big cock. He sat down at my table and we talked for about an hour. Then I left and went back to my hotel which I think was a Hyatt. – Guy Sands

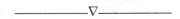

Beverley Hills, CA

When I was twelve years old, I was riding my bicycle and I saw a friend of my parents and he was walking with Groucho Marx. I had no idea who he was at the time. He introduced me to Groucho and Groucho said, "You know what kid, there's two things I hate most. Kids and kids on bicycles." I was devastated. – Randy

New York, NY

Quentin Crisp. I was walking on a Sunday in New York City and he was coming toward me at Washington Square and we stopped and talked for a while and we went back to his place. We just sat and talked. He was the most calmly outrageous person I've ever met. He knew his life and what he wanted. He lived his life and not let anybody change it. He just lived his life. He lived his truth. He was just amazing. As soon as you see him, you know he's a celebrity. That was really fascinating. – David Hardy

—————▽—————

Los Angeles, CA

Roddy McDowell was very gay-friendly. I was working in a lighting store and he asked me to bring what he bought to his house. We were sitting on his patio talking and he said, "Do you want a blow job?" So I dated him for a while. – John "Smokey" Condon

—————▽—————

Los Angeles, CA

I was walking down Sunset Boulevard, near Vine, and this woman stopped me and said, "Can you direct me to the Pacific Cinerama Dome?" I said, "Yes, it's the next block on the other side of the street." She walked away and half a block later, I said to myself, "That was Bette Davis." She was little, tiny. I lived with a guy and we rented movies in Hollywood and we watched *Of Human Bondage* a lot. That's how I recognized her. – John "Smokey" Condon

—————▽—————

Chicago, IL

I met Anne Bancroft on the night of the World Premier of *The Producers*, the musical. I was on loan to the event company that was producing the after party. The night of the premier I was introduced to all of the principles and their spouses. There was a guest who was unable to attend that night and rather than have a noticeable empty seat in row F, I was asked to seat fill. I was seated next to Anne Bancroft. I was reluctant to say anything but she immediately engaged me in small talk. At intermission she asked me to escort her to the drinks station in the lobby where I got to tell her my favorite movie of hers was *84 Charing Cross Road*. Her face lit, not expecting me to pick that particular movie. "Darling," she said with a huge smile, "I think Mel and I were the only ones who ever saw that movie. Let's have gin!"

Later at the after party, following the most thunderous standing ovation I have ever experienced. When I was directing guests, having resumed my duties with the event planner, she tugged on my sleeve and asked me to join her in a quiet corner where I got a hug and an autograph in thanks for me making her feel at ease on such a fraught night. – Mike Martinez

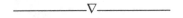

New York, NY

When I lived in New York, I used to go down to the bars on Christopher Street. I walked into a bar one day and there was this man and I sat down next to him. We sat and talked for quite a while and he got up and left. The bartender says, "Do you realize that was Divine?" I'm going, "No!" He was the sweetest person. Absolutely adorable. – David Hardy

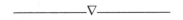

Chicago, IL

It was at MS lounge in Chicago, a bar I ran. One night my bartender told me to come to the front bar. Right there was Rusty Warren of Knockers Up! and Frances Faye. Her brother, Marty Faye, was a DJ here in Chicago and did not like that his sister was out to everyone, so she sang a song, *Frances Faye is Gay*. I gave them both a t-shirt we had for sale. It was 2 women symbols and below it, it said "We've come a long way baby." – Marge Summit

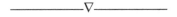

Chicago, IL

Yes, back in the late '80s I was meeting a friend in the lobby of the Intercontinental Hotel on Michigan Avenue. I was early. I noticed this blond guy sitting at the bar. He looked very familiar but I wasn't certain why at first. Then it occurred to me that I had seen him in a gay porn. We locked eyes briefly, but I quickly looked away and walked back over by the entrance and looked out the front window. I tried my best to casually look over at this guy again and he was still looking, so I smiled. He got up and walk over to me and asked, "Are you leaving already?" "Nope, I chuckled, waiting for a friend but I'm sorta early." "How early?" he asked smiling. "Why do you ask?" I said. "Why don't you follow me to the men's room and find out," he responded. He turned and started to walk. Gee, he was cute but for whatever reason, I froze. He turned, looked over his shoulder, and motioned with a nod to follow him. I took a deep breath and followed. Just outside the men's room door he paused, leaned closely towards me and

said in a hushed voice, "Change your mind?" I looked down at his pants and he was rock hard. I came right out and said, "Aren't you a porno star? I think I watched you in a movie where you had sex in a sauna." "Oh sure," he said, "That was with Kevin Williams ... I'm S_____ R_____ but I'm not into talkin' bout that stuff. I just need you to suck my cock." I sucked his dick in the last stall. He didn't reciprocate. He didn't speak nor did I. No other words were spoken. I got myself together and returned to the lobby to wait for my friend. Ah, man-to-man sex is so ... special.
I also met and chatted briefly with Liza Minnelli at a meet n' greet at Northwestern University but good lord, she's no porn star. – Deschicago

—————▽—————

Chicago, IL

I've met quite a few famous people – and I'm assuming that many of the ones I've met are gay-friendly (Ellen Burstyn, Colleen Dewhurst, Richard Dreyfuss, Sigourney Weaver, to name a few). I met Anderson Cooper at his book signing. I went to school with Scott McPherson – I still miss him. – David

—————▽—————

St. Louis, MO

As a flight attendant I had all the greats on my flights, especially to Europe working First Class. The worst was Anthony Perkins. What an ass! His way of getting our attention was to put his plates on the floor. Never said thank you. He pointed at the menu. (In those days we had menu's). Never would speak. Looking back, he must have been very ill at the time. Ray Milland was wonderful. Pure class. Dressed perfectly. Oh, the stories I could tell about the stars. – T.C. Burfield

—————▽—————

Chicago, IL

I had a mutual jerk-off/suck-off with a major '80s half of a musical duo in his hotel room ... the dark one with curly mop hair. We met as I was walking back home from school and he was leaving the Artist's Cafe on Michigan Ave. Side note: was the first time anyone ever swallowed my load ... I didn't know that was a "thing" until then. – Malone Sizelove

219

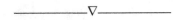

Chicago, IL

In 1990 I had gone to see Erasure in concert. Later that night I was at Berlin bar and saw Andy ordering a drink at the bar. I basically jumped on his back and told him how much I enjoyed his show and that I thought he was cute. He politely thanked me and then moved to another side of the bar. I was obnoxious when I was 20 (still using my fake ID). – Ruben Cruz

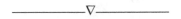

Chicago, IL

I met my hero Shirley Manson, the lead singer of the band Garbage, who's always been a hugely outspoken advocate of the LGBTQ community. She was gorgeous and lovely and very generous. – James Conley

New York, NY
Las Vegas, NV
Los Angeles, CA

As someone who has covered pop culture and entertainment for publications from *Out* magazine to *The New York Times* – and someone who did celebrity interviews on the radio for a dozen years – I've met everyone I've ever wanted to meet … or at least I've been in the same room with him or her. The only person that I desperately wanted to meet but never did was Liberace, but, years from now, I'm hoping to meet him in hell.

Anyway, back in the Nineties, in one banner year, I met and interviewed both Elton John and Bette Midler within a few weeks of each other. They were at the tippy top of my list from the time I was, like, ten years old. After that, I kept telling everyone, "I never need to leave my apartment again. Who am I going to meet that'll top those two?"

Well, flash forward to 2017. We were in Las Vegas – I was doing stand-up as the opening act for Lisa Lampanelli – and my husband, Jim Colucci, decided we needed to go see Cher in her new show, "Classic Cher." Who would argue with that?

So we bought tickets and went. To add to our good fortune, there was a mix-up at the box office and we got even BETTER seats than we expected. That night, I don't know how to express what happened other than to say, I came unglued. It was one of the greatest shows I'd ever seen, and I went out of my mind with delight. I'd seen Cher several times before that, but this show was it.

A couple of weeks later, I heard that Cher was going to be on *The Talk*, the afternoon chat show which happens to tape right near our apartment in LA. Jim had been on the show with his *Golden Girls Forever* book a few months before that, so I said, "You know the booker! You get us in to that taping!" and he did!

So we go to the broadcast and it's great – Cher, Bob Mackie, Chad Michaels in drag, heaven.

Afterwards, we're filing out and Jim said, "Just follow me and don't say a word." We broke off from the crowd and went to the dressing room area looking for Cher.

We were hanging around waiting for her and security came over and said, "Why are you here?" I said, "Oh we're going to say hello to Bob Mackie. I wrote his book and he's expecting us." With that, Bob came out and saw me and said, "Frank!" and gave me a big hug, and I knew we were golden. A few minutes later, Cher came out and, as you can imagine, everyone wanted a picture. Her poor, harried publicist was trying to get her into her limo and it didn't look like we'd get our picture.

But then some crazy lady from the audience yelled, "Cher, you promised me a picture!!!" and because she's Cher, she obliged. That was all we needed. Jim said, "Cher, I interviewed you for my book!" and her friend said, "Give me your phone!"

I didn't want to just jump in, but then I thought, hell, I'm not getting left out of this moment. I said, "Cher, I wrote the Bob Mackie book!" and she put her hand on my shoulder and pulled me into the shot. It was the moment I'd been waiting almost fifty years for. I became a Cher fan at a VERY young age.

Long story short, that's how we got the greatest Christmas card ever. It's a picture of Jim, Cher, and me with the word BELIEVE written on it in gold leaf. When I think back on that day, I remember this most: I got so worked up meeting Cher that afterwards I had to go home and take a three-hour nap. I think that's how she stays so young. She sucks the life right out of you. But my fan-fatigue was a very, very small price to pay for such an enormous thrill, and all the joy she's brought me and so many others over the years. – Frank DeCaro

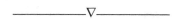

Chicago, IL

Too many to list, but I did get to work with Liberace several times and when Paul Lynde did a Neil Simon Suite, I was his dresser. They were two incredible human beings. When Cyndi Lauper did the Oprah show with *Too Wong Foo*, I got to work with her for two days and appear on the season opening with the three leads, backing her up on *Girls Just Want to Have Fun*. She is a monster talent. – Honey West

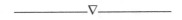

New York, NY

In 1981, strolling down Manhattan's Second Avenue, I saw a circle of uniformed police officers curbside. Cautiously, I approached, and saw in their midst the unmistakable figure of the great raconteur, Quentin Crisp, he of the bravura black hat and blue hair. Quietly, I asked Mister Crisp if he required any assistance. Gesturing at the policemen, he replied, "Oh, you probably mean these gentlemen here. No, no, no, this is America. They only want my autograph!" – Robert Patrick

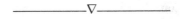

San Francisco, CA

In 1991, I was nominated for a Cable Car Award for the birthday party for Rita Rockett, Al Parker [real name Andrew Robert Okun], and myself at the Eagle. Drew and Rita and I met in the Castro that night to ride together in his van. Drew and I found seats in an empty upper balcony and watched Rita present an award. The stage was so far below that Rita was just a dot of red and blonde. Drew and I were wasted on some hash that we'd smoked in his van on the way over there.

I confessed that I had never seen any of his movies. I said, "I hope you're not insulted. It's just that I think of you as Drew, as a friend that Rita and I share a birthday with and how cool it is that we can help raise money for her brunches at the AIDS ward."

"I know. Isn't she amazing? Look at her down there, such good energy!"

"Yeah," I agreed. "Amazing, but if I saw your movies, I think I'd have a hard time talking to you like this. I am so stoned."

"Yeah, that was some good stuff? I think I know what you mean, though. I was just back east visiting my dad a while ago and when I got home to San Francisco I was really horny, so I went out and ended up meeting this really hot guy at the Badlands. I was sure he didn't recognize me, so I went home with him. Everything was great until he turned on the VCR in his bedroom with one of my movies already in it!"

"What did you do?"

"I got dressed and went home! What a bummer! I just couldn't deal with it."

"Bummer," I agreed. "Something similar happened to me a while back."

"Oh, yeah?"

"Yeah, but the guy turned on one of his movies, and I didn't recognize him. I think he was insulted. He was hotter in the movie than in person, even in the dark. It must have been a pretty old movie. Hey, I can't believe I missed you on the *Merv Griffin Show* and now your foreskin surgery is all over Herb Caen's column. What's up with that? He's been writing about you every other week. "

"Only three or four times."

"Still, it's interesting. Where did the extra skin come from? Did it hurt a lot?"

"It didn't hurt at the time, not until later when it was healing and the first time I got hard, whoa-ho!"

"Ooooh, ouch! I don't really want to know."

"They bring the skin up from the base. The surgeon had never done anything like it, but he was cool. I had it done at Children's Hospital. They sort of loosen the skin so it can slide further down the shaft, and it looks like I was never circumcised at all. I can't wait to make another movie with it. You know, I never really celebrated my birthday before I met you and Rita. I'm glad you got me into it for a good cause and all."

"Me, too. You've always been a good sport about it. So, how did Herb Caen find out all about your foreskin surgery?"

"Mostly over the phone, but he didn't print everything I told him, like how much it cost. I told him that was a lot of money to pay for cheese."

We both cracked up, and I said, "That must be the most expensive cheese in town."

"I know. That's exactly what I told Herb Caen, but he wouldn't print that part!"

We saw Rita coming toward us from the elevator. "Come on, you guys. I've been looking all over for you two. It's almost time for our award. We've got to hurry downstairs. We're going to win, you know. It's a public vote in our category, and those two drag queen events will cancel each other out. You guys are stoned! What's so funny?"

"Cheese!" we both said at the same time, and I was still laughing about smegma as the two of them pulled me toward the elevator.

Afterward, Drew and I smoked another bowl of hash in the van as he drove us back to the Castro. Rita said we should stop for a beer somewhere and show off our new Cable Car award. Drew suggested going to the Pendulum. He'd worn a black fur jacket over a skin-tight white t-shirt and even tighter Levis. When we got out of the van, he said, "Wait! I'm not dressed right!" and he turned his reversible jacket inside out to reveal basic black leather. Whenever he was worried about what to wear, I reminded him that no one who recognized him would have seen him before with his clothes on anyway! – Mark Abramson

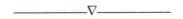

Chicago, IL

My wife and I, in 2006, were very heavy sponsors/ supporters of The Gay Games. We bought/sponsored a table at the Soldier Field Clubhouse for the fundraising gala. Thom Bierdz was creating a painting on-site in the huge room. It was a large canvas separated into 4 sections. He was painting a puppy dog in one of the quad's squares. It was absolutely adorable. It just happened that one of my friends at our table actually owned a custom piece by Thom! He told me to go up and introduce myself – I did, we totally clicked and he was a sweetheart. We decided to collaborate and promote his artwork and his autobiography through my business contacts. His first show sold out and we did two very successful book signings! We still remain friends – Thom resides in California and has amassed an amazing art career! – Anonymous

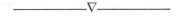

San Francisco, CA

My love for Edie [Massey], aside from her movies, went back to when she performed at the Woods Resort. I'd produced "Leather Weekend at the Russian River" with Edie as the final act on a Monday night. After her performance, I ended up spending the rest of the evening in the room adjacent to hers in a threesome with Edie's manager and his boyfriend who was acting as her "tour photographer."

In the morning, I took the two of them and Edie to breakfast at the little café that was perched over Fife's Creek. I ordered an omelet and Edie had pancakes. She said, "You know, Mark … I don't even like eggs. That egg-lady thing was just for the movies. That was John's idea."

I will never forget that amazing voice of hers, a nasal high-pitched shriek. That morning at breakfast, she also told me, "You know, Mark … I could afford to get teeth now, but John said it might ruin my image."

Edie's trip to the Woods had been a year or two earlier, but I'd held onto her phone number and address. I wanted to get her to entertain at Chaps in San Francisco. Edie was thrilled to perform for me for yet another Monday gig. She didn't get many offers for Monday nights. She told me she would be in Phoenix that weekend, so I arranged a flight for her which was due to arrive at SFO.

A couple of weeks before Labor Day someone called and said we had to cancel everything. The event wouldn't be happening. Evidently, someone had seen our ad for a "Blue Collar Bash" and reported to the authorities that Chaps was planning to have live entertainment without the proper licenses and permits.

When I first heard this, I thought they were joking, but they were dead serious. This was a disaster. Someone had filed a formal complaint against us, so the police were obligated to act on it. I called everyone except Edith Massey. I didn't know how to reach her in Phoenix, and I couldn't get hold of her at home either because she was already "on tour."

Then I got an idea. If we couldn't cancel Edie, we would just have to make the best of it. If she didn't sing, we wouldn't get in trouble with the authorities. Edie couldn't really sing, anyway. People would come to see Edie just because they wanted to see her in person. In those days, Sunday afternoons south of Market meant hundreds of people at the Eagle beer bust and good crowds at all the other leather bars too, especially when that Sunday was part of a three-day weekend. It also meant hundreds of motorcycles. I got cards printed up that said:

If you would like to be part of a motorcycle escort from SFO for "Edie, the Egg Lady" wear your leather and show up with your bike tomorrow morning at 11am at Chaps, 375 – 11th Street FREE Bloody Marys!

We tucked a card on every motorcycle in the SOMA that afternoon. I had no idea what to expect. I needn't have worried. At least two-dozen men in full leather regalia showed up on their hogs and Hondas. For being part of the motorcycle escort, they each got a free drink or two before we took off for the airport. Someone we knew had a big old chrome-encrusted pink Pontiac convertible with giant tail fins. Edie would ride in that. We decorated the bikes with rainbow flags and American flags, maybe flags with the Chaps logo.

The motorcycles rode two abreast, half in front of the car and half behind it. We roared into the airport, pulled up to the terminal. I ran inside and found Edie, gave her a quick hug, grabbed her bags and told her I had a big surprise waiting for her outside. She couldn't believe her eyes.

"All this for me?" she screamed. I perched her on the backseat for our drive through the airport. The motorcycles roared their engines, and we started to slowly move. Edie sat above it all wearing a big floppy hat, sunglasses, and a faded print housedress. Other passengers stopped and stared. Cab drivers hooted and whistled. Edie waved at the throngs of strangers and yelled out, "Yes, it's really me! I'm a movie star! It's me! I'm Bette Davis! (Which she pronounced "Bet" as one syllable, a la Midler) I'm a movie star!"

I pulled her down into the back seat with me just before we got onto the freeway to head back into the city. We pulled up to Chaps for more drinks and for all the guys in her cavalcade to get their pictures taken with Edie and visit with her for a little while. Since everyone was having so much fun, I thought we might as well continue. The leather men got back on their bikes, and we returned Edie to her backseat perch. Kym slapped together some pasteboard signs we taped to both sides that said:

Edie the "Egg Lady"
Join us tonight - 9pm
CHAPS Bar – 375 - 11th

We took Edie up and down all the major gay streets of the city. This time she yelled out, "Yes, it's me! It's Edie! Come and see me tonight at the leather bar!" When people asked for autographs, she told them, "Come and see me tonight at the leather bar, and I'll sign anything you want!" I smiled. Edie was far more clever than she looked.

That evening the owner of the pink Pontiac took me to pick up Edie at the Atherton Hotel where she introduced me to her old friend Ruth, who would be coming along to keep her company. They had been reminiscing all afternoon. Edie yelled from the bathroom, "I'll be right out. I just have to put on my glamour wig."

In the car on the way to Chaps, I listened to Ruth and Edie in the back seat talk about all the Tenderloin bars they recognized from back in World War II. In those days, Edie and Ruth had been B-girls together. They would sit in bars and entertain gentlemen, flirt with them and get them to buy drinks. The house would charge the men top-shelf prices, serve the B-girls juice or soda water and split the profits later.

"Oh Edie … look! We got out through the back door of that place more than once or twice!"

Then Edie would laugh and point to a bar in the next block. "Remember the sailors we met in there?"

At Chaps, I propped up Edie on a bar stool near the stage so that she was visible to everyone. Soon the line was out the door and down the block. She had a huge stack of postcards from various John Waters' films. Anyone who wanted her autograph had to buy one of those first for a dollar. Once they did, she'd sign anything else the person wanted signed as well, from a VHS tape to a plaster cast to a bare butt.

It must have been past midnight when Edie called me over. "Mark, do you still think the cops will come tonight?"

I said, "No, I don't think so, Edie. Why do you ask?"

"Because I could still do the songs on my tape." She pulled a cassette from her purse. "You got me all this way to sing, so I could at least give them a couple of numbers, can't I?"

"Okay, Edie." We had the soundman cue up her tape, propped Edie up on the stage in a spotlight, and she did *Big Girls Don't Cry* and *Punks! Get Off the Grass!*"

Only a few weeks later, I was riding the #8 Market bus home from the Castro one afternoon when my truck was in the shop. Reading the afternoon *San Francisco Examiner,* I saw Edith Massey's obituary. She had died of cancer on October 24, 1984. I stuck the paper in my backpack and trudged the rest of the way home that afternoon with thoughts and fond memories of dear Edie.

When I got there, I opened my mailbox and found a letter addressed to me in crayon that looked like it was written by a drunken child. I was amazed that the US Post Office had even been able to get it to the right address. Inside was a one-page note from Edie, thanking me again for such a swell time in San Francisco. She wrote that she wanted me to send her "love to all those nice boys down at the leather bar."

I brought her letter to Chaps that weekend. We decided to put it up on the bulletin board in the office for all the bar staff to see. Someone stole it. – Mark Abramson

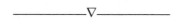

St. John, VI

I spent an entire day on St. John (US Virgin Island) with Mel Brooks and Anne Bancroft. They were truly charming, worldly, generous and kind people. I said to Ms. Bancroft, at one point, "As a gay man, I'd be remiss if I didn't tell you that *The Turning Point* changed my DNA." She winked and kissed me on the cheek and said, "That was a good one, wasn't it?" Swoon! And later we all toasted to the recently departed Madeline Kahn. – Mitchell Fain

DO YOU RECALL WHEN YOU FIRST HEARD ABOUT STONEWALL?

Chicago, IL

I did not know about Stonewall before I came out of the closet. I don't remember the exact moment I heard about it, but it was soon after I came out in 1999, in the form of a magazine article or essay I read about "post-Stonewall literature," which also introduced me to *Dancer from the Dance* and *Faggots*, which I immediately read. But I also recall reading about the Compton's Cafeteria riot in San Francisco very soon afterward and thinking "this is really the first gay riot, how come this doesn't have the same recognition as Stonewall?" I understand why of course, but I've always considered myself to be on Team Compton. – Shane K

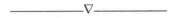

Chicago, IL

It would have been either when stumbling across a broadcast on WTTW of *Word is Out*, or going to the library after watching *Word is Out* to find out more. I remember crying while watching the film because I had figured I was the only person in the world who was attracted to the same gender, and that there must be something wrong with me. The people in *Word is Out* showed me otherwise, and it made me so happy to know that I wasn't crazy or evil or dangerous. – Allan

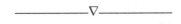

Chicago, IL

In college, I was being recruited by a Queer Nation ACTUP chapter when I was told about the history of Queer revolts in the US. They convinced me to join that afternoon. The fact that he had an English North Country accent and grey eyes was not a factor. – Mike Martinez

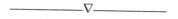

St. Louis, MO

June 28, 1969. The day of the riots and also the day of my birthday. I was only six years old, and saw something on the news. I didn't understand why it happened, just that it involved "those homosexuals." Being a child in the Midwest back then, the basic view of gays in my part of the US was usually spoken with disdain. Since I knew I liked to look at men already, I just kept my mouth shut. – Todd Jaeger

Central Illinois

When I was still in high school, I did as much reading of gay books and magazines that I could get hold of. That's when I first read about Stonewall. I had a lot of anger because of anti-gay attitudes. Many years later, I was able to see a documentary about it and was impressed that my queers would dare to stand up and fight back. – Paxton Anthony Murphy

Chicago, IL

1978. My first "serious" boyfriend was older than I was and he was very wise and was so very good to make sure that I was not just an airhead gay boy/man. He was also involved with *Gay Life* newspaper, news type of items were important to him. I was in my first parade, in 1977, but I really did not understand what the parade was commemorating. As I recall it was just a fun party. I was one of those "young and dumb and full of cum" in my early years. I dated bartenders, bar owners and was just enjoying the ride. I did not recognize the need to be fighting for our rights, because I never experienced anything more than name calling and such. As a kid I was kind of used to it as it had been a part of my life always. I did not even think of it being something that was not normal, or that was something that I would not experience always. When I was in my first parade, I rode with Elly Cook who owned Crystal Blinkers. He was married to a woman, but he was dating me. It never struck me that this was not accepted. I never went anywhere with him and felt that I was not safe or treated well. We drank well, we ate well, people were kind to us. But what I do remember most of the parade, was that we were in a white limo, and the windows were tinted, and you could not see in. We would just wave our hands out, but no one knew who was in the car. Elly did tell me that it had to be that way because of his wife, and because it was not safe to be identified at that time. It was the next year that Michael taught me what Stonewall was all about and then it made me angry that we had ridden in the parade hiding. I think that was a big realization and made me think about how we needed to stand up for rights that clearly were not available to us. – Dean Ogren

———————▽———————

San Francisco, CA

I didn't really hear about it until the parades started. I think it was two years later that San Francisco had their first Gay Pride Parade and I was there for that. – Steve

———————▽———————

Lafayette, IN

I heard about Stonewall in passing initially in college around the time of coming out and getting politically active on campus. It really wasn't until I took a formal gay and lesbian course at Purdue that I learned about Stonewall and its impact on bringing the LGBT community into life and out of closets, back rooms, and dive bars. The course was my first exposure to two of my heroes, Marsha P. Johnson and Sylvia Rivera. – Cody Las Vegas

———————▽———————

New York, NY

I first heard about Stonewall when I was 12. I was living in New York City and it was all over the papers. I first heard about it when my mom was having a conversation around the table with her girlfriends. They were talking about gays and all these women friends were talking about how disgusting and how could they do that? And my mother said, "Why can't you just let people be who they are? What have they done to you? They should be allowed to live how they want. They were born this way. There is no reason why anybody should discriminate against any other human being. Why do you all have a problem with this?" That enlightened me about being gay, although I wasn't sure what I was at the time. But it was important to me and how my mother reacted was very important to me. – Randy Warren

———————▽———————

USA

Maybe 10th or 11th grade. A history teacher briefly mentioned some riot that happened in New York after Judy Garland died. It seemed like a strange thing to have a riot over (even if she was a beloved icon of the community). Of course, a trip to the library and the newspaper archive there quickly revealed the true reasons. I raise a glass each June to Storme DeLarverie and Marsha P. Johnson. Both were fierce warriors who belong in high school history books. It was a defining moment where I realized one needs to defiantly claim one's history and never accept what someone tells you. – Misha Davenport

———————▽———————

Denver, CO

Not exactly. But I was part of Denver Gay Liberation, so certainly by the early '70s. – Steve Lafreniere

———————▽———————

Vermont

In 1969 when it happened. – Neil Cooper

———————▽———————

Chicago, IL

Yes, when I was 18 years old. They spoke about it during a pride celebration on TV. – Giovanni

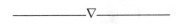

Lima, Peru

It's not widely talked about down here in Latin America, not because it's hush-hush or anything, it's just ... not that much of a cornerstone for LGBT rights as it is in North America. I think I learned about it in my late teens, when I was 17 or 18. I don't think we have an equivalent of Stonewall, and if we do, it's probably not a protest but a massacre. In the case of Peru, there's the terrorism era during the '80s, which was a dark time for LGBT people. There were several occasions where gay men and trans women were butchered in public by terrorists, which became the spark for the first LGBT movement in the country to be born, the MHOL (Movimiento Homosexual de Lima; Lima Homosexual Movement). My girlfriend's dad was actually a big ally in its foundation. – Robb

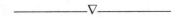

Chicago, IL

When it happened. Although I didn't know I was a lesbian yet, I was active in both the second wave women's movement and the anti-war movement. Information about all the different struggles moved through my circle of friends. – Anonymous

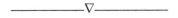

Chicago, IL

When I first came to Chicago on a visit about 1988/89 New Years, there was a *Gay Chicago* magazine that had a front page of Stonewall Anniversary. I asked, "What's Stonewall?" Being from NY I got a lot of surprised looks. I was a new gay at 22. – Anonymous

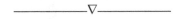

Chicago, IL

The day after it happened it was covered by the national media in 1969. I later met individuals who were there over that weekend. They weren't involved directly, but they went down to Christopher St. to see what was going on. I was in NYC to celebrate at the 25th anniversary march in June 1994, the day after the closing ceremonies of the Gay Games. From celebrating in Yankee Stadium to marching the streets literally overnight. The most moving part was the moment of silence at 3:00 PM. The sound of the roar coming down the Manhattan canyons afterward still gives me goose bumps. – Anonymous

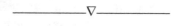

New York, NY

I had been to the Stonewall a couple of times in 1968 and early 1969. It was unlike the few other gay bars I'd been to, because there were "go-go-boys" wearing nothing but a tiny g-string dancing atop the bar. I couldn't believe it! It seemed so daring to be allowing this. Then, my boyfriend and I spent the summer of 1969 traveling across Europe – what in those days was called a "Europe-on-$5-dollars-a-day" trip. We ended our travels in Paris in late August 1969, and wandering around the city, we noticed a copy of *The Village Voice* being sold at a newsstand. The issue was from late June/early July and it reported about the Stonewall raid and the riots that went on. We both thought – "Oh my God, what will this lead to?" And, of course, it led to a lot. – John D'Emilio

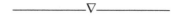

Chicago, IL

It's too difficult for me to pinpoint where I heard about it first because, obviously, it was never formally taught to me. Some documentary (probably whitewashed or trans-exclusionary) is the likely place I first learned about our history and fight for rights. How sad and terrifying it is when one's own history is so diluted and kept-quiet. That ultimately taught me the importance of community. – Jordan

Boston, MA

As 1994 approached, so did "Stonewall 25" – 25 years since the infamous Stonewall Riots. The gay social club that I was a part of often met in someone's home since a highlight of the meeting was often the watching of a VHS video. The video was a kind of news and variety show about gay culture, legal issues, the quest for visibility, hope for AIDS and related Quilt stagings, and whatever else was deemed every homo needed to know. Since there wasn't an LGBT cable channel, you could subscribe and get these videos sent to your home. The term "Stonewall 25" is indelibly printed on my mind as it was worked into the show's material for a good year-and-a-half leading up to the actual anniversary.

The irony of Stonewall, of course, is that there were Trans people who rallied together and fought the good fight. But acceptance of Trans people remained elusive, sadly, for another 25 years. 2019 will be "Stonewall 50," and I want all Trans people to know that your time has finally come. And I, as a homosexual, vow to treat you with the respect and inclusivity that you've deserved all along. There is a T in LGBTQ and I will no longer pretend that any one letter is more important than another. And I'd like to thank all Trans people for their courage to do nothing more than just be themselves. – Anonymous

———————▽———————

Sydney, Australia

In the mid-late '70s when I was a student. I took part in the first Sydney Stonewall March in 1978. – Susan H

———————▽———————

New York, NY

I don't, actually. I was a nut for gay history at a young age – and when I visited New York (before moving there for school and, as it happens, life) in the winter of 1985, I went and had a bagel at the bagel place it had become at that point, because it felt important to visit hallowed ground. It's hard to imagine that night, and that life – but sometimes I stand outside of it and look at the familiar architecture from the photos of those riot nights and try to conjure it. – David Zinn

———————▽———————

Chicago, IL

Within a day or so, a friend told me about a big riot at a gay bar in Greenwich Village. At first, it didn't appear to me to be such a big deal. I'd witnessed antiwar demonstrators fighting with the police during the Democratic National Convention the previous summer. And resistance during bar raids wasn't new to me either. The latest one I was in, some other customers and I refused to flee as fast as our feet could take us when the cops showed up. We continued drinking and chatting and made the kind of remarks you'd expect when the cops patted us down for concealed weapons. "I've got one in my ass." "I'd love one in my ass!" Then we heard some enraged higher-up tell the officers on their walkie-talkies to "get the hell out of that place!" The embarrassed mob-connected owners of "that place" assured us they'd paid the proper amount of money to the proper people. The police had also recently attempted to raid a party I was hosting in my apartment. At the door, I told them they had no search warrant or probable cause to make an arrest, and they therefore had no right to come into my home. The mere fact that my guests and I were queer and had no clothes on, I huffed, had nothing to do with it. If they persisted, I said, they'd face a devastating civil rights suit in federal court. Rather than deal with that kind of crazy pervert, they left. – Ron Fritsch

————————▽————————

Chicago, IL

Here is a bittersweet memory. I became aware of the significance of the Stonewall Riots in the early nineties when I was still heavily closeted. Since the twenty-fifth anniversary was approaching, I read quite a bit about the Riots in gay magazines, like *Out*. In honor of the anniversary, a giant pride flag was commissioned for the 1994 New York City Pride Parade. People were encouraged to donate money for the flag; donors were also invited to help carry the flag at the parade, and later a piece of the flag would be given to all donors as a memento. I made a sizable donation and made plans to travel to New York to be one of the flag-bearers. When controversy arose about the parade and the flag (I forget why) I wrote a letter of defense to *Out*, which was published with my full name and the city in which I lived (hadn't really counted on that!). Surprisingly, I received a couple of congratulatory phone calls from local gay men, all strangers, who appreciated the sentiment and who, perhaps, like me, felt as though they were the only gay men in the far west Chicago suburbs. A day or two before the parade, I had my airline ticket, my hotel reservations, and my limo lined up. As I was packing my bag the morning of my departure, I found myself tossing a box of condoms into my suitcase, wedging it between my Lands' End khakis and pink polo shirt. At that moment, I had a major anxiety attack; I knew that, for some reason, this was a journey I just wasn't ready to take. It just wasn't my time. So I erased the whole trip: I cancelled all my reservations, unpacked my suitcase, called a dear friend, and had a good cry. Passing up the chance to be a part of this moment in gay history has remained one of my biggest regrets.

A few weeks after the parade, I received in the mail a strip of the flag; I was embarrassed to get it. I kept it, though, in its original envelope until three years ago. After finding it tucked away in a downstairs closet, I presented it as a gift to a dear, younger queer friend of mine who had been lovingly supportive in my late-life coming out drama. As a thirty-something immigrant, he knew little about American gay history, so I had some explaining to do. A few weeks later I attended a party at my friend's house and discovered that he had fastened the long strip of rainbow along the living room walls, just below the ceiling. Several of the younger party-goers asked their host about it; my friend always directed them to me for answers. I spent quite a bit of time that evening explaining to a few young queer men the significance of Stonewall and explaining that the rainbow strip surrounding us had been a part of a very special Pride Parade in 1994. The personal, regretful part of the story I kept to myself. – Bill

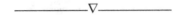

Florida

Thankfully again to my mentor, I remember hearing about Stonewall at an early age (about 15-16). It was 1983 then. I did research at libraries (most of the gay books were stolen) and looked through the reference books and "microfiche" of old newspapers. – Eric Andrews-Katz

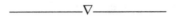

Normal, IL
New York, NY

1972. I was an under-graduate at Illinois State University, still closeted at the time, side-eyeing those Midwest farm boys in the showers.

I think I saw a copy of *Life* or *Look* magazine in the school library that referenced it and I knew that I would one day make a pilgrimage.

Five years later, I was living in Chelsea (back when it was a slum) and I remember walking by the Stonewall Inn. At the time, I think it was shuttered. – David Clayton

Chicago, IL

Being at my grandparents' house, watching on a black and white TV and the first Chicago Gay Pride parade. He couldn't hear, but I remember hearing him say, "What are those guys protesting for? It was 1970. I was 10. – David Plambeck

Do you recall when you first heard about Stonewall?

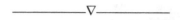

Atlanta, GA

It has always been there in the background, kind of like Gettysburg or Appomattox. – Roy Felts

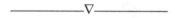

Detroit, MI

I actually remember seeing the article in *Life* magazine, a story about the pride parade in 1970. The one with the banner. I zeroed in on the striped bell-bottoms worn by one of those happy, happy men, and I'm happy to say that the person wearing them, Jim Fouratt, is a friend of mine. – Terence Smith

Davis, CA

Probably around 1979 in Davis, CA. There was even a class offered in Gay History at Davis by a Sacramento State University Psychology Professor and it might have been either then or just on my own. – Paul Harris

Long Beach, CA

Yes. I was 16 during 1978 and had just moved in with my friend Michael who was also 16. He was born to an American mother and South African/Afrikaner father who had taken most of the family back to South Africa. Michael and his 20-year-old brother got an apartment in Long Beach and continued on with their lives. Michael had a small library of gay books and one of them was a thick book called *Gay American History* published during 1976. I borrowed it and read it from cover to cover and it discussed Stonewall. I remember being impressed, but as I learned about the lives and history of transpeople, cisgender women, and people of color in later years, I began to doubt how the story had been told in the book, especially after meeting a transwoman named Miss Majors who was at Stonewall. I think we would laugh at that book today because the entire book was from a white, non-Latino, cisgender, gay male perspective ... so it was all about the

237

gay white boys who started the Stonewall riots … NOT! … all about all the lesbians who dressed as men to fight in various wars … NOT! They were transgender first and who knows who they loved and fucked … and so on and so on. It was similar to my feelings when Randy Shilts came out with the book *And the Band Played On* during 1987 where he blamed a solitary figure, a French-Canadian airline attendant Gaetan Dugas, for passing HIV to every infected gay man on the west coast of the US. We knew it wasn't true. The irony in my life has been accepting the fact that the left will sell us as many lies about life and history as the right does and I often become the one brave voice in the room willing to argue what is authentic history and what is not with people who are supposed to be supporting the same civil rights imperatives that I do. – Regalos Urban (Born cisgender female during 1962. Transitioned to male at 26 during 1988.)

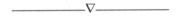

New York, NY

Shortly after it happened, I was in NYC with my sister and we went by where the riot happened. – Art Healey

Northlake, IL

I first heard about Stonewall in real time. It was summer 1969, Judy Garland had just died, and the news was reporting about a series of riots started by homosexuals in Greenwich Village. I knew in my bones, at 12 years old, that this was my Tribe and a very important moment in the struggle for equal rights and gay history was unfolding and I had to be part of the fight. The struggle continues. – Paul Mikos

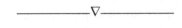

Detroit, MI

I heard about the Stonewall riots shortly after they happened. It was reported somewhat in the *Detroit Free Press*. I remember my Dad saying something to the effect of, "Just a bunch of queers being idiots." Looking back on it, that was interesting coming from a man who raised two queer sons. Lol. – Guy Sands

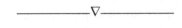

Chicago, IL

The 1971 Year in Pictures edition of *Life Magazine*. Life-changing! – Gregg Shapiro

—————▽—————

Chicago, IL

Maybe not until the movie *Before Stonewall* in 1985. I knew about gay liberation much earlier, however. My dad thought it would be "a riot" to watch the "queer parade" in 1972, which was like the second or third Pride Parade in this city. – R. M. Schultz

—————▽—————

Chicago, IL

I remember reading about the Stonewall riots when I first came out in 1976. – Rick Karlin

—————▽—————

New York, NY

I made myself dinner and I went down to the Stonewall. I didn't go down with friends. I went on my own. I drove down. I had a car with CD [corps diplomatique] plates on it, so I could park anywhere I wanted. They couldn't tow me. I'd been to the Stonewall before once. I remember it was one of the few places you could dance, and I enjoyed slow-dancing with guys. So, I went down there. Of course, in New York, nothing started until 10 of 11, so it was late when I got there. I met this guy soon after ordering a beer. It was a small bar and we went to the back and we were making out. That's when all the commotion started. We noticed the police were running through and we looked at each other and thought, "Maybe it's time to go." We knew there were raids. There were always raids in those days. I'd just come to the country, in 1968. I didn't know the ropes really. In those days you couldn't look at a guy, or touch a guy, without being arrested.

We stayed at the back of the bar and didn't do anything for a while. We thought we could ride it out. Then we noticed people were either being taken out or were leaving. So we decided to get out and see what was happening. We went out the back door, which went out to a little alley, then made our way around to Sheridan Square. That's when we saw the paddy wagons and people being loaded on. We stood there for a moment. We swapped phone numbers and he went his way and I went mine. I went back to pick up the car and drove home. Next morning my next door neighbor came around with a *Village Voice*. He said, "Did you see what happened last night?" And I thought, "I was there." I didn't see the drag queens being loaded onto the paddy wagons, but I remember hearing a lot of screaming. It took a while for me to piece it all together. But the real thing that connected it all was going down to Sheridan Square on June 29, congregating and going off on that march. That's when it all came together for me. It wasn't the raid that made us a community. There were raids on bars all the time. Why did this one make such a big fuss? It was different because it got a lot of press in the Village papers. But with the march, I knew that we were never going back into the closet again. This is it, we've come out. – Richard Pass

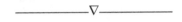

San Francisco, CA

Again, I wasn't really radicalized until I got to San Francisco in 1985 at the age of 22. Then I started reading all the histories of gay organizations because of the books provided to me by the San Francisco Public Library. That's when I started to identify as a gay writer. – Alec Holland

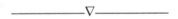

Chicago, IL

I believe when I was in high school in the '90s. My American History teacher didn't believe in only teaching out of the textbooks because she told us they were all written by wealthy white men and left a lot of history out. We talked about Stonewall when we discussed the '60s and '70s and that was the only time I'd heard of Stonewall before I took queer history courses in college. – James Conley

Chicago, IL

Yes. In 1975 I was introduced by a co-worker to an older Jewish gentleman from Brooklyn, NY, straight, married, children, grandchildren. When discovering I was gay, he inquired if I was familiar with the Stonewall riots and what I thought about what happened there. I shook my head that I did not know anything about it and that I hadn't been out for very long. He proceeded to give me a comprehensive gay history lesson along with a, "I hope you can appreciate the significance of what happened there, young man," remark. I thought it was quite remarkable that this straight married man knew so much about gay history. Later, I pulled my co-worker aside and asked her about it. She laughed and said, "Oh my god, he's as queer as a two dollar bill."

"But what about his wife and kids?" I said in disbelief.

"Oh grow up," she said, "Him and his wife adopted two kids from Thailand back in the day. He was a big-wig at Sears before he retired and, face it, you don't get promoted if you're queer." Never judge a book ... – Deschicago

————▽————

New York, NY

I used to hang out at the Monster in the '90s when I would visit New York – so I was right across the street from the Stonewall Inn – but it was later (maybe late '90s or the turn of the millennium) when I really was aware of the Stonewall riots. Growing up in a small farm town, I was 15 the summer of Judy Garland's death and the Stonewall riots; I read the paper pretty regularly, but somehow those two events didn't make it onto the front page of the *Omaha World-Herald*. Trying to think back to what I was doing that summer, I realized I was teaching little girls to twirl a baton. So, I guess I was doing my part (there never were any little boys who wanted to learn how to twirl, which I'm sorry about). – David

————▽————

Atlanta, GA

Yes, probably in the 1970's. I remember reading a paperback book about Bette Midler and it mentioned the Stonewall riots. As a young gay it gave me hope and let me know that I wasn't alone. – Daniel Goss

————▽————

Los Angeles, CA

I've seen this low-budget film called *Stonewall* starring Guillermo Diaz at Outfest. He was one of the first openly gay actors I'd seen star in a movie.

He was so good and the idea that he was really a gay man was so powerful to me. I remember the quote that Harvey Milk made about why straight people don't want to see gay folks in powerful positions. I'm paraphrasing ... "A gay person in power, now that's scary." – Jason Stuart

———————▽———————

North Carolina

My first Pride march, my junior year of college. I had two gay friends who were like my "parents" that schooled me as to why we marched and how it started. – Bill

———————▽———————

Milwaukee, WI

I first heard of Stonewall when the riots were happening because it was big news at the time. I became really aware of the significance of Stonewall in 1971 when I participated in Milwaukee's Gay Pride Parade. – Pat Cummings

———————▽———————

Chicago, IL

I think the first time I heard about it was in high school, the night of the protests following the death of Harvey Milk. Cleve Jones or a news report compared the protest to Stonewall. Being the bookworm I was, I went to the library and looked up what little I could about it. – Bernard

———————▽———————

New York, NY

As it happened. People ran into the Old Reliable Theatre Tavern on the East Side where I was directing a show, with fresh news-breaks. I must say, I and my cast, totally absorbed in our work, did not realize the event's importance. Off-Off Broadway playwright Doric Wilson lived next door to the Stonewall. He was totally unpolitical until he walked out of his building into the major landmark event of the gay rights movement. He became so politicized that he started the first openly gay theatre troupe, T.O.S.O.S. (*The Other Side of Silence*) and wrote a great play about the origin of the riots, *The West Street Gang*. – Robert Patrick

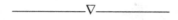

New York, NY

I first heard of the Stonewall Inn after attending an Encounter Workshops (a combination of Esalen and Gestalt Therapy). After the session a couple of us decided to go to Greenwich Village for dinner. In passing by the Stonewall, we began to comment on the people entering and the music & energy that came out every time the door opened. A few days later I decided to check it out for myself. That was a couple of years before the Stonewall Riots and by that time I had become a frequent visitor. Although I was not at the bar for the raid all the activity and commotion on Christopher Street soon had me down there. It was as if an emergency alarm had gone off throughout the Village. – Philip Raia

Denver, CO

I think I first heard about it the fall of 1969. When Stonewall happened, in June '69, I was spending the summer after my freshman year of college in Denver with my brother and his family. I don't recall hearing about Stonewall then, but when I got back to college the following fall, I learned about it. – Albert Williams

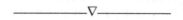

Chicago, IL

I don't recall when I first learned about the riots. But I do recall the first time I learned about Marsha P. Johnson, who is a very important piece of that story. But most people who tell the story of Stonewall to young queer kids leave her out. Gay men especially tend to leave out that the riots were led by trans women of color. I didn't learn about Marsha until I was 23 and heard her mentioned on a podcast – long after I knew about the riots. – Devlyn Camp

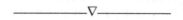

HOW DID YOUR PARENTS REACT WHEN YOU "CAME OUT" TO THEM?

Chicago, IL

I don't think we ever sat down and had the chat. Some I think was obvious, some was sort of understood with the rarity of girls in my life and those who were only pals not close and possibly it was the late teen poster trio of Frank N Furter, Greg Lougains, and Boy George on my walls. Much later in life when I was caring for my terminally ill Dad, we sort of broached the subject after a particularly rough day for him and he said, "When you pick someone to be with after I'm gone, make sure he deserves to know you better than I ever did."

My mother on the other hand, still refuses to believe Liberace was gay, so there's still hope I will have to tell her all about being gay someday. – Mike Martinez

————————▽————————

St. Louis, MO

While I was in college, some time in 1982 or '83. Instead of staying at my family's home during a summer break, I stayed at my partner Ron's apartment. Of course, my parents were going to drop by at some point, and they tried to not show astonishment when they saw he was 20 years older than me. Nothing was really said, it was just understood. It was some years later in 1987 when he was dying that dialogue was more open about it all. – Todd Jaeger

————————▽————————

Texas

My parents had separated when I was in high school. I came out to my mother at 19, a few months after coming out to my best friend. I knew she wouldn't be happy but I was always very close to her growing up, so I wanted her blessing. I left a note in her purse and went to work. When I came home she was on the porch, crying. She wouldn't listen to a word I had to say. She just kept telling me that I was not gay, and that I was going to go to a psychiatrist. Our relationship changed forever that day. We had many yelling matches over the next couple of years. She finally came around about 10 years later. The same summer I came out to my mother, I went to see my Dad in Atlanta, and came out to him. He had a similar reaction as my Mom but he listened to me, and at the end of the conversation he just told me that all that was important was my happiness. Today they are both pretty accepting. – Brent

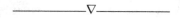

San Francisco, CA

They both reacted rather badly. I told my mother at 15. Her response was, "You'll never go to San Francisco again." My fathers was, "Let me pay for a prostitute." All I had to do was experience a prostitute and that'll repair me. My mother and father were divorced at the time. I was living with my mother. So, I spent the next two or three years convincing my mother I was not gay and it was a phase. That was a favorite thing in the 1960s, it was just a phase. So I could continue to pal around with my college age friends and go to San Francisco." – Bill Barrick

New York, NY

It was on my 21st birthday and I had just moved into Manhattan from Queens. I was there for a few months, and my parents came into the city to take me out to dinner. I decided that night, when we came back to my apartment, that I was going to come out. The night before I came out I was telling my mother about something-or-other and she said, 'Well whatever makes you happy.' So when they came back to my apartment, I said to my mom, "What you said last night about whatever makes me happy, will make you happy. Well I'm gay and happy." She said, "If you're happy that's fine. I support you. You're my son. I love you. Not a problem." I asked dad how he felt and he said, "I feel just like your mother. When I took them to the elevator, my mother turned around and said, "Just be careful." Got in the elevator and went back to Queens. – Randy Warren

——————▽——————

Chicago, IL

My father passed away before I even knew I was gay and my mother was more upset about the fact that she wouldn't be a grandmother than the fact I was gay. – Jack Delaney

——————▽——————

USA

I was 17. I had already been outed by a jerk at high school who saw me at one of the gay clubs (why no one asked him what he was doing there, I'll never know). The town I grew up in was super small in both area and mindset and I knew I would have to come clean to my mom that night. I was crying and trying to get the words out. She just hugged me and told me she knew the minute she first held me in the hospital after giving birth. It didn't matter to her and she joked that she knew I would always make sure she was dressed well and photographed in only the best light.

My father died before I came out to him, but I suspect he also knew from an early age. One Christmas after the divorce, my parents had a huge fight because I had asked for a GI Joe action figure and my dad didn't want my mom to buy it because he didn't want me playing with dolls. I ended up commandeering my sister's Easy Bake Oven that Christmas instead and proceeded to perfect creme brulee, brownies and a host of other things in it. Yeah, should have bought me the doll, dad. – Misha Davenport

——————▽——————

USA

My parents were both about 40 when I was born and their formative years were in the 1950s. That was a time when being homosexual, or being a communist for that matter, literally ruined people's lives and made them outcasts. My own formative years being in the 1980s and having the support of a strong and organized LGBT youth group in Boston – BAGLY – were completely different. I felt that there was hope and things were getting better every day. We were the "new gay generation" – more visible, out earlier, and pushing forward. In fact, BAGLY guided us so strictly that we were told we were not "allowed to get AIDS" (this was before the term HIV Positive was used), and those of us, like me, who were the first openly out members of our school and community were given grand names by BAGLY's founder Grace Sterling Stowell. Grace named me "Matthew, Dowager Empress of the Western Shires" since I was from Westborough Massachusetts.

It was definitely a clash of culture between my own Boy George and Annie Lennox loving self and my parents' idea of how one should behave and what was expected. My mother was afraid that it would be a very hard life for me. My dad dis-enrolled me from the Catholic high school I was about to start at and instead I moved to my mom's house and started at the local high school there. That was very rough, obviously, but I think it turned out truly for the best as I was able to be myself in Westborough. – Matt

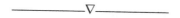

British Columbia, Canada

My dad died before that. But he was very loving and tolerant in general, so I doubt it would have been a huge thing. With my mother, we were hiking in a forest in British Columbia, and she was taking photographs of trees and wildlife. In conversation she mentioned something about a friend's son coming out, so I took the opportunity to join him. She paused a milisecond and then said, "Oh, well, I've always thought that was probably the case." At that very moment a beautiful dark green bird flitted by: "Oh my goodness, look at that!" We grabbed the camera bag and went running after it. And that was that. – Steve Lafreniere

Chicago, IL

My father died before I realized I was gay. He wouldn't have taken it well. I remember when I was maybe 12 years old, we were walking through a parking lot one evening to get to the entrance of a restaurant and he pointed at a small group of men standing under a light (street light? alley light? parking lot light? light at the back entrance of the restaurant?) and talking, and he said to me, "That guy's a fag. You can tell by the way he holds his cigarette." I couldn't figure which of the men he meant, and I'd never heard the word "fag" before, so I didn't understand it.

In 1979 I took a trip from Boston back to Chicago to come out to my mother. My sister had just sustained an injury in rugby practice and was in the hospital. I asked my mother for some private time with my sister, and as she left the room she said, "No fooling around, you two." That was a very uncharacteristic comment.

When I was done telling my sister I called my mother back and told her I was gay. She tried hard not to cry, and she said, "I hoped this wouldn't happen." I don't know if "this" meant my being gay, or my telling her. By the time I thought to ask her about that, years later, she didn't remember. Also, years later, I learned that she thought that by coming out I was telling her Goodbye Forever. She knows better than that now. – Rick

————————▽————————

Chicago, IL

My father's response was typically blasé. He told me he didn't approve, but it was *my* life. Mother on the other hand, was high drama. When I told her, she burst into tears and cried all night. Then she became the Grand Inquisitor, and wanted to know how I *knew* I was gay? Things got so toxic that I moved to the Lake Hotel on Broadway. That was in the summer of 1986, when I was 22. I didn't speak to them again for a year. – Corey Black

————————▽————————

Atlanta, GA

I came out to my parents at my house after my first partner, Nick, passed away from AIDS. They wanted to move to Atlanta to take care of me. – Tom

————————▽————————

Chicago, IL

Both cried and said terrible things. They eventually got over it. – Anonymous

————————▽————————

Chicago, IL

They were fine with it, not surprised, but more relieved. – Giovanni

Chicago, IL

I was messing around with another boy when I was in between 8th grade and freshman year. The other boy's mother was listening to our calls and called my parents with the news. It did not go over well. I was so young. They sent me to Catholic Charities for counseling for 6 months and I was cured. LOL. A few years later they were much more accepting and understanding when it came up again. It still makes me laugh that they sent me to a priest for counseling. – Kbro

New York, NY

Not happy. I got kicked out one night and slept on my sister's couch. My parents then insisted I go to some psychiatrist way out on Long Island. Since they were paying for my college and I was living under their roof, I had to comply, but left the very day of college graduation for Chicago. Didn't speak to them for several years after. – Frederick

Chicago, IL

I made them ask rather than tell them, thinking I was protecting them. They did so when I was 32. We lived in separate cities. It went very well. We talked all night, and my mother shared parts of her upbringing that were secret from us when we were growing up. It was very revealing on both sides and brought us closer together. – Anonymous

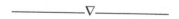

Chicago, IL

My father seemed to know I was gay before I knew I was gay. I was being pressured by friends and family to get fixed up with girls. I kept saying, "No, I'm not interested." My father firmly told well intentioned friends and family, "Stop that! Not everyone wants to date girls." My mother introduced my boyfriend at family events by saying, "I'd like you to meet —— who is a member of our family." – Bob

Chicago, IL

Here's what you need to know. My mother lived in Hawaii for 15 years as the secretary and book keeper to the owner of the original Hamburger Mary's. She worked in that restaurant and Dirty Mary's Bar until the gay men around her started dying of AIDS. She helped many of them as they died, becoming their "adopted" mother when their own parents shunned them. My father was married to a woman who was a lesbian until they met. Here's the only thing my parents cared about – that my partner and I loved each other and treated each other with kindness. What more could a child ask for? – Anonymous

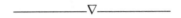

New York, NY

I was about 26, it was 1974, and I had been leading up to it, dropping hints over several visits home for dinner, until one evening, when I came home, my mother looked up from cooking and asked, "John, I want you to tell me the truth. Are you a gay person?" I was so relieved, I said "Yes" with a big smile, and then she changed the subject as if I had never answered. Then, my dad got home from work, we're eating dinner, and he looks up from his plate and says, "John, I want you to tell me the truth. Are you a gay person?" Again, I said yes, he went totally pale and started saying "No, no," and then my mother interrupted and said, "Yes, he is, he told me the same thing." What followed was three hours of intense conversation in which they asked me a million questions. I didn't lose my calm and kept answering. Finally, I needed to go home, but we agreed I'd come back in a few days to talk some more about it.

We had a couple more of these evenings – they weren't hostile or angry, but they didn't seem happy – and then finally I came home for another, and they said, "John, I hope you won't mind, but we really feel like we have to tell the family." In this case, "family" meant 15 to 20 aunts, uncles, and cousins of mine and theirs. Of course, I was thrilled – they were going to do the coming out for me – and I said, "Yes, you can."

Over the next weeks, I heard about the visits and the responses, and they all seemed to be okay which, by implication, meant to me that my parents were doing well with this revelation about their son. Finally, on one of the visits home, they were being noticeably silent, and I asked what was going on. They looked at each other, with a strange smile on their faces, and then proceeded to tell me about a visit to my dad's two sisters and a brother-in-law. Over dinner, they said, "There's something we have to tell you about John," and before they could say anything my two aunts both became hysterical and starting screaming "Oh my god, oh my god, what's wrong? He has cancer. He's doing drugs. He's been arrested. He's been in a car accident." And as my parents are now describing this, my mom says, "So finally we started screaming back at them and said, "No, no, everything's okay, nothing's wrong, he's just gay." And I thought, "Nothing wrong? Just gay? Hmm. I think this has turned out okay."

And truly, the whole family, working-class immigrant heritage Italians, have been completely accepting of me, treated my long-term partner as a member of the family. Considering how long ago this was, I consider it a miracle! – John D'Emilio

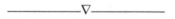

USA

Terribly. They literally locked me in my room for weeks and I had to deny everything just to live a normal life. I was very resentful and did not speak to them for 17 years after that. Surprisingly I have a good and honest relationship with both of them now and they both have come and stayed with me in the Castro in San Francisco. – Eric Kuznof

Los Angeles, CA

I came out to them in a letter. I was madly in love with a beautiful man and I wanted to shout it from the rooftops. Alas, the letter arrived shortly before Christmas (I've always been a master of timing.) My mother wrote back saying that she would rather I had died. She wanted to know if I "blamed her for this." And if so, she rejected that out of hand. She took down every gift I'd ever given her and was in mourning as though I was dead. My father, a CPA, wanted to know if this was just another form of "rebellion" or was this who I really was deep down inside? He offered that he deeply loved his fraternity brothers from college (all of whom were like uncles to me) but that he'd never imagined having sex with them. I told him that was how I felt about women. After a relatively brief time, my mother came around. She was nothing if not loyal. Over the years I have come home with several of my boyfriends. My husband is treated as a member of the family on equal standing with my sisters-in-law. – Bo Young

Hickory, NC

I had to come out three times (to my parents). I lived in a somewhat broken home. I had a mother, a father and a step mother. When I was 12, I told my mother, who was okay with it. She asked me questions like are you planning on being safe, do you have any crushes, things like that.

However, when I told my stepmother, she stopped talking to me for two whole weeks straight. I would speak to her and she would outright ignore me. After about two weeks I asked what her problem was, that I was the same kid I was two weeks ago. She said she just had to get used to it and had a lot to think about. My aunty describes her reaction quite well by saying that my stepmother lives in this little bubble and when something like that shows up on her viewscreen on the bubble she has to try to clean it off, and if she can't, it takes time to accept that it's going to be there.

My father was quite unusual. I entirely expected him to react angrily or upset. However, when I told him he asked me if I had any boyfriends yet and to let him know before bringing them over, and then we continued watching football (it was on a Sunday, and despite me not really liking sports, I'd watch them with my dad to spend time with him.) – Christian Bane

Chicago, IL

I was sitting on a bed in a hotel room. My mom lived in a single room occupancy hotel room. The Bel-Park Hotel. I told my mom and she cried. That was the last time we really talked about it. – Joseph G

Chicago, IL

I never really officially came out. I was more found out when my mother searched through my room and found letters and notes from a young woman I had dated in college. I noticed my things had been disturbed and my mom was acting angry and cold towards me. I put it together and decided to move out as I found an apartment I could afford. She's now okay with me being gay and, I think, loves my wife more than me (LOL). – Chicago T

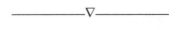

Newton, MA

They had me followed by a detective because I was underage. I had moved out of the house when I was 16 almost 17 as it was a horrible household.

It was a blame game and a phase to them. My mother even tried to blame me being gay as to the cause to my father's fatal heart attack in 1978. She was always just an evil woman. – James S

———————∇———————

Portland, ME

I never came out to my parents. But I did come out to my sister in the late 1990s. I had realized she was a lesbian long before, with her obviously butch women friends who also never had any men in their lives. I was surprised she had never figured out MY story – I mean, given there were almost no women in my life other than coworkers. So, when I came out to my sister, she said in great surprise, "You too?" – Jeff

———————∇———————

Utica, NY

Very poorly. It ended our relationship. – Dave Russo

———————∇———————

Chicago, IL

My apartment in Chicago's Ravenswood neighborhood.

Mom cried. I asked why she was crying. "Oh," she sobbed, "I know they say you're not supposed to think this, but I can't help but feel it's because of something I did."

"Don't cry," I replied. "Besides, I'm thinking it's pretty much Dad's fault."

My Dad groaned and buried his face in his hands. I laughed. Mom shook her head.

"It's nothing either of you did or didn't do," I reassured them. "Shall we get some lunch? I've been dating a guy named Robert. You'll love him."

And the four of us went to lunch. And, sure enough, they fell in love with him.

Mom died in 2006. She was quite fond of Robert, who was with my

Father and me at my Mother's bedside when she passed. And, these days, my 89-year-old Dad refers to Robert as "my other Son." – Michael Burke

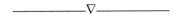

New York, NY

It's a sweet story that I didn't really appreciate as sweet at the time, but they did most of the work for me. I was out to everyone, basically, except them, and when my mom took me to the airport to begin my second year at NYU she – well, first she cried a lot but then she said she and my dad knew I was gay, and it was alright with them. And she'd wished I could have talked to them about it. It was a huge step for her, and a big moment of connection between us. I remain incredibly grateful for her bridging that enormous gulf. – David Zinn

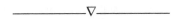

Australia

My mother took me to a psychiatrist, who was very understanding. I was 17 years old and he told me I might change my mind or might not, but he was not judgmental. My father didn't say anything. I think maybe my mother didn't tell him, and I didn't talk to him about it. – Susan H

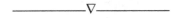

Chicago, IL

My brother was the one who brought that about. My partner and I had been together for 25 years, lived together the whole time, started businesses together, and always assumed my parents knew. My brother was visiting them and our mother was going on about whether I would get married, etc. My brother looked at both my parents and said something on the order of "He and Owen have been in a gay relationship for 25 years." They were actually surprised. He never told me he had done that until later, but the week after that conversation I got a lovely letter from my parents, signed by both of them, that said they were surprised, but grateful I had found someone who was dear to them as well, and all they wanted was for us to be happy. We never talked about it again, but it made a real difference in honesty and openness that we hadn't even realized had been a problem. – Ripley

San Francisco, CA

I came out to my parents to protect them from hearing about me from any outside source. My first partner had been outed to his parents, and I didn't want that to be the route for me. I sat them down after dinner and told them that I had something to tell them. They took the information without any great concern. My dad commented that, "At least you won't be contributing to the population problem" – I don't think my mother was pleased with that remark! I found out later that they had gone to see a psychologist about me and were told that I seemed, from their description of me, like a very well-adjusted young man. We never really discussed the subject after that which I think was too bad. After my dad passed away, my mother and I created two quilts for the quilt project to honor two of my friends – one of whom I was romantically involved with. Even at that point, we didn't really talk much about my sexuality. – Brian

Madison, WI
San Francisco, CA

I came out to my mom in 1999, at 19 years old. I was in college at UW-Madison at the time. I lured her out to dinner, promising "important news" which made her very anxious. As soon as we ordered food, she started questioning me. Did I get a girl pregnant? Am I dropping out of college? Am I gay? I told her I was gay. She nervously talked about "the perfect potato salad" for about 5 minutes before sighing and exclaiming "Don't you ever tell your father." Though she didn't tell me at the time, for years she thought (or was hoping) my gayness was a phase, and one year later when I told her that I went on a date with someone she asked me, "What's her name?"

In 2002 I came out to my father. I was in San Francisco on a trip at the time, and my dad lived outside of Oakland. I called him because I thought maybe we could meet up to talk. It wasn't going to work out, so I told him over the phone that I was gay. There was silence. He asked me if I was sure, I said yes. Then he said that he would rather that I be dying of cancer than be gay and hung up. We haven't spoken since. – Shane K

Iowa

Not good. Disgusted. But they accept and tolerate me now the best way they know how. – Anonymous

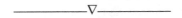

Lima, Peru

They didn't cry or anything, but I didn't come out "properly" either, I just told them, "Hey this girl is my girlfriend." My mom was quite neutral about it, but she kept thinking I'm a lesbian (I'm bisexual) and trying to groom me into a more femme aesthetic (I like to present myself androgynously, leaning towards masc). My dad keeps coming up with excuses for not liking my girlfriends, even though he absolutely loved the time I brought home a boyfriend and invited him for lunch on the first week. The first thing he said to me when I told him about my first girlfriend was, "I don't like it." Well, shit, sucks to be you. – Robb

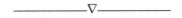

Chicago, IL

I told them when I was 32, and was so nervous, as they were well established and recognized conservative society people. I told them, and their response was, "Thank God, we knew since you were five, we thought you'd never figure it out, and we weren't sure what to do. Big day of anxiety was a bust! – Robert

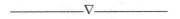

Perth, Australia

As for coming out. Like so many of us, I told my mother first. She seemed to take it well, asked me a few questions, such as did I want to be a girl. I said no. She asked if I had ever slept with a girl, I said no. She asked me how I knew I was gay if I had never slept with a girl. I then asked her if she had ever slept with a girl. She said no. I said how do you know you wouldn't like it. She said she knew she wouldn't. I said, well. It's the same for me. I know I wouldn't. However, after she thought about it some more, she got a bit cagey about it. If I brought up anything gay-related in conversation, she would quickly change the topic. Or if she was on the phone, make up an excuse to get off. Over the years she has become more comfortable with it. I don't blame her at all for her reaction. She is a product of her generation. And I know it's not what she would have wanted ideally, so I understand. She told my father, so I don't know what his reaction was, although I could imagine. – Mansfield

——————∇——————

OTHER BOOKS BY ...

ST SUKIE DE LA CROIX

Chicago Whispers: The History of LGBT Chicago Before Stonewall
The Blue Spong and the Flight from Mediocrity
The Memoir of a Groucho Marxist: A Very British Fairy Tale
Out of the Underground: Homosexuals, the Radical Press, and the Rise and
Fall of the Gay Liberation Front

OWEN KEEHNEN

The LGBTQ Book of Days: Revised 2019 Edition
Dugan's Bistro and the Legend of the Bearded Lady
Night Visitors
Love Underground
The Matinee Idol
Young Digby Swank
Vernita Gray: From Woodstock to the White House – with Tracy Baim
The LGBT Book of Days
Gay Press, Gay Power – contributor
The Sand Bar
We're Here, We're Queer
Jim Flint: The Boy From Peoria – with Tracy Baim
Leatherman: The Legend of Chuck Renslow – with Tracy Baim
Doorway Unto Darkness
Nothing Personal:
Chronicles of Chicago's LGBTQ Community 1977-1997 – co-editor
Rising Starz
Ultimate Starz
Out and Proud in Chicago – contributor
More Starz
Starz

CPSIA information can be obtained
at www.ICGtesting.com
Printed in the USA
LVHW091431241220
675092LV00025B/204